"This book is an exceptional example of how to combat deficit thinking about students with disabilities. The authors provide salient and practical ways for educators to become *true advocates* for their success. This is a must read for anyone who is serious about the educational, social, and economic success of our students in our schools."

- Bruce G. Barnett, Professor of Educational Leadership and Policy Studies, University of Texas at San Antonio

"*Unifying Educational Systems* offers a blueprint for imagining schooling that embraces student capabilities and promise. It proposes an entirely new, but eminently possible, transformation of special education. The authors unmask basic flaws in current structures and policies and point to how leadership can bring clarity and vision that will hold."

- Douglas Biklen, Dean of the School of Education, Syracuse University

"This book is an important resource for leaders committed to social justice reforms in education. It questions conventional special education and offers an alternative vision of a unified system that better serves the egalitarian ideals of public education."

- Tom Skrtic, Department of Special Education, University of Kansas

UNIFYING EDUCATIONAL SYSTEMS

Unifying Educational Systems encourages leaders to move beyond the forms and rituals of leadership for special education that are caught within traditional definitions of a continuum of services. Grounded in public policy debates, research on teaching and learning, and an emerging consensus throughout the leadership community that calls into question our current practices, chapters in this volume provide a discussion of the purpose, principles, and paradoxes extant in the implementation of current special education policy. Chapter authors discuss how students are currently served, the feasibility of re-conceptualizing special education leadership in the current policy context, and the challenges for the future. Ultimately, this book calls for a new policy framework to integrate special education within the larger instructional support system in schools, in order to support a social justice and inclusive practices agenda.

Leonard C. Burrello is Professor and Chair of Educational Leadership and Policy Studies at University of South Florida, USA.

Wayne Sailor is Professor of Special Education, 2012 Budig Teaching Professor, and Co-Associate Director of the Beach Center on Disability at University of Kansas, USA.

Jeannie Kleinhammer-Tramill is Professor and Doctoral Program Coordinator for the Department of Special Education at University of South Florida, USA.

UNIFYING EDUCATIONAL SYSTEMS

Leadership and Policy Perspectives

Edited by
Leonard C. Burrello
Wayne Sailor
Jeannie Kleinhammer-Tramill

 Routledge
Taylor & Francis Group

NEW YORK AND LONDON

First published 2013
by Routledge
711 Third Avenue, New York, NY 10017

Simultaneously published in the UK
by Routledge
2 Park Square, Milton Park, Abingdon, Oxon OX14 4RN

Routledge is an imprint of the Taylor & Francis Group, an informa business

Library of Congress Cataloging-in-Publication Data

Unifying educational systems : leadership and policy perspectives /
edited by Leonard C. Burrello, Wayne Sailor, and Jeannie
Kleinhammer-Tramill
    p. cm.
    Includes bibliographical references and index.
1. Inclusive education.   2. Special education.   3. Educational leadership.
4. School management and organization.   I. Burrello, Leonard C., 1942–
II. Sailor, Wayne.   III. Kleinhammer-Tramill, Jeannie.
    LC1200.U65   2012
    371.9'046—dc23   2012026899

ISBN: 978-0-415-52468-1 (hbk)
ISBN: 978-0-415-52469-8 (pbk)
ISBN: 978-0-203-12028-6 (ebk)

Typeset in Bembo
by Apex CoVantage, LLC

Printed and bound in the United States of America on sustainably sourced
paper by IBT Global.

CONTENTS

PART I

Introduction and the Proposal for Unifying Systems

1

SPECIAL EDUCATION

A Critical Perspective on Reframing Public Policy for Students With Disabilities

Jeannie Kleinhammer-Tramill, Leonard C. Burrello, and Wayne Sailor

This book proposes a new policy frame for special education that is intended to remove the praxis of our efforts to serve students with disabilities from an insular system of services, bound within its own rules and regulations, and to pose a new vision for a system that is fully integrated within the larger context of education. We propose to reconceptualize special education as a temporally bounded instructional support system for any student in the public schools who might need support to achieve his or her full capabilities. It is our intent to describe and propose an instructionally oriented discourse and accompanying system that is centered on the learner and the ecology of learning that includes the home, the community, and the school itself (Lashley, 1994; Burrello, Lashley, & Beatty, 2001; Sailor, 2009).

The nation can ill afford to continue to support an educational system that accumulates failure upon failure for students who have different learning needs because of disabilities, cultural or racial diversity, language differences, poverty, or the need for different types of instruction at different points in their educational experience (Kirkpatrick, 1994). Further, we can no longer support a set of service delivery options that expose children with disabilities to the harmful effects of seclusion and restraint (Amos, 2004; Fogt, 2002). The requisite knowledge and technology needed to accelerate student learning exist, but applying them requires a transformational reexamination of the purpose and principles, as well as the culture, of schools in relation to the diverse characteristics of our students and communities.

Our intent, then, with this chapter is to provide the groundwork for a critical reconceptualization of special education. The guiding principle throughout this volume is that we believe that moral leadership, by its nature, is inclusive. We fully embrace the commitments of P.L. 94-142, the Education of All Handicapped

Children Act of 1975, and its subsequent reauthorizations as the Individuals With Disabilities Education Act (IDEA, 2004), to ensure the right of children with disabilities to a Free Appropriate Public Education (FAPE). Likewise, we fully appreciate the circumstances and advocacy that led to incorporation of procedural safeguards that ensure due process and education of children in the Least Restrictive Environment.

While we would like to believe that policy maturation has occurred—that all students with disabilities have access to education and are provided with social and academic opportunities that will enable them to fully participate in the environments they select and in the ways that they choose, we believe that the potential for the field of special education has not been fully realized. As we anticipate the forthcoming reauthorization of the Elementary and Secondary Education Act (ESEA) and IDEA, we find that the operationalization of IDEA often remains ceremonious rather than meaningful—caught in habits of interpretation that Skrtic (1991, 2005) and others have referred to as machine bureaucracies that are suited for performing certain functions in routinized ways as if all "clients" of special education need particular types of services (those provided by the bureaucracy) rather than responding to the real and ever-changing needs of real, live children.

We see the field of special education as caught in something of a crisis as it tries to respond to demands for accountability, to the competing demands of compliance versus outcomes, and to efforts to move toward new strategies for policy implementation such as Response to Intervention (RtI). Each of these policy imperatives challenges the bureaucratic form and professional customs of what we currently term *special education* and raises the question of whether current ways of implementing special education policy serve to improve the lives and learning of children or to buttress the existing system.

We believe that a number of paradoxes exist in the implementation of current special education policy, including:

1. The field of special education continues to espouse the ideal of LRE while maintaining rigid adherence to the concept of a continuum of services. This means, *ipso facto,* that some children must be placed at various stages of the continuum, and away from general education, for the continuum to exist.

2. The field of special education continues to espouse alignment of IDEA with standards-based education, provision of the opportunities and curricular enrichment associated with high expectations, and the commitment to hold schools accountable for the progress of all students, while at the same time using the standards-based assessment and accountability system to track students with significant support needs into alternate assessment or accountability-exempt statuses.

3. The field of special education continues to espouse the goal of graduation while narrowing graduation options and tracking students—particularly those who take alternate assessments—into nonstandard diplomas.

4. The field continues to espouse the goal of preparing all children to fully participate in a democratic society but fails to hold schools accountable for postschool outcomes related to that goal.
5. The field acknowledges the promise of special education to provide data-driven, individualized learning opportunities for students but continues to focus on special education as a place rather than as a service.
6. Finally, the field of special education espouses innovation to better serve children while interpreting new paradigms such as Response to Intervention (RtI) as threats to the very foundations of the field.

We believe that the nexus of these paradoxes, the identity crisis of special education, and, conceivably a shifting policy environment, provide the occasion and opportunity for a critical reconceptualization of special education policy and practice.

The principles undergirding our vision for a new and more responsive form of special education necessitate several shifts in perspective regarding the nature of schooling and the organization of supports necessary for children to learn. These shifts include the following, (1) a shift from a human capital agenda for education to a human capabilities agenda, (2) a shift in the purpose of special education from that of sheltering a select group of children from their regular education classmates to the conception of special education as "experimental education" (Burrello, Tracy, & Schultz, 1973), or what we would now term *innovative education*, that brings an array of diverse expertise to bear on the full range of learning problems encountered by all children, (3) a shift from a narrowed vision of what children should learn to a critical pedagogy, (4) a shift from a closed system that occurs within the confines of the schoolhouse to an open system that is interdependent with the community; and, finally, (5) a shift from accountability focused on rules and normative assessments to accountability based on values and a moral commitment to schools, communities, families, and children. This chapter provides a broad overview of these shifts, and the chapters that follow provide a more detailed vision of what we see as a critical reconceptualization of special education.

Shifting From a Human Capital Agenda to a Human Capabilities Agenda

From the inception of the common school movement in the late 19th century until now, preparation of youth for the workforce has been a primary rationale for universal, public education in America. While building an educated citizenry capable of participating in a democratic society has perhaps been the ideal of education, development of human capital, consisting of trained workers, has been an underlying, or, often, explicit agenda for education, what Postman (1995) called, the economic imperative of public education. Frequently, the human capital agenda is tied not only to work, but to national defense, as was the case when the National Defense Education Act was passed in 1957 (Tyack & Hansot, 1982). From the *Nation at Risk* report (NCEE, 1983) until the present, the need for development of a new labor force with the 21st-century skills necessary to succeed in the knowledge economy that employers value has been the primary political argument and policy lever for school reform. Marshall Smith, a primary architect of standards-based reform and the policies that supported it during the mid-1990s, addressed the human capital agenda of Goals 2000 explicitly. Smith and Scoll (1995) state:

> The demand for attention to education and training issues in 1992 was fueled by three broad arguments. . . . The primary public rationale, however, for the concern about human capital was based on the ever-present challenges of international economic competition and a changing workplace. . . . As machines replace more and more manual workers, the demand for low-skilled jobs has shrunk. Higher skill jobs not only bring higher wages, they also hold more promise of stability. All jobs, however, require workers who can adapt to changing conditions and the constant evolution of technology and the world economy. Job stability, like that for industry, depends on flexibility and adaptability and these, in turn, depend on training and experience. (pp. 390–391)

While No Child Left Behind (NCLB) was publicly presented as a renewed effort to achieve equity, Apple (2006) and others have critiqued what they perceive as a neoliberal agenda with a feverish commitment to markets, privatization, and commodification of education. Apple feared the hidden implications of this movement are only slowly emerging, which could lead to a separate system of private and public charters serving students with disabilities in separate, segregated settings. Moreover, current discussions of reauthorization of the ESEA (e.g., U.S. Department of Education, 2010) have reemphasized the link between education and employment.

Not coincidentally, the history of services for persons with disabilities has also focused on the goal of human capital development. More enlightened forms of institutionalization for persons with emotional and cognitive disabilities focused on habilitating them for employment (Sarason & Doris, 1979). Likewise, while P.L. 94-142 did not explicitly address transition or employment outcomes as a goal for education of students with disabilities until the 1990 reauthorization of IDEA as P.L. 101-476, preparation of personnel to provide vocational and, later, transition services has been a priority for discretionary funding authorized by disability legislation in most years from 1958 to 1992, and, again, in 2010 (Kleinhammer-Tramill, Tramill, & Brace, 2010; Morningstar, Kleinhammer-Tramill, & Lattin, 1999).

Preparing youth to be employable may well be a worthy goal that engenders independence, self-determination, and, most important, human dignity; however, an increasing body of thought from the critical disabilities perspective points out that employment, independence, and self-determination are distinctly Western values that may not reflect an individual's goals or the cultural norms or values for all groups (Zhang, 2006). While we embrace these goals as worthy outcomes that are likely to promote the well-being and dignity of persons whose lives *are* contextualized by Western culture, we would argue that a human capabilities approach provides a more robust argument for the value of education and a richer context for considering these goals as valuable postschool outcomes.

Sen (1992) describes the capabilities approach in the following: "A person's capability to achieve functioning that he or she has reason to value provides a general evaluation of social arrangements, and this yields a particular way of viewing the assessment of equality and inequality" (p. 5). Alkire and Deneulin (2009) elaborate, "the key idea of the capability approach is that social arrangements should aim to expand people's capabilities—their freedom to promote or achieve what they value doing and being." An essential test of development is whether people have greater freedoms today than they did in the past. Sen describes the human capabilities approach as a triad consisting of functioning, freedom, and agency, or the pursuit of goals that the person values or has reason to value (Sen, 1985). Sen's concept of agency is similar to other approaches that speak to self-determination, authentic participation, voice, participation in one's own plan making, and acting out those values in one's life. Based on the work of Alkire and Deneukin, Sen offers four attributes of agency, including: (1) agency goes beyond individual power and direct control to participating in collective or group interests, (2) agency may mean pursuing other goals beyond the self that include the environment, civil rights, or more family- or community-oriented goals, (3) agency is tested by its degree of reasonableness and does not include goals that might harm or hinder another's progress or pursuit of other valuable goals, and (4) agency requires an evaluation of what is created or sustained to determine how one's responsibility as an agent is enacted (pp. 37–38).

Nussbaum (2006) provides a theory of social justice and human capability that explicitly includes persons with disabilities. She discusses her assumptions regarding human dignity and disability as core principles within the human capabilities approach in the following: "The role of the species norm in thinking about dignity is discussed, and it is argued that dignity does not rest on some actual property of persons, such as the possession of reason or other specific abilities; this account represents a shift from some earlier discussions of 'basic capabilities.' It is also argued that dignity is not a value independent of the capabilities, but that the articulation of the political principles involving capability are (partial) articulations of the notion of a life with human dignity" (p. 7). Nussbaum argues for the utility of the capabilities approach as a means to ensure children and their families all the attributes and rights of human beings, including participation in what constitutes the common good. She identifies 10 uniquely human capabilities that apply to all, including a long life, good health, emotional engagement, bodily integrity, senses, imagination and thought, practical reasoning, affiliation, enjoyment of other species and nature; play; and control over one's environment (politically and materially). She describes these as comprehensive "possibilities" so as not to preclude other values a person may hold or wish to pursue. Nussbaum stresses that these capabilities are not a *means* to lead a life with human dignity; she does not view them as processes to reach an end. In her view, "they are understood, instead, as ways of *realizing* a life with human dignity, in all of the different areas of life in which human beings typically engage" (p. 161).

She distinguishes her theory from other social contract theories such as that of Rawls, which, according to Nussbaum, views the social contract as existing between "equals" and, thereby, excludes persons with disabilities from consideration as participants in the contract.

She enjoins the discussion of the human development and capabilities approach in her words as, "an improved account of the language of human rights" and places mutual respect, reciprocity, and the social basis of self-respect as central to our understanding of what supports the development of human dignity. In her view, then, social policy is evaluated in terms of how it assists each person to become what he or she wishes to become, and that is in her words "the principle of each person as an end; in other words, the person not the group, is the primary subject of political justice, and policies that improve the lot of a group are to be rejected unless they deliver the central capabilities to each and every person" (p. 216).

Differences matter within Nussbaum's theory, and she recognizes variability among all children and, for that matter, adults. Nussbaum (2006) states it flatly: "the problem of variability of need is pervasive" (p. 125), and she adds "so the question of variability cannot be postponed, it is omni-present" (p. 165). However, variability does not negate the essential rights of persons with disabilities.

We argue then for replacing the dominant human capital educational agenda with a human development and capabilities approach that sees education as fulfilling three roles of liberation, empowerment, and participation. We acknowledge the political pragmatism associated with the human capital agenda argument, and we believe that liberating individuals and acknowledging their agency may well include and even enhance employability and other outcomes that are considered desirable for education. However, we see employability as one potential goal of education and means of agency within a broader spectrum of human capabilities.

Shifting the Context and Form of Special Education

Gilborn and Youdell (2000) argue that the architecture of schools is designed to serve two sets of students. They write: "The reality is that students are privileged or marginalized according to class, geographic location, ethnicity, and perceived notion of 'ability.'" In other words, the architecture of schooling becomes more distinctly tiered—sponsored schools for the achievers and residualized schools for the less deserving (Slee, 2009, p. 162).

Data on student achievement today bears out the prediction that students with special needs are at risk for becoming a permanent underclass (Conner & Ferri, 2007; Government Accounting Office, 2003; Mellard & Patterson, 2008). These findings lead to an essential moral issue: unless all students have equal membership in schools, they may suffer lasting harm. Under the guise of "specialness" tied to the construct of disability, a construct that locates educational problems solely within the individual, we have created an unjust and unfair parallel system of programs and services that result in poorer outcomes than those realized by students in the general education system. Slee (2009) contends that "epistemology distributes status and power unevenly; some are in, some others will always be others." Membership in a public school is a fundamental right. It implies that all students deserve full membership (Black & Burrello, 2010).

Our argument for shifting the form and purpose of special education—for a critical reconceptualization—is grounded in public policy debates, published research on teaching and learning, and an emerging consensus throughout the leadership community that calls into question not only our current continuum of services but also those services described under "full inclusion" practices. Research increasingly suggests that failure of students with special needs to progress at grade level can arise from a number of considerations including low expectations for student performance related to poverty; lack of parental support; discrimination on the basis of racial/ethnic identity; discrimination on the basis of primary spoken language; weak or inappropriate instruction; poor or incoherent curricula; inexperienced teachers (particularly in impacted urban settings); and/or physical, emotional, or cognitive conditions that affect students' ability to learn. We believe that these factors have not yet been fully addressed in educational policy. Further, since most of this lies outside the child, a new organizing framework for policy in education that can move us beyond the disability construct without sacrificing needed supports and services for students is warranted.

This argument also requires a new way of thinking about human development and social patterns that have segregated students in special education. How students come to know what they want and how they participate in determining their future with their families and school personnel are at the heart and start of the issue. It also calls into question who is to serve them, how will they be served, and the role they and their families play in determining what services are needed and desired to support their becoming the persons they seek to be.

Since learning is highly individual and challenging at different times and for different reasons in human development, children may need assistance to benefit from the social and cognitive opportunities presented by schools. Assistance for learners may necessitate inquiry into the learning schemata for individual children and innovative approaches to instructional or behavioral pedagogy to promote development and the learning of new capabilities. Since all children and youth have this common need, we believe it is neither necessary nor desirable to view the need for assistance as pathological or intrinsic to the child, or as chronic and/or intractable. Rather we believe that learning challenges can be thought of as questions of how to educate each child and facilitate his or her progress within a given social and curricular context and at a given moment in time. The educational challenge is to present opportunities for professionals with a variety of expertise to pool their knowledge and skills so as to find unique solutions to the unique challenges individual children bring to education.

What if we stop asking whether or not a given child has a disability and instead start asking what a child needs to succeed educationally in light of his or her post-school goals? As special educators, parents, advocates, and professionals coalesced to prepare testimony for FAPE in 1975, Burrello and colleagues (Burrello, Tracy, & Schultz, 1973) argued that a new conceptualization for special education, described as *experimental education*, better addressed the promise of the law than did creation of a second system of education. They argued that special education was not intended to take responsibility for individual students away from general education and that the burden of labeling children for eligibility should be avoided (Mercer, 1973). Students with disabilities, they argued, should not lose the benefits of membership as well as opportunities to learn with and from their typical peers who might be key members of their social network in adulthood (Brown-Chidsey & Steege, 2005). Burrello and colleagues also argued that the potential usefulness of special education rested in determining how and why students learn the way they do and under what conditions they can learn to be independent, self-sustaining adults who work, play, and participate in the community—or, in Nussbaum's terms, under what conditions they can experience and be recognized as having human capability.

In summary, we believe that special education should be reconceptualized as a dynamic response system that is fully embedded within general education. Within this reconceptualization, the expertise of special educators is available to all children, based on their needs at a particular point in time. The services provided within this system are open-ended and may be provided in a variety of ways ranging from consultation to direct instruction, but a key assumption is that children will flow in and out of these services according to their support needs at particular points in time or curricular contexts. While all school personnel as well as family members might provide solutions to a child's contemporaneous learning challenges, the unique contribution of special educators would be that of what Burrello and colleagues termed *experimental education*. That is, special educators would bring their pedagogical expertise to bear by using data to adapt or develop approaches that are unique to the instructional context, assessing their effectiveness in helping a child progress, and making decisions about the efficacy of the approach based on the child's response. This process is displayed in Figure 1.1 and

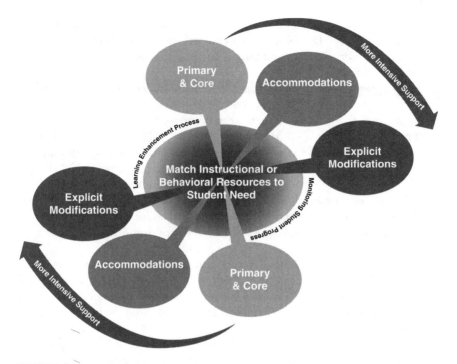

FIGURE 1.1

reflects in dynamic fashion the constant flow of data to indicate what is working and not working.

As illustrated by Figure 1.1, assistance to students and teachers may vary given the intensity of support needed to provide instructional and behavior support. The figure suggests how the team support moves from a single classroom teacher to collaborative intervention efforts starting with and based in a typical classroom with both accommodations and more explicit modifications being added as necessary to support all students including those with the most significant needs. While the process is similar to that involved in RtI, there are two distinguishing characteristics. First, there are no "tiers" of intervention but, rather, the use of data to determine what works for an individual child at a particular point in time. Second, we envision the process to be part of a normalized regular education system that allows children to freely move in and out of the purview of specialized expertise without the threat of being perceived or treated as a "tier 1, 2, or 3 child." The most important similarity to RtI would be the ongoing interactions of *ad hoc* problem-solving teams, consisting of professionals, family members, or others who might provide or implement recommendations for ensuring that children learn.

Beyond this, we offer some guiding principles and values for how such a reconceptualized system of special education might be constituted, including:

1. Education has unitary purposes that might result in different outcomes for different students. Desirable outcomes reflect student and family preferences, natural environments, and cultures. Education is responsible for all students and all services.

2. At any given point in time, some teachers and students will need assistance to ensure access to meaningful content, relevant curriculum, and innovative approaches to pedagogy. It is neither necessary nor desirable to view the need for assistance as chronic, intrinsic to the child, or intractable. Rather, educational challenges present opportunities for professionals with differing expertise to pool their knowledge so as to solve problems. The challenge, then, is to identify what configurations of expertise, time, and accommodations and/or modifications need to be in place so that the student can learn developmentally appropriate and culturally relevant social and academic concepts and to provide instruction that is responsive to student progress in learning.

3. Problem-solving approaches demand creative solutions that may or may not yet be identified. The focus of problem-solving teams should be on implementing research-based practices, adapting these practices, and/or creating new practices—to "try another way," and to find group or individual solutions for learning challenges.

4. The contributions of students and families should be acknowledged, and they should have full membership in problem-solving teams.

5. Special educators, as well as all other educational personnel, would play a critical role in bringing expertise to problem-solving teams. Ideal problem-solving teams would include individuals with expertise in social skills development, curriculum, pedagogy, and school and classroom ecology.

6. A primary role for special educators would be to serve as "innovative educators" who are prepared to work toward desired goals first, and then, within problem-solving teams to devise and help implement creative responses to individual student and teacher needs.

7. Problem-solving teams are best viewed as groups of educators who convene on an ad hoc basis, and with *ad hoc* membership who come together because of their knowledge of particular strategies to address unique student needs for a limited time period.

8. The formal structures and processes of what is currently known as special education would no longer be necessary; however, the need for special education would continue:

    - IDEA's guarantee of a free and appropriate public education would continue.
    - Processes such as eligibility determination would no longer be necessary. Every child would have access to services and a problem-solving team for assistance in long- or short-term problems.
    - The strategies derived from service providers and problem-solving teams would be individualized but would be challenging, coherent, and

reflect access to the general education curriculum as well as the child's and family's preferences and applicability in natural environments.

- Services/recommendations provided by a service provider and a problem-solving team would be time-limited and would be delivered in general education environments.
- The problem-solving process together with frequent informal and formal assessment processes (state or national assessments; end-of-course assessments) would replace triannual evaluations.
- All children, including those with the most significant support needs, would be served in their neighborhood schools and in proportion to their theoretical incidence in the general population.
- A hold-harmless approach to funding special education would be instituted to prevent sudden gaps in state/federal support. Such an approach might involve providing every school with funds that would normally be available if 13% of its children had disabilities. The percentage allocated for incidental benefit in IDEA would expand from 15% to 100%, with some building-level discretion as to use, based on the assumption that all children would at some point need assistance from problem-solving teams. Special education funding streams would be available only to LEAs (Local Education Agencies) and schools that serve all of their students.
- The preparation of both general and special educators would need to include foci on specific areas of expertise (i.e., curriculum, social integration and behavior, career preparation, longitudinal planning, and instruction). While special educators would need advanced skills in instructional adaptations and modifications, general education teachers would, likewise, need an expanded repertoire of curricular and instructional knowledge and skills. All educators would need both practical experience and formal preparation for participation in problem-solving teams.

Shifting From a Narrowed Vision of What Children Should Learn to a Critical Pedagogy

A fundamental design principle, the principle of relevance, revolves around the issue of school purpose. Why guarantee the provision of K-12 education for any child? If goals for student learning need to change for individual students, what is the goal that informs that change? While the goals of literacy and numeracy, in some form, associated with NCLB are important to achieving human capabilities and agency, implementation of standards-based reform has too often been associated with narrowing and decontextualizing curriculum as well as neglecting the social dimensions of education. The aim of standards-based reform—to hold high expectations for all students, to align curriculum and instruction with standards that reflect these expectations, and to hold schools accountable for student progress in meeting these standards—held promise for focusing attention on the learning needs of groups of students who are typically disenfranchised from education, or worse, stereotypically blamed for their own academic failures. Whether by intent or neglect, implementation of the policy has often taken a perverse turn in the form of the belief that standards define the boundaries of curriculum and that only those instructional foci and practices that produce success on assessments associated with the standards are valued. Thus, connections between academic instruction and its applications to real-world problems may be lost, and opportunities for critical discourse between teachers and students may be put aside to ensure that time is devoted to skill acquisition that produces positive assessment results. Likewise, while the use of assessment data to identify contextual barriers to learning holds the potential for closing gaps in learning, the current accountability system operates as if students' lives and learning processes end with high school. Paradoxically, while the human capital agenda, described earlier, has been a foundational argument for standards-based reform, efforts to assess post-school success in terms of employment, community participation, relationships, leisure activities, continued learning, agency, or general life satisfaction are minimal and are not used as a tool for accountability. Thus, the pedagogy designed to focus on outcomes rather than inputs (in this case K–12 education) largely neglects accountability for what it aims to achieve.

Consistent with a human development and capabilities approach, we argue for explicitly broadening the aims of education to incorporate not only literacy and numeracy goals but also their application to improving society. If access to literature is, for example, the goal, then education should open to students its expository and/or artistic intent and should fully contextualize its arguments and symbolism within the social, philosophical, moral, or political arguments it was intended to expose and should encourage interpretation, reinterpretation, and integration into current social, philosophical, and/or political contexts. This means that educators would be released from what may now be a piecemeal approach to literary analysis that happens to be aligned with an assessment and would empower students to think and act in ways that may reinforce or disrupt social norms. The teacher's role, in this conception, is to encourage students' multiple perspectives and to assist every student—regardless of varying needs—to find contradictory or complimentary relevance to his or her life. Likewise, if mathematics is the goal of education, educators might focus, in natural settings, on a range of applications from price comparisons (number recognition and numeration) to calculation of the costs of Annual Percentage Rates on credit purchases.

Walker (2009) draws on the work of Freire to argue for a critical and humanizing pedagogy. She states, "we want students to experience democracy and equality in their learning experience, not inequality or injustice" (p. 334). Further she reminds us that what is taught, while important, must be accompanied by equal consideration of who is teaching, who is being taught, and how they are being taught. Walker refers to Freire (1970, 1985), who envisioned pedagogy as a more humanizing endeavor. The educator's responsibility is to fully engage the learner in the constructing and coconstructing of his or her knowledge. Becoming in the world occurs through engagement of the world and is potentially a vehicle to transform the world. "This means that history, participation, and mutual engagement, connecting experiences to the learning encounter and a process of inquiry, critical dialogue, and dissent might ensue" (Walker, 2009, p. 336). Through praxis, individuals realize their full humanity. Freire advocates an interrogation of the powerful and, in education, an examination of how power is used to oppress and dominate through selection and sorting mechanisms that control access to the good life.

We recognize the challenges inherent in shifting the focus of education to such a critical pedagogy—particularly for students with significant intellectual disabilities, but we believe that critical pedagogy holds the promise of reciprocal benefit for all students, including those with disabilities. As described by Nussbaum, differences matter—thus, we don't negate the concept of disability or difference of any kind but rather acknowledge the different perspectives and contributions that derive from disability, race, or language difference as essential voices within democracy. From this perspective, critical pedagogy entails critiquing the hegemonic belief in "normalcy," celebrating difference, and building community through praxis.

Schools as Open Systems Rather Than Closed Systems

If schools are to shift toward a critical pedagogy, we believe that, as Gilborn and Youdell (2000) suggest, the basic "architecture" of schools must likewise change. Historically, the nature of the social contract between citizens and schools is that parents have entrusted and given over authority for educating their children to the schools and expert educators in return for the investment of tax dollars. Thus, at least hypothetically, schools and families interact in much the same way that citizens commission other local bureaucracies such as fire and police departments to perform services that are more easily and efficiently provided through a collective effort. Paradoxically, while school systems are enfranchised to operate more or less independently under the direction of expert educators, their role as a universal access point for families has been used, politically, as a method for enacting social change. From vaccination requirements to civil rights, the schools have been the primary, if not the only, lever for policy implementation (Wells, 2009).

While schools have served as formal levers for macro-level social policy, their roles in communities have been comparatively minimal. Our contention is that schools have as their purpose "to create a public" (Postman, 1995), and, thus, must play a key role in the infrastructure of their communities. To do so, schools must open their doors in more than symbolic ways to families, businesses, and other community members so that reciprocal relationships are developed. A number of excellent models for such relationships exist, such as Full-Service Schools (Dryfoos, 1994). Currently, critical instructional resources and teaching opportunities are wasted by failure to engage community members and families in educating children, in pursuing adult education, in learning parenting skills, or in being connected to primary social, health, or mental health services. While parents are still blamed for lack of interest when they miss parent-teacher conferences or Individualized Educational Plan, IEP meetings, schools often operate in a nonwelcoming fashion and provide only token opportunities for family participation (Sailor et al., 1996).

Shifting Accountability From a Legalistic and Policy Frame to a Moral and Ethical Frame

As discussed earlier, we believe the aim of standards-based reform falls somewhat short of its aim toward meaningful outcomes because of implementation focused on narrowed academic aims within K–12 education and because of its neglect of how individuals ultimately use education to improve their lives as participating citizens. Skrtic (1991) proposes a broader framework for accountability in education that is based on a moral and ethical framework. This framework shifts the emphasis of accountability from *legal compliance*, consistent with a critical structuralist and functionalist view of the means and ends of schooling, to emphasis on *morality and ethics*, consistent with a critical humanist view. Whereas legal compliance depends on a bureaucratic infrastructure and demands regularity and transparency, moral and ethical compliance depends on political and discursive activity that is uncertain and interpretivist in nature. Within this framework, one might argue that schools are ethically accountable for educating all children and morally accountable for producing citizens who live, work, and recreate as full participants in society. We believe that exploration of new frameworks for accountability is essential to achieving policy maturation.

Where Do We Go From Here?

In this chapter, we have set forth a broad agenda for a critical reconceptualization of special education, based on our vision for unifying educational systems. At the heart of this agenda is the notion that special education might better be viewed as *experimental* or *innovative education* than as a separate bureaucracy that serves a few children who are deemed eligible for its services and who are all too often disenfranchised from full membership because of their very eligibility. Realization of this agenda depends on several shifts in perspective as to the purposes of education, the nature of curriculum and pedagogy, the relationship of schools to their families and communities, and models for accountability. We recognize that this is not a modest agenda, but we believe that it is both timely, in view of the pending reauthorization of ESEA, and essential if we are to maintain the current body of expertise that special educators can bring to bear on solving educational challenges. We also believe that there is a moral imperative both to ensure full participation, agency, and capabilities of children and adults with disabilities and to engage them and their peers in critical discourse aimed at removing social barriers and creating social bridges to full participation.

As we have suggested in this chapter, several promising approaches to reconceptualizing special education already exist. In Chapter Two of Part One of the book, Wayne Sailor and Leonard Burrello describe progress in whole-school reform that has been achieved through integrating special education and general education systems of support and organizing all educational interventions under behavioral and academic response to intervention. In doing so, Sailor and Burrello provide a new perspective on how schools are organized as democratic, data-driven, problem-solving systems.

As discussed earlier, we believe that the guarantees of P.L. 94-142 and its subsequent reauthorizations as IDEA—the guarantee of a Free Appropriate Public Education for all children with disabilities—must be upheld. At the same time, the policy landscape built on standards-based reform is currently shifting to turnaround school concepts, or what Richard Riley referred to as "existence-proofs" of school excellence (Riley, 2005). Likewise, "systems change" as a strategy for policy implementation appears to be overshadowed by what we would call *systems disruption*. Efforts to weaken the teachers' unions or change their agenda, to promote charter schools, and to promote alternative routes for teacher preparation are examples of such systems disruption. We are convinced that this changing policy environment provides both the context and the urgent need to reconceptualize special education policy.

Part Two of the book provides a legal and fiscal framework for enacting a unified system. In Chapter Three, Carl Lashley discusses the possibilities and promise of unifying systems so as to reframe educational policy in terms of human capability. Shana Haines and Rud Turnbull, in Chapter Four, provide a legal perspective of the possibilities and barriers to our thinking that ensures both advocacy and due process for the concerns of parents and providers alike. As discussed earlier, during and after the transition to a reconceptualized form of special education, it will be critical to ensure that IDEA funds continue to be available to provide specialized supports. The need to rethink special education funding is already evident, in fact, as the population of children identified for special education services diminishes as a result of RtI implementation. In Chapter Five, Anthony Rolle, Pakethia Harris, and Leonard Burrello discuss how IDEA funding patterns might change to ensure continuity of services for children who need them.

Part Three of the text is devoted to addressing the realities of practice within a unified system of education. In Chapter Six, Todd Gravois provides a vision for a more responsive and aligned service delivery system that will be essential in a unified system. Diane Ryndak, Ann-Marie Orlando, and Debra Duran describe in Chapter Seven the moral imperative and practical strategies for providing full membership and participation for students with significant disabilities. Mary Morningstar, Gregory Knollman, Sarah Semon, and Jeannie Kleinhammer-Tramill provide a model for the benefit of school/community partnerships in the transition process for all students and discuss how educational accountability systems might be expanded to include a broad range of postschool outcomes.

Part Four of the book focuses on leading diversity within a unified system. Julia White brings a critical disabilities studies perspective to this challenge in Chapter Nine. In Chapter Ten, Amy L-M. Toson and Elise Frattura expand our interpretation of a human capabilities approach particularly with regard to district leadership and its enactment. Elizabeth Kozleski, Alfredo Artiles, and Lisa Lacy deconstruct the role that systems plan in marginalizing students who are labeled as different and proceed to illustrate how and in what ways that happens, calling for a change in policy and practice in Chapter Eleven.

The final part, Chapter Twelve, of the book provides the editors' perspective on unifying educational systems and human capability. While public law ensuring free and appropriate public education for children and youth with disabilities has existed for 35 years, we see little evidence of policy maturation. That is, special education services are not yet universally provided under ideal circumstances in that many children still attend special schools or are placed for all or part of the day in special classes. Many students with IEPs are excluded from standards-based accountability systems and, thus, for all intents and purposes, *don't count* in the current context. Many families are still told that their children must fit existing services rather than that educators will work with them to meet their child's needs. School districts and states operate with a careful eye toward compliance to the letter of the law rather than its promise, and current policy and litigative history provide little room for shifting the focus to quality of services, as might be expected in a mature policy environment. These contexts create an urgency about the need to reconceptualize special education in the form of unified policy systems and day-to-day operating practices in the classroom.

References

Akire, S., & Deneulin, S. (2009). The human capabilities approach. In S. Deneulin with Lida Shahani (eds). *An Introduction to Human Development and Capability Approach*. Londan: Earthscan.

Amos, P.A. (2004). New considerations in the prevention of aversives, restraint, and seclusion: Incorporating the role of relationships into an ecological perspective. *Research and Practice for Persons with Severe Disabilities, 29*(4), 263–272.

Apple, M. (2006). *Educating the "right" way: Markets, standards, god, and inequality*. New York: Taylor & Francis.

Black, W., & Burrello, L.C. (2010). Towards the cultivation of full membership in schools. *Journal of Ethics and Values in Educational Administration, 11*(2).

Brown-Chidsey, R., & Steege, M.W. (2005). Response to intervention: Principles and strategies for effective practice. In W. Merrell (Ed.), *The Guilford practical intervention in the schools series*. New York: Guilford Press.

Burrello, L.C., Lashley, C., & Beatty, E.E. (2001). *Educating all students together*. Thousand Oaks, CA: Corwin Press.

Burrello, L.C., Tracy, M.L., & Schultz, E.W. (1973). Special education as experimental education: A new conceptualization. *Exceptional Children, 40*(1), 29–31.

Connor, D., & Ferri, B. (2007, January). The conflict within: Resistance to inclusion and other paradoxes in special education. *Disability & Society, 22*(1), 63–77.

Dryfoos, J.G. (1994). *Full-service schools: A revolution in health and social services for children, youth, and families.* San Francisco, CA: Jossey Bass.

Eber, L., Hyde, K., Rose, J., Breen, K., McDonald, D., & Lewandowski, H. (2009). Completing the continuum of schoolwide positive behavior support: Wraparound as a tertiary-level intervention. In W. Sailor, G. Dunlap, & R. Horner (Eds.), *Handbook of positive behavior support* (pp. 671–703). New York: Springer.

Friere, P. (1970). *Pedagogy of the oppressed.* New York: Herder & Herder.

Friere, P. (1985). *The politics of education.* Westport, CT: Bergin & Garvey Publishers, Inc.

Gilborn, D., & Youdell, D. (2000). *Rationing education: Policy, practice, reform, and equity.* Buckingham: Open University Press.

Government Accounting Office. (2003). *Special education: Clearer guidance would enhance implementation of federal disciplinary provisions.* (Publication No. 03–550). Washington, DC: Author.

Hall, S.L. (2008). *Implementing response to intervention.* Thousand Oaks, CA: Corwin Press.

Individuals With Disabilities Education Act Amendments of 2004, P.L. 20 U.S.C. § 1400 *et seq.*

Kirkpatrick, P. (1994). Triple jeopardy: Disability, race, and poverty in America. *Poverty and Race, 3*(3), 1–2, 8.

Kleinhammer-Tramill, P.J., Tramill, J.L., & Brace, H. (2010). Contexts, funding history, and implications for evaluating the Office of Special Education Program's investment in personnel preparation. *Journal of Special Education, 43*(4), 195–205.

Lashley, C. (1994). Criticizing special education as a social practice. *Special Education Leadership Review, 2*(1), 40–58.

Mellard, D. F., & Patterson, M.B. (2008). Contrasting adult literacy learners with and without specific learning disabilities. *Remedial and Special Education, 29*(3): 133–144.

Morningstar, M., Kleinhammer-Tramill, P.J., & Lattin, D. (1999). Using successful models of student-centered transition planning and services for adolescents with disabilities. *Focus on Exceptional Children, 31*(9), 1–19.

NCEE (National Commission on Excellence in Education). (1983). *A nation at risk: The Imperative for educational reform.* Portland, OR: USA Research.

Nussbaum, M.C. (2006). *Frontiers of justice: Disability, nationality, and species membership.* Cambridge, MA: Harvard University Press.

Postman, N. (1995). *The end of education: Redefining the value of school.* New York: Knopf.

(2007). *Problem -based learning handbook.* Novato, CA: Buck Educational Institute.

Rogoff, B. (2003). *The cultural nature of human development.* New York: Oxford University Press.

Riley, R. (2005). Reflections on Goals 2000. *Teachers College Record,* 96(3), 380–388.

Sailor, W., Kleinhammer-Tramill, J., Skrtic, T., & Oas, B.K. (1996). Family participation in New Community Schools. In G.H.S. Singer, L.E. Powers, & A.L. Olson (Eds.), *Redefining family support: Innovations in public–private partnerships* (pp. 313–332). Baltimore: Paul H. Brookes.

Sarason, S., & Doris, J. (1979). *Educational handicap, public policy making, and social history.* New York: Free Press.

Sen, A.K. (1985). Well-being agency and freedom: The Dewey Lectures 1984, *Journal of Philosophy, 82*(4), 169–221.

Sen, A. (1992). *Inequality reexamined*. Oxford: Oxford University Press.

Skrtic, T.M. (1991). *Behind special education: A critical analysis of professional culture and school organization*. Denver, CO: Love.

Skrtic, T.M. (2005). A political economy of learning disabilities. *Learning Disabilities Quarterly, 28*(2), 149–155.

Slee, R. (2009). Inclusive school as a means and end of education. In L. Florian (Ed.), *The Sage handbook of special education* (pp. 160–170). Thousands Oaks, CA: Sage.

Smith, M. S., & Scoll, B. (1995). The Clinton human capital agenda. *Teachers College Record, 96*(3), 389–404.

Tyack, D.B., & Hansot, E. (1982). *Managers of virtue: Public school leadership in America, 1820–1980*. New York: Basic Books.

U.S. Department of Education. (2010). *Elementary and secondary education: A blueprint for reform*. Retrieved from http://www2.ed.gov/policy/elsec/leg/blueprint/publication toc.html

Walker, M. (2009). Teaching the human development and capability approach: Some pedagogical implications. In S. Deneulin and L. Shahani (Eds.), An introduction to the human development and capabilities approach: Freedom and agency. London: Earthscan, Dunstan House.

Wells, A.S. (2009). "Our children's burden": A history of federal education policies that ask (now require) our public schools to solve societal inequality. In M.A. Rebell and J.R. Wolff (eds.), NCLB at the Crossroads: Reexamining the Federal Effort to Close the Achievement Gap. New York: Teachers College, Columbia University.

Zhang, D. (2006). Parent practices in facilitating self-determination skills: The influences of culture, socioeconomic status, and children's special education status. *Research and Practice for Persons with Severe Disabilities, 30*, 154–162.

2

SHIFTING PERSPECTIVE TO FRAME DISABILITY POLICY

Wayne Sailor and Leonard C. Burrello

We have argued in Chapter One that a human development and capabilities perspective is more useful not only to replace what has been largely a human rights and advocacy approach but to provide insights into what might constitute a new practice, a social justice practice. As a social justice practice, a human capabilities approach offers guidance about how we conceptualize our practice as professionals in relation to students, families, and staff. For example, Sailor (2009) argues for a shifting policy context away from a "handicapped" or disability frame toward determining the best instructional resource matches needed to achieve valued individual student goals at the highest level for all students regardless of reasons for needing extra supports and/or services. The shift can occur through a combination of high-quality and appropriate curriculum that connects students to their own learning and instruction, augmented by specialized supports as needed. Education is not about doing something to others but about helping individuals find their human potential; their unique pathways to their aspirations in a diverse historical-social-political-economic context. "What I think we know so far is that any new frame on education resource need-match policy will likely move away from an exclusive focus on various limiting characteristics of the individual, in favor of greater attention to the ecology of the individual's learning situation and life circumstances" (p. 31). Since most of these factors lie outside the child, a new organizing framework for policy in education that can move us beyond the disability construct seems timely and necessary.

Whatever the human development and capabilities that lie within a student's repertoire, our policy statements and praxis need to exercise and perhaps embrace the student's and his or her family's valued goals. Learning results from enhancing current competence through a rich and diverse curriculum and the process of effective instruction. Bernstein's (2000) concept of confidence applies, for example, and includes staff as well as students increasing their capacity to act independently with assurance that they can pursue desired goals. Thus confidence arises from increased functioning and increased belief in the efficacy of one's work in pursuit of mutual (i.e., teacher- and student-designed) goals.

Inclusion here is defined as the right to participation in the age-appropriate academic and social curriculum offered to any student in the school and community. It requires recognition that learning occurs in reciprocity with one's peers and is best accomplished when students requiring extra supports and services are represented in accordance with their natural proportion (i.e., usually about 10%) in school, class, and community settings (Brown-Chidsey & Steege, 2005). Anytime, Bernstein argues, you overload a system, "it spits you out." The natural ecology of the class, school, and community requires balance and proportion as the community pursues goals for all of its members. He argues from a sociological perspective that individual rights include enhancement of confidence, social inclusion, and participation. In Bernstein's model, participation has the most overlap with Nussbaum's (2006) view that a human development and capabilities approach is largely a social justice phenomenon. Participation engages the community in a discourse about equality and equity. Do persons with disproportionate needs (i.e., physical, emotional, and/or cognitive conditions that may affect their education or progress through adulthood) deserve disproportionate resources to be as successful as possible in the school and community? The question is loaded with values considerations that policy makers must address in order to pursue a policy and funding structure that increases levels of independence, offering meaningful supports when needed. The social justice discourse is not based upon the proportionality argument alone but in seeing in the individual the inherent value of becoming all that the person aspires to be.

Four Policy Education Initiatives

Since the initial passage of Public Law 94-142 in 1975, there have been four special education policy initiatives that have attempted to stem or reverse the movement of the praxis away from general education. Each of these special education initiatives was largely needed then, as well as now, in order to obtain the commitment of general educators to consider educating labeled students in general education classrooms and other integrated settings in the schools that they would attend if they were not so labeled.

The four initiatives were:

1. The Regular Education In-service Projects (REGI)—The Regular Education In-service Initiative existed largely as a personnel preparation funding program designed to train educational professionals to learn to work with "disabled" populations across the mild disability spectrum for much of the school day in typical classrooms.

2. The Regular Education Preservice Grants (REGP)—These dean's grants targeted teacher preparation programs in universities and colleges of education for support in educating general education teachers with prerequisite skills to effectively serve students with disabilities in the general education classroom.

3. The Regular Education Initiative (REI)—Here an inclusive learning philosophy was promoted as a means to reintegrate all students across the disability spectrum into general education classrooms. This initiative added students with more "severe" disabilities into the mix of students with learning disabilities originally tagged for the first time in the REGI initiative.

4. The Response to Intervention Initiative (RtI)—The RtI initiative was added in 2004 legislation. The "standard protocol" form of RtI serves as a means of prevention, to determine if a failing student is more a casualty of poor or insufficient classroom instruction that can be addressed through providing access to intensified levels of instruction rather than having a "disability" that qualifies the student for services under the Individuals with Disability Education Act (IDEA). A broader concept of "problem solving" or a "schoolwide" form of RtI (cf. Sailor, 2009) creates systems of assessment designed to measure student response to classroom instruction (and other interventions) for any student falling below benchmark performance in the grade level curriculum. It also provides two additional levels of increasingly intensive support for students failing to respond to grade-level "interventions" provided to all students. Under schoolwide RtI increasingly also referred to as multi-tiered systems of support (MTSS), protocols and problem-solving strategies are provided to assist teachers in the redesign of more successful instructional processes and in the provision of larger amounts of more intensive support if needed.

Each of these four initiatives was designed to serve students who require additional supports and services from within a "continuum of services structure" codified in P.L. 94-142 (IDEA) and maintained in all the legislation through today. The first three have clearly failed and the fourth, RtI, at least the "standard protocol" special education version, still depends upon securing "parallel" educational resources tied to the disability construct that are subject to the statutory "continuum of services" and "least restrictive environment (LRE)" provisions that drive the separate educational system (Fuchs & Fuchs, 1993; Gersten & Woodward, 1990; Kleinhammer-Trammill, 2003; McKinney & Hocutt, 1998; Pugach & Sapon-Shevin, 1987; Slavin, 1990).

This continuum of services paradigm is rooted in the deficit thinking of the 1950s, maintained by professionals and parents to protect both a way of preserving autonomous practices (with little accountability) and to safeguard students from a larger and impersonal system of educational opportunities and standards. It has worked in opposition to each of the failed initiatives above and is what Robert Fritz (1999) calls structural tension. He argues if a system cannot resolve the structural tension between opposing forces, the system will oscillate forward and backward like a rocking chair but never move toward the desired end result: in this case, full participation in the school community. Fritz (1999) goes on to suggest that establishment of purposes and principles or priorities helps set the order of values to be pursued. The development of facilitating structures then follows.

Special Education and Its Moral Imperative

The Principle of Full Class Membership and Ways to Measure Participation

What if we stop asking whether or not a given child has a disability and instead start asking, what does a child need to succeed educationally? Burrello, Tracy, and Schultz (1973) argued more than three decades ago that unless the essential design principle that *general education is as responsible for the education of students with disabilities as it is for other students* is upheld, then a separate class of students and their families would become marginalized in some significant ways that would clearly impact their academic, personal, and social growth and, ultimately, their postschool success. These students would forever be doomed within "the continuum of services paradigm" to receive a second-class education; their postschool outcomes would suffer, and they would remain a perpetual outcast group of individuals in need of public life support for their entire private lives. Students with disabilities, they argued, should not lose the benefits of membership as well as opportunities to learn with and from their typical peers who might be key members of their support system into adulthood (Certo et al., 2008; Black, Grant, & Burrello, 2010). Burrello, Tracy, and Schultz (1973) also argued that a proper role for special education was to determine how and why students learn the way they do and under what conditions they learn to be independent, self-sustaining adults who work, play, and participate in the community without continuous adult paid supervision.

Data on student achievement today bear out the prediction that students with special needs would become a permanent underclass (Connor & Ferri, 2007; Government Accounting Office (GAO), 2003). This design principle or value is connected to an essential moral issue: unless all students have equal membership in schools they will suffer incalculable harm. Under the guise of "specialness" tied to the construct of disability, a construct that locates educational problems solely within the individual, we have created an unjust and unfair parallel system of programs and services that results in less efficacious outcomes than those realized by students in the general education system. Slee (2009) contends that:

> the regular school/special school (regular student or *class;* special student or *class; or resource room*) binaries deflect from the epistemic weight of normality and abnormality. Epistemology distributes status and power unevenly: some are in, some others will always be others. (p. 164)

Membership in a public school is a fundamental right or, as Bernstein (2000) offers, a pedagogical right. It implies we're all equal and deserving of full membership and participation regardless of who we are. This seems to us to apply to any child as secured by Public Law 94-142 in 1975. While we all want to seem "more the same than different," the differences in what and how we learn are important and need to be recognized and accommodated. Black, Grant, and Burrello (2010) discuss how cultural redesign is now a key dimension of what school leaders do. They use resources to guarantee full membership for all students. According to Anderson (2009), a key structural dynamic today is that standards-based accountability reduces variability. Grade-level standards are often too gross a metric to measure growth of students who require more time and alternative instructional conditions within classrooms to learn what is valued and desired. One administrator remarked, "In our system of 68,000 students we have 1,000 elementary students still failing to learn to read by fifth grade. We are punishing them and their teachers as failures but the system is failing them."

A human capabilities approach supports the concept of full membership. All children need to be seen to be as much a member of the community as any other child. When the child enters the community school that he or she should attend, the first question should be what can he or she do and what is next? What new capability is valued and desired? The first measure of membership is how will the child be accepted as a member of the community, and how will we enhance his or her learning by emphasizing what is valued and desired? Where and how the child learns what is needed to achieve the valued or desired capability is influenced by whom the child interacts with. If a child enters school with communication as a goal, a rich and abundant source of language models might be a key resource for learning that capability. We should be held accountable as educators for arranging the conditions for that new capability to be enhanced. We always assume some capacity is there. One of us remembers a high school Spanish teacher who said to his special education colleagues, "We do not need a sixteen-page referral form to inform us about each child who enters our classes. What is needed is a one-page form that tells us what the child can do. Then we can begin to determine how to proceed with him."

The Principle of Relevance

Another design principle, the *principle of relevance*, revolves around the purposes and goals to be pursued for each individual and the good of the collective community. Why guarantee the provision of K–12 education for any child? If goals for student learning need to change for individual students, what are the conditions that inform that change? Proximately, from a human capabilities approach, what goals need to be established that increase the child's freedom to function, with more freedom to pursue new capabilities? More distally, we contend that the process should be focused on postschool success. Can a student enter college prepared to compete successfully in a more advanced curriculum of his or her own choosing? Can a student enter the workforce with a high school education and earn at least the minimum wage and secure the benefits provided by his or her employer? Can the student enter the military and function successfully? Can the student live independently, or at least interdependently, having meaningful social relations with typical peers? Whatever the valued distal goals, they require consideration in the present. For in the present, the very human relationships that are developed become part of the new capabilities that some students may need to support those goals in the longer term. The nature of the social purposes of education, we believe, include learning to be a compassionate and caring member of one's community committed to the welfare of all of its members.

Standards-based reform, a continuing federal policy initiative based upon annual grade-level quantitative assessments, easily misses the full range of outcomes that we ought to be pursuing when we consider all students' postschool success. An appropriate curriculum and instructional procedures and assessments for all students, not just students with special needs, should be guided, at least in part, by student interest (Sailor, 2009). Starratt (2009) notes that students need to believe that what they study is important and so compelling that they connect with it in a meaningful and personal way. Not everyone is likely to choose to enter a two-year college or a four-year institution of higher education. Some students should be provided a curriculum that has work or military service as a more proximate goal. For some, a job that enables them to achieve independence and earn sustenance is a desirable and positive postschool outcome.

Structural Flaws in Contemporary Educational Policy

Four structural flaws are worthy of consideration in the context of this chapter. The first structural flaw is that school improvement efforts embodied in the four policy initiatives discussed above have largely failed to consider the significance of individual school and district cultures and their values as reflected by their respective professional communities. Further, they have failed as well to consider the goals of the larger community for the districts' schools and their operations. Sarason (1971) reflected in his book *The Process of Change and the Culture of Schools* that unless the "program regularities" of schooling are open to improvement, schools will largely continue to be impervious to change. Unless, for example, a school's professional community collectively finds ways to expand its capacity to serve students no matter what levels and intensity of support are required, it will essentially co-opt any change initiative and continue to maintain the status quo. It will merely embrace the change initiative symbolically because of the political necessity of district or state mandates, but change will not be sustained (Skrtic, 2005). Schools will continue to create separate programs to insulate the whole from its less successful parts. It has often been argued that separate, parallel systems afford a more efficient and cheaper way to run schools, but as a growing body of research indicates, it is not a way to effectively prepare all students for postschool success.

A second flaw is revealed when separate structures are created for a common goal, in this case, education. Separate programs tend ultimately to pursue separate purposes and aims. Educators, for example, who are identified with special education generally lose perspective and social currency with their general education peers since they consider the work of grade-level teachers as distinct and not comparable to their own work. Conversely, general education teachers come to view children with special needs as the responsibility of special educators, the inevitable result of binary thinking and practice as we know it.

A third structural flaw arises from the fact that the parallel supportive services system is itself fractionated and largely guided by federal policy that again does not consider the unique culture and context of individual districts or schools. Special education and other supportive services are largely implemented by categorically trained specialists with their own subcultures, standards, rules, and regulations that collectively fail to embrace and enhance a holistic view of the student and family within the context of the school and community (Lawson & Sailor, 2000).

A fourth structural flaw arises from the fact that much of special education innovation has been focused lately on micro-technical improvements and changes. As noted by Berman (1980), technical or programmatic change requires stability of leadership, clarity and constancy of purpose, low levels of conflict between change agents and implementers, and a clear core technology to be present in order to make the changes stick. These conditions have been absent in the evolution of special services since 1975. Special education is contested terrain and continues to strain the systems of response to any initiative that requires the general system to grow and develop new capacity to serve all students more effectively, including students with extensive special support needs.

Ultimately, all systems change initiatives integrating general and special education are doomed to fail unless the school board, superintendent, principals, and key central staff believe in and are committed to a higher moral purpose (Fullan, 1991; Sergiovanni, 1992). This moral purpose assumes that (1) all students deserve equal membership in schools; (2) schools are committed to educate their communities to garner support for change; and (3) schools are committed to take steps to put into place infrastructure, resources, and assessments directed to differentiating goals and practices for individual students that match their instructional or behavioral needs.

In our view, any initiative to succeed where the others have failed requires (1) school leadership, both principal and teachers, to be committed to a value-guided vision of the district focused on supporting any student who needs a customized instructional or behavioral match to be successful academically and socially; (2) a community committed to partner with the school district to do whatever it takes for each student to be successful academically and socially (Lawson & Sailor, 2000); (3) leadership that is committed to collaborative rather than separate instruction; and (4) leadership that is committed to bring coherence to curriculum, instruction, and assessments through ongoing formative processes that differentiate and reformulate instruction while providing an instructional match of needed supports and services to facilitate student learning (Sailor, 2009).

A Theory of Change

Paul Curtis (2009), a curriculum architect of New Tech Network of high schools, argues for a holistic community to be developed using the principles of backward design (Wiggins & McTigue, 2005) and project-based learning (Buck Educational Institute, 2007). Unless the total community is brought together to consider its vision and values according to this perspective, it cannot collectively discover the principles and purposes that will ultimately guide its work. Our contention is that schools, in representing their entire populations, have as their purpose "to create a public" (Postman, 1995). Each community of practice within a school needs multiple means to successfully educate all of its students. But it first starts with a vision and a set of values that drives the purpose coupled with a means to evaluate progress toward realizing the vision (i.e., Fetterman, Kaftarian, & Wandersman, 1996; Fullan, 1991). This cultural building process has been missing except in a few cases where the leadership is committed to serving all students under the banner of general education with collaborative support from categorical programs such as special education (Sailor & Roger, 2005; Sailor, 2009; Sailor, Dunlap, Sugai, & Horner, 2009). Toson, Burrello and Knollman (2012) studied system leaders' values, orientation, and respective frames on setting district direction and infrastructure in three large urban and two suburban schools engaged in merging all resources for all student learning into fully integrated settings. Their intent was to create a more integrated and higher-performing set of system initiatives for all students' learning.

Integrated setting is defined here as adherence to the principle of "natural proportion." If 12% of students at a school have individual educational plans (IEPs), then no more than 1.2% (one or two students) would be integrated within classrooms or other educational environments such as special purpose rooms.

We agree with Curtis (2009) that unless there is a systemwide policy operating at the level of the schools that supports all students in integrated settings, including grade-level classrooms, then we can never achieve equal membership and parity for students requiring special assistance. Figure 2.1 captures the essence of Curtis's conception for a new direction for high schools.

An end to the marginalization of students needing special assistance and the fragmentation of services within special education and between special and general educational structures requires a cultural redesign (Black, Grant, & Burrello, 2010). Change initiatives come and go, and measures of student achievement

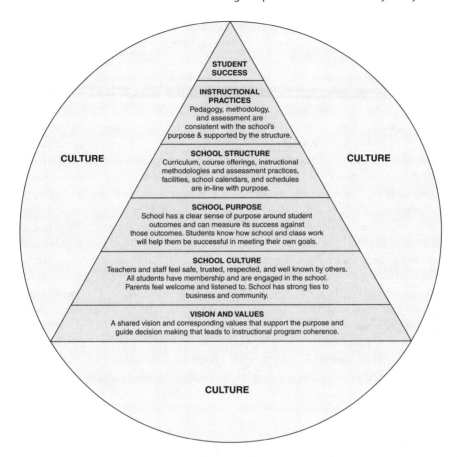

FIGURE 2.1

reflect largely dismal results (GAO, 2003; Lipsky & Gartner, 1996; Pullin, 1994). We may get temporary structural changes for as long as a particular initiative is funded and the leadership agency backs it, but we will not get the kind of acceptance and engagement of all students that is needed until we have some consensus around full membership, equity of need leading to equity of outcomes, and support for enabling the adults in the system to implement it.

School-level leadership, with or without district support, can pursue a similar pathway to more integrated delivery of instruction that includes all students. Leaders can confront the faculty with data on student progress and behavior and ask if there is a better way to combine resources to serve all students more effectively. Highly imaginative principals who have a history or familiarity with people with special needs and their siblings or family members have always seen students with disabilities as interesting people with a variety of capabilities others do not see (Black, Grant, & Burrello, 2010). Together with their staffs they build local expertise and experience and engage their colleagues within grade-level teams or departments within middle and high schools. Cultural redesign is officially underway. Lisa Grant (Black, Grant, & Burrello, 2010) shows us a typical model of practice that illustrates this pattern of school integration work today. So we see movement up through the Curtis triangle (Figure 2.1) with a set of individual cases, with individual teachers and teacher teams occurring one at a time. There is no wholesale dumping of students into integrated settings. It is a classroom or department-by-department level initiation within an emerging direction of integration for all of that proportion of the school day that can lead to new, valued capabilities for each student. The mistake we want to avoid is the jump to new structures and instructional practices without the deliberation of values and purpose; without the consideration of new possibilities with a core of believers and practitioners who can provide the pathway to success for teachers and students so that others can follow. This is what one superintendent leader, Ron Barnes, called evolution not revolution. But district leadership cannot accomplish change alone; school-level leadership needs to step up to make it happen. While we have more school leaders answering the call, district leadership has lagged behind and has not led the evolution to more inclusive schools.

So we are proposing a new general education (rather than special education) initiative. We are proposing that general education take control of a set of entrenched categorical systems of support through a schoolwide adaptation of the three-tiered RtI system proposed in the 2004 reauthorization of IDEA. This proposal is outlined below.

Schoolwide Instructional Support Match Systems as a Basis for New Educational Policy

We propose that education leadership at the district level consider a vision and corollary set of values embracing the need to create equal membership for all students as well as all staff who work within the school to support all students' learning. Those values might well, for example, support the vision of schools suggested by Cuban (2003) and earlier by Dewey (1966); preparing all students to be literate, civic-minded, and critical and independent thinkers who are socially and ethically responsible in order to create and sustain a democratic society that is committed to the benefit of all Americans. This means each student is prepared for a postschool life that leads, to the maximum extent possible, to work for pay, further education if desired, military service if desired, independent or interdependent living, and healthy democratic communities.

Guiding Values

Sailor and Roger (2005) articulated six values that ensure full membership and relevance of curriculum that leads to more freedom and agency for each student with a special need. Each district and school community needs to consider these values in order to implement a fully unified educational system.

One: The General Education System Should Guide All Students' Learning

A fully merged and integrated system of curriculum, instruction, and assessment should be put into place to guide all students' learning. The unified system is based upon five requirements: (1) all students attend their regularly assigned school; (2) all students have membership in their assigned classrooms in that school; (3) general education teachers and school-based leaders are responsible for all student learning; (4) all students are prepared within the district curriculum with appropriate adaptations and supports as needed; and (5) all staff are fully aware of teacher and student rights and capabilities, have the freedom to pursue what is important to them and their families, and have due process protections under law.

Two: All School Resources Should Be Configured to Benefit All Students

The key requirements regarding access to resources and benefits are: (1) all students are included in all activities; (2) all resources are integrated, configured, and delivered in a focused way that potentially benefits all students; and (3) resources are matched to learning enhancement and development goals for each student.

Three: Schools Should Directly Address Social Development and Citizenship

The key requirement here is that the school has a social development program that is explicated and tied to development of social capital among all students. Each student comes to know what is expected of him or her as a student and as a member of a community and the world. Sailor and Roger (2005) propose using the three-level schoolwide positive behavioral interventions and support (PBIS) system for this purpose (Sailor et al., 2009) since it can be easily integrated with academic interventions within a schoolwide MTSS/RtI system (Sailor et al., 2009).

Four: Schools Should Be Democratically Organized, Data-Driven, Learning Enhancement Systems

Five key requirements are included here: (1) the school operates a team structure, including grade-level teams and a leadership team, that considers reliable and valid sources of data to determine instructional matches (i.e., services, supports, levels of intensity, etc.); (2) all staff (i.e., all school employees) participate in at least some way in the teaching and learning process; (3) the school employs a noncategorical lexicon (i.e., special education labels are not used in school discourse); (4) the school is guided by distributed leadership (i.e., teacher leaders assume some key leadership functions); and (5) each school has one or more learning enhancement teams that bring together the resident expertise of the school, its partnerships, and district personnel when needed to design conditions that increase student learning possibilities within and outside the school as appropriate to learning new functionings.

Five: Schools Should Have Open Boundaries in Relation to Their Families and Communities

Three requirements exist at present: (1) schools have working substantive partnerships with their students' families (i.e., beyond just meetings of parent-teacher association groups and toward participation of parents in school governance and decision making); and (2) schools have meaningful partnerships with local businesses, their neighborhoods, and their service providers (i.e., formal partnerships, for example, with the community mental health agency for the provision of wraparound services as part of a tertiary-level RtI intervention (Eber et al., 2009)); and (3) schools have collaborative arrangements to support student learning on community training sites and work settings.

Six: Schools Must Have District Support for Undertaking Transformative Systems-Change Efforts

The key requirement here is for each school undergoing a transformation to fully integrate instructional and behavioral systems of practices under schoolwide learning enhancement teams. The district must provide the required levels of system support (i.e., school prioritized professional development activities, consultation, and interagency support collaboration) to accomplish those changes in the school, its programs, and external relationships.

Designing an Instructional Schoolwide Support System

Sailor (2009) described an integrated student and teacher support system that merges academic and social development for grade-level achievement and postschool success. The match of specialized resources and supports to measured student need is decided through team processes on the basis of screening data (social and behavioral) and ongoing progress monitoring of students' response to instruction at various levels of intensity (viz., response to intervention).

This systems change model has all of the key ingredients with which to reframe policy directed to matching instructional resources to identified student needs. As a schoolwide problem-solving model, it embraces the following in a single system of prevention: potential or actual problem identification, targeted interventions at three levels of intensity, accountability for tracking results from interventions, a socio-behavioral focus integrated with an academic focus, attention to information processing and learning schemas, transdisciplinary problem-solving teams to match resources to measured needs, and the eventual development of decision rules grounded in evidence that can help educators to select particular interventions (curriculum and instruction) with which to address specific identified problems. What is essential is that all interventions start in grade-level classrooms and are carried out, as needed, in fully integrated (i.e., general education) environments.

Whereas the frame of disability has led to most of the assessments undertaken to address an emerging problem in, say, reading, to be directed to personal characteristics, the schoolwide problem-solving approach directs assessments toward environmental factors. More important, it examines the interaction of personal factors with environmental circumstances in analyzing educational and/or behavioral problems. For example, assessments of a child who has a problem learning to read (increasingly informed by breakthroughs in neuroscience) yield personal information that has direct implications for selecting both curricula and type of instructional interventions. Coupling these data with data from environmental assessments leads us ultimately to the possibility of selecting among some general decision rules, grounded in evidence from rigorous investigations, that will assist teachers to better match learning resources to identified needs.

All of this implies a major shift of focus. Its basis is fueled by scientific breakthroughs in both personal attributes (e.g., brain theory) and in environmental modifications (e.g., schoolwide positive behavior support). The question becomes: Can instructional support systems, as we know them today, become fully integrated into an organizational structure bringing all of the elements together that are needed to take American education to a new level? Consider each of the following two key components, a system of increasing intensive support and team-driven processes, to see if an answer in the affirmative may be warranted.

A System of Increasing Intensity Support. What structures need to be in place to make fully integrated instructional supports within a schoolwide problem-solving framework an alternative to the continuum of services or full inclusion approaches? Controversy continues to swirl over when does special education check into the support system and where are specialized services delivered? We argue that the intensity of instructional support services should be largely determined by assessments indicating *when an appropriate instructional match* is found. The general education classroom is often the setting for interventions (behavioral, academic, or combinations of the two). Increases in the intensity of instruction are accompanied by increases in the accommodations required to make the instructional and behavioral matches. The most intense interventions are likely to require explicit modification in curriculum, instruction, and assessment aimed at desirable postschool outcomes for each student, particularly when a student reaches transition planning age in school years (about age 14). Intensive interventions, often individualized to a degree, may occur outside of the grade-level classroom (but not in a special class or special education resource room). The important point is that specialized education can and should be provided at each level of intensity through collaborative instruction between general education and special education teachers (who are liberated from the isolation of a self-contained or resource special education-led classrooms).

As described in the literature on RtI, a three-tiered system is lodged within IDEA (2004), but in language and in practice it tends to be confined to eligibility determination for special education. What is needed is a way to think about the originally depicted three tiers within a context of a fully integrated education system of supports and services that includes special education, second-language learner programs, and so on at all levels of intervention; hence the term *schoolwide MTSS/RtI*. This system presents a conceptual model for a schoolwide learning enhancement approach providing levels of intensity directed to matches of instructional practices to identified student need. Universal instruction is applicable to all students. The key integrative concept here is that all instructional interventions are embedded and extend from the primary instructional core, led and directed by the classroom teacher. We call them *primary (meaning first option for all students under the direction of the classroom teacher designed to deliver the instructional core)* as they are expected to be learned by all learners at the first stage. Our second stage, referred to as *more intensive academic and behavioral accommodations*, is designed to match smaller groups of students' assessed needs. Our third stage refers to *individualized, highly intensive, explicit modifications* that are directed to a few students for whom accommodations to the primary instructional core are insufficient. The stages are never tied to specific, separate places but always refer to designated interventions at varying levels of intensity. The objective is to identify an actual or potential risk factor that presently impedes the child's ability to maximally benefit from the teaching/learning process. A successful stage-explicit modification is intended to return a student to academic success under conditions related to primary or secondary accommodations. Similarly, the goal of providing accommodations to the primary interventions provided to all students is to enable students to succeed under the levels of intensity provided all students in the general education environment. Space limitations prevent us from providing detailed examples in application, but readers are referred to books by Sailor (2009), Hall (2008), and Brown-Chidsey and Steege (2005) for examples of these processes in application.

The breakthrough in "standard protocol" RtI, the special education version, is in the addition of scientifically valid and reliable measures that are curriculum-based rather than referenced against normative distributions that are divorced from the immediate curriculum, such as IQ tests, for disability determination. Schoolwide MTSS/RtI or a Learning Enhancement Approach, which we advocate for here, applies these processes to all students as a way to match instructional resources and supports to all students' measured educational needs in order to be successful.

Team-Driven Processes. Rosenfeld and Gravois (1996) write that their intent is to create and maintain student success within the general education environment by supporting the classroom teacher. The Instructional Consultation Team (ICT) serves as a delivery system with which to inform school teams (Rosenfeld, 1987; Gravois & Rosenfeld, 2002). By focusing both on the *content* (i.e., curriculum-based assessment, evidence-based academic and behavioral interventions) and the *process* (i.e., data collection, problem-solving steps, the reflective relationship established for the classroom teacher), instructional consultation seeks to enhance student achievement through improving teacher performance. It is the explicit emphasis on supporting teachers' professional capacity to develop and deliver effective instruction in the general education classroom that distinguishes instructional consultation from other forms of consultation and teaming. The IC structure is based on the premise that quality instructional and management programming, matched to a student's assessed entry skills, increases student success, reduces behavioral difficulties, and avoids the need for special education evaluation and placement (Gravois & Rosenfeld, 2006).

Gravois and Rosenfeld (2006) and Sailor (2009) both focus on whole school structures in support of individual teacher capacity-building. These authors argue for team-driven, collaborative problem solving and identifying individual instructional needs with uses of data to monitor interventions to enhance students' progress. They also argue for the use of the entire array of professionals and other staff available to schools to provide assessment, problem identification, and problem-solving interventions, and to monitor and evaluate intervention success.

Instructional practices that emerge from these team problem-solving processes are steeped in evidence-based practices. The process starts with screening for risk; these assessments usually take place early in the school year, often in September. The result of screening usually determines the percentage of children in a classroom who are at some level of risk for failing to respond to grade-level performance on high-quality instruction (using a science-grounded curriculum directed to all of the children in the classroom). For some of the identified children, a simple adjustment at the primary stage may suffice to remove the child from risk consideration. This might include differentiating instruction, for example, or withholding attention for inappropriate behavior.

For some children at risk, an accommodation stage may become warranted on the basis of careful monitoring of the child's progress in the risk-determined area. In a few cases, more explicit modifications through the intensive stage may become warranted. Researchers have estimated some gross percentages of children who are likely to require interventions at each of the three stages. These are 80% in the primary stage, 15% at the accommodation stage, and 5% at the most intensive stage (Batsche, Elliott, Graden, Grimes, Kovaleski, et al., 2005). Percentages at any one school, however, or for any single classroom may be strongly tied to community factors such as demographics, family income, or population density.

A critical element in selecting the right intervention is the fidelity with which any particular intervention, at any level, is implemented. Examples include assessment for fidelity of implementation of the Schoolwide Applications Model (SAM), conducted through a fidelity tool called the SAM Analysis System

(SAMAN—Sailor & Roger, 2005, 2006, 2009), and assessment of fidelity of implementation of schoolwide positive behavioral interventions and support (PBIS), conducted through the Schoolwide Evaluation Tool (SET—Horner et al., 2004).

The Problem of Practice

Poor student achievement results, as measured by increasing levels of standardized testing, poor graduation rates, and certainly dismal postschool success for students in special education, are energizing the present discourse on alternative systems of educational policy. No Child Left Behind (NCLB)'s contribution was to illuminate the poor results, since the law required all students to be assessed for the first time in 2004. The constant pressure for academic achievement results today (i.e., Adequate Yearly Progress—AYP) has caused many urban and suburban districts to send their students with special needs back into the continuum of services array of separate settings, because to do so alleviates some of the pressure for accountability for student success. Again, the only counterbalancing forces have been IDEIA 2004 and the Elementary and Secondary Education Act (ESEA) requiring more and more access to the general education curriculum in order to achieve at higher levels.

The bouncing ball of responsibility for serving all students in the general education classroom continues to move back and forth between grade-level or subject-matter teachers and special educators, who are often expected to support students in grade-level classrooms to ensure their success in the general education curriculum. The responsibility for the success of students who require specialized supports and services needs to rest with those responsible for teaching the general education curriculum but with collaborative support from special educators. In spite of multiple efforts to promote and implement co-teaching models, or into better prepare both through classroom consultation and teacher preparation programs, general and special educators to teach students with special needs, at the policy level, the effort has yielded equivocal results.

Summary

It is our contention that the assessment and sorting of students with special needs into 13 separate categories of disability has resulted in a parallel system of responsibility and care for these students. This parallel system is serviced by a cadre of specialists each with their own culture, roles, and expectations for their professional performance often characterized by lowered expectations for student outcomes and, unfortunately, poor postschool results. Parents are often the most informed and committed advocates for their children with special needs as these students advance from grade level to grade level without reflecting new skills and knowledge within our nation's schools. A parent shared this observation recently in a conversation with the first author.

The many meetings with school personnel often left us disillusioned and drained as we often heard statements like, "He does not belong" and "If the world were a Utopia, all children would go to the same school." We were told that if we chose to push for inclusion, he would be dropped from special education and could not go to school with his sister. We were trying to keep our family intact and trying to understand why there was so much resistance coming from the school system.

Inadvertently, we as a nation have, under the present education policy and system of practices, which locates responsibility for learning for different groups of students and their teachers or care-givers with different administrative and service/support units, created a perpetual struggle between school systems across the nation and their families of students.

Second, we as a nation have not confronted this culture of deference to the specialist, coupled with the abdication of responsibility under the guise of lack of expertise by the grade-level, general education teacher. Similarly, we have not addressed school-based leadership that collectively regards students with special needs as if they were an "endangered species" who happen to require special protections that take a law degree to understand.

Third, we as a nation have taken the path of least resistance and are meeting the cultural imperative to serve all students in the public schools largely through a separate and unequal system of supports in order to access the general education curriculum. So we have guaranteed access to schools but not access to the general education curriculum and the potential for resultant equity of outcomes for many students and families. Under present policy our specialized system of supports is fractionated and unconnected to the general education system. A district inclusion facilitator reported in her eight-year practice that resistance to coteaching or collaborative teaming has come primarily from special educators who do not have the skill set to differentiate instruction in a general education classroom (R. Calco, personal communication, 2009).

We believe there is a pathway to better policy that builds upon evidence-based practices garnered from decades of education and special education research. We are recommending that the integration of all supportive services for students with special needs come under the responsibility of district- and school-based general education leadership. We recommend further that new policy be focused on a system of outcomes that requires differentiating instruction and that holds school districts accountable for producing positive differences in rates and level of performance under schoolwide commitment to learning within a human development and capabilities approach. Finally, professional capacity building is a fundamental leadership responsibility. Creating a culture of responsibility and authenticity precedes a culture of competence. The forthcoming Congressional hearings on reauthorization of both IDEA and ESEA will set the stage for policy-level discourse on the structure and form of educational supports and services to special needs populations. We advance the proposition that now is a good time to consider the continued usefulness of the construct of disability and the resultant medical-model–driven conception of a continuum of services as a basis for educating some students. There are other populations of students, inner-city children of color in high-poverty communities, for example, or children of non-English-speaking families who also require specialized supports and services, many of which are completely continuous with those provided through special education. Perhaps now is the time to seriously consider merging ESEA and IDEA into a single, coherent set of policies that support a system of school-level education delivered in a MTSS/RtI framework. Such a merged policy structure would need to ensure that students with families who counted on IDEA 2004 for support are not shortchanged, but rather are afforded a better framework for postschool outcomes than is presently available.

References

Anderson, G. (2009). *Advocacy leadership*. New York: Routledge.

Batsche, G., Elliott, J., Graden, J.L., Grimes, J., Kovaleski, J.F., Prasse, D., . . . Tilly, W.D. (2005). *Response to intervention: Policy considerations and implementation*. Alexandria, VA: National Association of State Directors of Special Education.

Berman, P. (1980). Thinking about programmed and adaptive implementation: Matching strategies to situations. In H. Ingram & D. Mann (Eds.), *Why policies succeed or fail* (pp. 205–227). Santa Monica, CA: RAND.

Bernstein, B. (2000). *Pedagogy, symbolic control and identity*. London: Rowman and Littlefield.

Black, W., Grant, L., & Burrello, L.C. (2010). Cultivating full membership in schools: Supporting students with disabilities through moral literacy, ethical leadership, and cultural design. *Journal of Ethics and Values in Educational Administration, 11*(2).

Brown-Chidsey, R., & Steege, M.W. (2005). Response to intervention: Principles and strategies for effective practice. In W. Merrell (Ed.), *The Guilford practical intervention in the schools series*. New York: Guilford Press.

Buck Educational Institute. (2007). *Project-based learning handbook*. Novato, CA: Author.

Burrello, L.C., Tracy, M.L., & Schultz, E.W. (1973). Special education as experimental education: A new conceptualization. *Exceptional Children, 40*(1), 29–31.

Certo, N.J., Luecking, R.G., Murphy, S., Brown, L., Courey, S., & Belanger, D. (2008). Seamless transition and long-term support for individuals with severe intellectual disabilities. *Research and Practice for Persons With Severe Disabilities, 33*(3), 85–95.

Connor, D., & Ferri, B. (2007, January). The conflict within: Resistance to inclusion and other paradoxes in special education. *Disability & Society, 22*(1), 63–77.

Cuban, L. (2003). *Powerful reforms with shallow roots: Improving America's urban schools*. New York: Teachers College Press.

Curtis, P. (2009). The New Tech Foundation. Presentation at New Tech Foundation. Napa, CA.

Dewey, J. (1966). *Democracy and education: An introduction to the philosophy of education*. New York: Free Press. (Original work published in 1916.)

Eber, L., Hyde, K., Rose, J., Breen, K., McDonald, D., & Lewandowski, H. (2009). Completing the continuum of schoolwide positive behavior support: Wraparound as a tertiary-level intervention. In W. Sailor, G. Dunlap, & R. Horner (Eds.), *Handbook of positive behavior support* (pp. 671–703). New York: Springer.

Fetterman, D., Kaftarian, S., & Wandersman, A. (1996). *Empowerment evaluation: Knowledge tools for self-assessment and accountability.* Thousands Oaks, CA: Sage.

Fritz, R. (1999). *Path of least resistance for managers: Designing organizations to succeed.* San Francisco, CA: Berrett-Koehler.

Fuchs, D., & Fuchs, L.S. (1993, July). Inclusive schools movement and the radicalization of special education reform. (Report No. ED364046). 42pp.

Fullan, M. (1991). *The new meaning of educational change.* New York: Teachers College Press.

Gersten, R., & Woodward, J. (1990). Rethinking the regular education initiative: Focus on the classroom teacher. *Remedial and Special Education, 11,* 7–16.

Government Accounting Office. (2003). *Special education: Clearer guidance would enhance implementation of federal disciplinary provisions.* (Publication No. 03–550). Washington, DC: Author.

Gravois, T., & Rosenfeld, S. (2002). The multi-dimensional framework for evaluation of instructional consultation teams. *Journal of School Psychology, 19*(1), 5–29.

Gravois, T., & Rosenfeld, S. (2006). Impact of instructional consultation teams on the disproportionate referral and placement of minority students in special education. *Remedial and Special Education, 27*(1), 42–52.

Hall, S.L. (2008). *Implementing response to intervention.* Thousand Oaks, CA: Corwin Press.

Horner, R.H., Todd, A.W., Lewis-Palmer, T., Irvin, L.K., Sugai, G., & Boland, J.B. (2004). The School-wide Evaluation Tool (SET): A research instrument for assessing school-wide positive behavior support. *Journal of Positive Behavior Interventions, 6,* 3–12.

Individuals With Disabilities Education Act Amendments of 2004, P.L. 20 U.S.C. § 1400 *et seq.*

Kleinhammer-Tramill, J. (2003). An analysis of federal initiatives to prepare regular educators to serve students with disabilities: Deans' grants, REGI, and beyond. *Teacher Education and Special Education, 26*(3), 230.

Lawson, H., & Sailor, W. (2000). Integrating services, collaborating, and developing connections with schools. *Focus on Exceptional Children, 3*(2), 1–22.

Lipsky, D.K., & Gartner, A. (1996). Inclusion, school restructuring, and the remaking of American society. *Harvard Educational Review, 66*(4), 762–796.

McKinney, J.D., & Hocutt, A.M. (1998). Policy issues in the evaluation of the regular education initiative. *Learning Disabilities Focus, 4,* 15–23.

Nussbaum, M.C. (2006). *Frontiers of justice: Disability, nationality, and species membership.* Cambridge, MA: Harvard University Press.

Postman, N. (1995). *The end of education: Redefining the value of school.* New York: Knopf.

Pugach, M., & Sapon-Shevin, M. (1987). New agendas for special education policy: What the national reports haven't said. *Exceptional Children, 53,* 295–299.

Pullin, D.C. (1994). Learning to work: The impact of curriculum and assessment standards on educational opportunity. *Harvard Educational Review, 64*(1), 31–54.

Rosenfeld, S., (1987). *Instruction consultation.* Hillsdale, NJ: Erlbaum.

Rosenfeld, S., & Gravios, T. (1996). *Instruction consultation teams: Collaborating for change.* New York: Guilford Press.

Sailor, W. (2009). *Making RtI work.* San Francisco, CA: Jossey-Bass.

Sailor, W., Dunlap, G., Sugai, G., & Horner, R. (2009). *Handbook of positive behavior support.* New York: Springer.

Sailor, W., & Roger, B. (2005). Rethinking inclusion: Schoolwide applications. *Phi Delta Kappan, 86*(7), 503–509.

Sailor, W., & Roger, B. (2006). Positive behavior support in the urban core. *TASH Connections, 32*(1/2), 23–24.

Sailor, W., & Roger, B. (2009). SAMAN: An instrument for analysis of critical features of the Schoolwide Applications Model (SAM). (Unpublished). (For more information contact Wayne Sailor at wsailor@ku.edu).

Sarason, S. (1971). *The process of change and the culture of schools.* Boston: Allyn-Bacon.

Sergiovanni, T. (1992). *Moral leadership: Getting to the heart of school improvement.* San Francisco, CA: Jossey-Bass.

Skrtic, T.M. (2005). A political economy of learning disabilities. *Learning Disabilities Quarterly, 28*(2), 149–155.

Slavin, R.E. (1990). General education under the regular education initiative: How must it change? *RASE: Remedial & Special Education. Special Issue: Perspectives on the REI: Views from general education, 11*(3), 40–50.

Slee, R. (2009). Inclusive school as a means and end of education. In L. Florian (Ed.), *The Sage handbook of special education* (pp. 160–170). Thousands Oaks, CA: Sage.

Starratt, R.J. (2009, October 3). *The moral completion of the process of knowing and its necessarily humble beginnings.* Paper presented at the Values and Leadership Conference at Penn State University.

Toson, A.L-M., Burrello, L.C., & Knollman, G. (2012). Educational justice for all: The capability approach and inclusive education leadership. *International Journal of Inclusive Education,* 1–17.

Wiggins, G., & McTigue, J. (2005). *Understanding by design* (2nd ed.). Alexandria, VA: Association of Supervision and Curriculum Development.

PART II

Legal and Financial Basis of Services for a Unified System

3

TOWARD A HUMAN CAPABILITIES EDUCATION POLICY

Carl Lashley

American public education has reached what Senge, Schwarmer, Jaworski, and Flowers (2004) call "a requiem scenario" (p. 21). Senge and his colleagues urge us to go on "an exploration of the unthinkable" (p. 24). They use two examples to illustrate what a requiem scenario is. The first is what might happen if we continue to despoil the earth through our ecologically unsustainable lifestyles; the second, discovering that death is near because of a terminal illness. When confronted with such requiem scenarios, people can simply give up, or they can "see the different future not as inevitable, but as one of genuine possibilities" (p. 25). Their book, *Presence: Human Purpose and the Field of the Future*, seeks out new perspectives by arguing that a deep turn inward is necessary before we, the organizations, and the communities in which we live and work can change. "When all is said and done, the only change that will make a difference is the transformation of the human heart" (p. 26).

Is American public education in a requiem scenario? Are we at a place where we need to think the unthinkable—that the school as we have known it, and as educators have often loved it, is no longer sustainable as an institution of learning? Today we hear arguments that the public school is an anachronism to be replaced by virtual schools, distance learning, private teaching and learning entrepreneurships, home schools, or publicly financed but independently operated corporate charters. Public school advocates argue in return that these alternatives would result in the public schools becoming institutions that serve only children and families who are poor, the difficult, or the outcast. Some say the upper and middle classes would abandon the public schools in part because they want better education and in part because they want to escape an increasingly diverse society. What are the "genuine possibilities" for educating all children in a learning environment that responds to children's needs and aspirations regardless of who they are or where they come from? Is education any longer the great equalizer, as Horace Mann argued in 1848?

Is American public education in a requiem scenario or simply in the doldrums brought on by an assortment of critics who brought us standardization, test-driven accountability, budget shortfalls and cuts, and bashing by an insecure public that doesn't recognize its schools any more. Whichever it is, American public education is in a crisis of confidence and a paralysis of purpose. The No Child Left Behind Act of 2001 (NCLB) has left its mark. On one hand, it has pointed out how many children we really do leave behind; on the other, it has helped to create schools that are at risk of becoming intellectually barren, mind-numbingly dull, and lacking heart. The Individuals With Disabilities Education Act (IDEA) (2004) has opened the schoolhouse and classroom door and created learning opportunities for 6 million children with disabilities every year, but it has also become a morass of time-, energy-, and morale-consuming paperwork and procedures that oftentimes distract teachers, administrators, and parents from the point—the education of a child. And increasingly, that education is aimed at only one thing—passing a standardized test brought to us by NCLB. The attacks on school we saw in Spring 2011 left teachers demoralized and confused, and then steep budget cuts took jobs and reporting test scores with teachers' names attached hit the newspapers.

What then shall we do? A requiem, a crisis, paralysis call us to imagine "genuine possibilities" (Senge et al. p. 25), to explore the unthinkable, to have a change of heart. In this chapter, we will explore the current status and requirements of NCLB and IDEA, imagine a possibility in which they are joined together to enhance the capabilities of all the diverse children of school age, and discuss how their current provisions can be transformed to bring about schools that are caring, mindful, thoughtful, and hopeful. Let's first turn to a short discussion of NCLB and IDEA as products of a theory of human capital development that has dominated educational discourse since 1983 and public discourse since at least World War II.

Public Education, NCLB, and IDEA as Human Capital Projects

At least since the passage of No Child Left Behind in 2001, and quite probably since the release of *A Nation at Risk* in 1983 (National Commission on Excellence and Education), the United States has cultivated an educational system and public perception that are rooted in the belief that the quality of a student's education is best indicated by the results of standardized tests. This may not be the way parents think about education when their children go to schools where students score pretty well on standardized tests. However, in schools where students do not score at acceptable levels on average, parents, students, educators, and the public are regularly reminded that these students are not learning.

Exacerbating the problem is the fact that many of these failing schools serve students from racially and ethnically multicultural families who live below the poverty line. NCLB purports to address the inequities in American education (Darling-Hammond, 2010). It has shined a light on the gaps in achievement that exist among groups of students. However, it has come up short in closing those gaps, and the strides that have been made have come at the price of a narrowed curriculum that hones in on back-to-basics reading and math skills and punishes schools where students do not achieve at required levels of proficiencies. In addition, the NCLB target of 100% proficiency by 2014 has resulted in many more schools coming close to being labeled failing because the target represents a very simplistic view of what it takes to teach the children of the 21st century.

Since the passage of the Education of All Handicapped Children Act of 1975 (EHA), American schools have been engaged in a negotiation about the degree to which students with disabilities should be educated. The law, reauthorized as the Individuals With Disabilities Education Act (IDEA), put forward a theory of practice that guided the development of a system of special education and related services for the approximately 6 million students with disabilities in U.S. schools. Embedded within that theory of practice was a variety of outcomes and expectations for these students. Most were expected to proceed in a curriculum toward a high school diploma, some had additional learning needs that required attention in order for them to be successful in school, and some had significantly different learning needs that had previously been seen as outside the purview of the public schools.

Implementation of EHA/IDEA has resulted in the creation of a subsystem of general and special education in American schools. In part, this is due to the structures that are required by the law, such as labeling of students, assessment practices, placement options in the Continuum of Services, and the design of the Individual Education Program. Other very influential factors are the culture of schools, the educational impact of deficit thinking, and the quality of special education teachers. The special education subsystem is well entrenched, even in schools that consider themselves to be inclusive.

The No Child Left Behind Act of 2001

Congress's rationale for NCLB, as stated in the statute (20 U.S.C. § 6301 *et seq.*), "is to ensure that all children have a fair, equal, and significant opportunity to obtain a high-quality education and reach, at a minimum, proficiency on challenging State academic achievement standards and state academic assessments." NCLB then is a codification of the standards-based reform idea that high educational standards for learning that are regularly measured by standardized tests will motivate students, teachers, and administrators to focus on student performance and will prompt investment in teaching, support programs, curriculum, and professional development necessary to enable all students to reach desired levels of proficiency (Darling-Hammond, 2010).

The equity vectors that are established under NCLB include.

- Accounting for results [20 U.S.C. § 6311 (2)];
- Informing the public about school performance [20 U.S.C. § 6311 (2) (B–C); (h) (1–3)]
- Illuminating the performance differences among various subgroups of students [20 U.S.C. § 6311 (C)]
- Utilizing data to inform educational decision making [20 U.S.C. § 6311]
- Redistributing resources to support the needs of groups of students who have historically been poorly served educationally [20 U.S.C. § 6321]

Accounting for Results

NCLB (2001) requires states to establish statewide standards and statewide assessments that measure student performance against the standards. States are then obligated to report the results of those statewide assessments annually for all schools and school districts. Instituting uniform standards, creating an assessment system, and informing the public of the performance of their schools were intended to ensure that all students had access to equal, challenging learning opportunities. Finally, NCLB indicates that teachers and principals are responsible for students' progress and that the public would be aware of the degree to which each school was meeting the prescribed goals.

The most important accountability mechanism in NCLB is Adequate Yearly Progress (AYP), a data point set by each state that reports what percentage of students have scored at proficient levels or above on the statewide assessments, which are aligned with the statewide standards (20 U.S.C. § 7325). States were expected to set these yearly data points beginning with 2001–2002 standardized test data and continuing in increments until 2013–2014, the goal by which all students would score at proficiency or higher. AYP also includes provisions that require schools to disaggregate their test data by subgroups of students who have traditionally not scored at proficiency on standardized tests: "economically disadvantaged students, students from major racial and ethnic groups, students with disabilities, and students with limited English proficiency" (20 U.S.C. § 6311).

NCLB (2001) installed a rigorous accountability system for Title I eligible schools that is based on the school's AYP status. If a school fails to make AYP two years in a row, it enters School Improvement, an escalating series of programs and interventions that can ultimately result in closing the school, turning it into a charter school, or otherwise substantially restructuring it. These measures, which are summarized in Table 3.1, reflect the bottom-line thinking that comes from a human capital approach to educational policy. Much like the results of an efficiency audit in a nonproductive factory, if a unit (the school) does not produce the desired results (high standardized test scores), it should be sanctioned (placed in School Improvement), and if results are then not forthcoming, it should be eliminated (closed, reconstituted, restructured).

TABLE 3.1. School Accountability Measures from NCLB

Year	School Status	Accountability Action
Year 1	School does not make AYP in reading, math, or both	District takes note; school prepares to enter School Improvement
Year 2	School does not make AYP in the same subject	School Improvement Parents are provided the choice for their children to transfer to another school.
Year 3	School does not make AYP in the same subject	School Improvement Choice to transfer School offers supplemental educational services to eligible students.
Year 4	School does not make AYP in the same subject	School Improvement Choice to transfer Supplemental Educational Services School enters corrective action, which includes one of the following: scientifically research-based professional development, instructional alignment, extended school day or year, replacement of staff, decreased management authority, appointment of outside experts, restructure the school.
Year 5	School does not make AYP in the same subject	School Improvement Choice to transfer Supplemental Educational Services School is restructured: Closed and reopened as a charter; replacing all or most of the staff; contracting with a private management company; state operation; reopening as a themed school; closing the school; and others.

Source: Adapted from North Carolina Department of Public Instruction, *NC NCLB Fact Sheets and Brochures*, http://www.ncpublicschools.org/nclb/communications/brochures/, 2008.

Informing the Public About School Performance

Beginning in 2002–2003, states, districts, and schools were required to publish an annual Report Card in which they would report in language accessible to parents and the public about the state of schools [20 U.S.C. § 6311 (h) (1–4)]. These Report Cards are required to contain the following:

- information about the performance of students in the various subgroups;
- comparisons between subgroup performance and the state's performance objectives;
- the percentage of students not tested;
- trends for student performance in each subject area and grade level;

- other indicators the state uses to configure AYP;
- graduation rates;
- information on the performance of Local Education Agencies (LEAs) related to AYP;
- the number and names of schools that are determined to be schools in need of improvement;
- qualifications of teachers, and the percentage of classes not taught by highly qualified teachers disaggregated by the poverty levels of schools.

States are also encouraged, but not required, to include the following:

- attendance rates;
- average class sizes;
- performance and improvement in English proficiency;
- information on school safety and discipline;
- information on parental involvement; and
- percentage of students who take advanced placement courses and the passing rate for the tests that yield credit for these courses.

School districts are also required to prepare and disseminate school Report Cards for each school and to include the information required on the state Report Card. District and school Report Cards must be distributed to all parents in the district and to the media. In addition, districts are obligated to report annually the following information:

- how many schools have been identified for school improvement and what percentage of all schools that constitutes;
- how students performed on statewide assessments and how that compares to the state.

Each school Report Card then includes all of the information above as well as whether the school has been identified as in need of improvement and how the school's students performed on statewide assessments. In addition, the school Report Card includes a statement of the school's AYP status in comparison to other schools in the district and the state.

Schools are also required to inform parents annually about the following:

- whether their child's teacher meets the state's standards for highly qualified in the grade level and subject areas he or she is teaching;
- whether the teacher has an emergency certificate;
- the teacher's major in his or her bachelor's degree and any graduate degree or certificate he or she holds;
- the qualifications of paraprofessionals who work with the child(ren); and
- information about the child's performance on statewide assessments.

Making information public about the performance of schools has the advantageous effect of letting the public know about the status of its schools and the progress of students. However, it also provides the opportunity for comparisons between schools, which can lead to controversy.

Illuminating Performance Differences Among Subgroups of Students

NCLB (2001) articulates "a goal of closing the achievement gap between high- and low-performing children, especially the achievement gaps between minority and nonminority students, and between disadvantaged children and their more advantaged peers" [20 U.S.C. § 6301 (3)]. The mechanism for determining whether the achievement gaps are closing is determining whether a school is meeting AYP. Although there are four categories of subgroups, the actual number of subgroups may vary from state to state. In North Carolina, which is relatively reflective of most states, the subgroups are (1) the whole school, (2) White students, (3) Black students, (4) Native American students, (5) Asian/Pacific Islander students, (6) Hispanic students, (7) Multiracial students, (8) Limited English proficient students, (9) Students with Disabilities, and (10) Economically Disadvantaged students. California adds Filipino students; Florida does not use Multiracial.

Since NCLB requires that a school's subgroups all meet the AYP standard for the school to make AYP, a school with several subgroups is more likely to miss the AYP proficiency standard. As the timeline for 100% student proficiency nears and higher percentages of students are expected to score above proficient on standardized tests, schools have begun to feel the AYP pinch. Secretary of Education Arne Duncan predicted in Spring 2011 (McNell, 2011, March) that as many as 82% of schools would not meet proficiency standards for the 2010–2011 school year. In fact, the number was nearer 48%, but still nearly one-half of American schools did not meet the standard, a sign that either the system is not working or schools are as bad as their critics say (McNell, 2011, December).

Utilizing Data

The emphasis on standardized testing and the interpretation of the data it yields has required teachers and principals to become data savvy. Public reporting of the schools' performance; the tight alignment of curriculum, assessment, and instruction; and a public narrowing of expectations for schools has led teachers and principals to focus on state test scores as the most important factor in a child's education. When schools use test data as one source of information about student learning, it can yield important insights and possibilities, and it can give teachers a place to start. However, focusing only on test scores soon degrades into figuring out how to look better on the student learning measures. By contrast, looking at student achievement results in conjunction with the context of the school and the processes that create the results gives teachers and administrators important information about what they need to do to improve learning for all students. (Bernhardt, 2003, p. 30)

Redistributing Resources

A stated goal of NCLB is "distributing and targeting resources sufficiently to make a difference to local educational agencies and schools where needs are greatest" [20 U.S.C. § 6301 (5)]. In fiscal 2011, the U.S. Department of Education distributed $14.5 billion in Title I and Grants to LEAs funds and an additional $535 million in School Turnaround Grants (Federal Education Budget Project, 2011). Schools in which 40% of the students come from families below the federal poverty level are eligible to receive these funds [20 U.S.C. § 6313]. NCLB includes a comparability requirement that students in Title I schools have access to similar services and opportunities that are available to students in non–Title I schools. A recent report from the U.S. Department of Education (Heuer & Stullich, 2011) indicates that 40% of Title I schools across the country have lower per-pupil expenditures on personnel than do the non–Title I schools in their districts. This inequity, which Title I funds are supposed to address, is caused by a definitional loophole in which teacher experience is discounted as a factor in school expenditures. High-poverty schools are more likely to employ inexperienced teachers whose salaries are lower, while higher-income schools are likely to employ more experience teachers whose salaries are higher. If teacher experience, and therefore teacher salaries, are held constant, then the schools appear to be more equitable in school funding terms. When teachers count the same for funding regardless of where they teach, the schools appear to be closer together on per-student expenditure (Bireda & Miller, 2010; Miller & Brown, 2011). As a result, it appears that funding inequities between higher- and lower-income schools are less significant.

Generally speaking, schools are institutions that operate to process groups of children through 13 years of education (K-12). The groups are established according to age, and the curriculum is divided into yearly sections that are intended to be developmentally appropriate for the ages of the students in that age group. The child's education is the responsibility of the teacher, the school, and the offices of the professional bureaucracy (Skrtic, 1991) that are in place to decide upon and support a variety of curricular, instructional, and assessment programs. The descriptions above of the NCLB policy vectors reflect this group-centered, bureaucratically hierarchical system. NCLB uses aggregate data on groups and subgroups of students to hold schools accountable for student performance. School districts are required to report those aggregate data to the public, and they use aggregate data to sanction schools for performance below proficiency. Resources are targeted toward schools on the basis of groups of students who are eligible for Title 1 services. The purpose of Title I funding and its approach to education is to provide motivation and support for students and sanctions for schools so they will reach proficiency standards. If NCLB works, 100% of students will reach proficiency in a uniform set of curricular requirements by 2014. That is, the inefficiencies and flawed products that result from failure to learn to read and do math will be eliminated by 2014. Focusing on reading and math performance will yield a workforce that can compete in a global economy.

The Individuals With Disabilities Education Act (2004)

The Individuals With Disabilities Education Act (20 U.S.C. §1400 *et seq.*), originally passed as the Education of All Handicapped Children Act (EHA) in 1975, requires school districts to develop a system of special education that is in compliance with the Act's provision in exchange for federal funding. Implementation of IDEA has resulted in the identification of approximately 6 million school-aged children in 13 categories of disability. Students who are eligible for services under IDEA are also protected from discrimination by Section 504 of the Vocational Rehabilitation Act of 1973 (Yell, 2012). In addition, approximately 1.2% of all students (Holler & Zirkel, 2008) have disabilities under the definition prescribed in Section 504 and are protected from discrimination on the grounds of disability. Congress's purpose in passing the Act in 1975 was "to ensure that all children with disabilities have available to them a free appropriate public education that emphasizes special education and related services designed to meet their unique needs and prepare them for further education, employment, and independent living" [20 U.S.C. § 1400 (d) (1) (A)].

The implementation of IDEA has introduced individualization and empowerment policy vectors into American schools. IDEA focuses on the unique needs of students with disabilities, codifies them in an Individual Education Plan, and involves parents and teachers in the design and delivery of the student's educational program. In addition, IDEA provides civil rights protection that allows parents to object to a school's actions through formal complaint processes that include due process hearings and litigation in court. These policy vectors can best be understood by a brief discussion of these aspects of IDEA. Included in these discussions will be allusions to NCLB in an effort to show the contrasts between the two policies:

- The Individual Education Program
- Individualized assessment and decision making
- Parents as partners in educating their children
- Parental involvement in decision making
- Challenges to decision making through due process provisions.

The Individual Education Program [20 U.S.C. § 1400 (d)]

The Individual Education Program (IEP) is "a written statement for each child with a disability that is developed, reviewed, and revised in accordance with section 614(d)" of IDEA [20 U.S.C. § 1400 (d)]. The IEP must include the following:

- the student's present level of academic and functional performance;
- measurable annual academic and functional goals;
- methods for measuring the student's progress toward the annual goals and provisions for periodic reporting to parents;
- a description of the special education, related services, and supplementary aids and services the students will receive;
- the degree to which the student will not participate in general education with students without disabilities;
- a statement of testing accommodations or reasons why the student will participate in alternate assessments;
- projected dates for beginning services and the frequency location and duration of services;
- a statement of postsecondary goals and transition services necessary for the student to meet those goals.

A particularly important element on the IEP is information about what the student's status shall be in participating in statewide assessments. First, this decision shapes the discussion of the curriculum and placement of the student, since access to the general education curriculum upon which the statewide assessments is based is critical, if the student is to gain the knowledge necessary to score at a proficient level on the test. Second, the decision determines where the student will be educated and by whom, since the general education classroom and the general education teacher are most likely to have the content knowledge and the pedagogical applications necessary to differentiate instruction to allow the student with a disability to learn what is necessary to be proficient.

Individualized Assessment and Decision Making (20 U.S.C. § 1414)

IDEA requires "a full and individual initial evaluation .... Before the initial provision of special education and related services" (20 U.S.C. § 1414). The evaluation must be interdisciplinary in that a variety of assessment approaches must be used, and no single criterion can be used to make a decision about the child's program. Assessments must be nondiscriminatory and administered in a form most likely to yield useful information about the child's academic, developmental, and functional needs. Personnel who are to administer and interpret the assessments must be properly trained and qualified. The assessment must also include information provided by the parent (20 U.S.C. § 1414).

After the completion of the individualized assessment the school convenes the educational professionals who are most knowledgeable about the child, those who have conducted the individualized assessments, administrative personnel, and the child's parent to determine eligibility for special education and related services and the content of the IEP (20 U.S.C. § 1414). From these deliberations about the education of the individual child comes a decision about the provision of a Free Appropriate Public Education (FAPE) for this student with a disability (20 U.S.C. § 1401; *Hendrik Hudson District Board of Education v. Rowley*, 1982).

Making decisions about individual children using individual evaluation data and providing FAPE for individual students has been a striking step forward for American schools. Schools are comfortable with processes and decisions that address the needs of groups of students. In addition, learning a new language of individualization and translating it into practice has proved to be continually challenging.

Parents as Partners in Educating Their Children (20 U.S.C. § 1414)

In IDEA, Congress stated that an important goal of the Act is "strengthening the role and responsibility of parents and ensuring that families of such children have meaningful opportunities to participate in the education of their children at school and at home" (20 U.S.C. § 1400). Schools first invite parents of students suspected of having disabilities into the decision-making process when they pursue consent for initial assessment. Parents are partners in the assessment process when they provide information about their child. If the student qualifies for special education and related services, the parent must give written consent for those services to be implemented. School systems are obligated to prepare documents that explain parents' rights and to provide training for parents about their rights and the education of their student with a disability.

The act of asking parents to work with school personnel as partners in the education of their children gets a lot of attention, but schools have not proved to be able to do it very well. Schools operate as professional silos in which the intrusion of even another school professional into a teacher's classroom is considered a breach of etiquette. Inviting parents to provide their knowledge about their child is usually considered to be a token, rather than a genuine effort to bring the parent into the educational community.

Parental Involvement in Decision Making

Congress intended that the power to make educational decisions about individual children with disabilities should be shared with their parents. Parents must have access to the information that has been gathered about their child, be asked to contribute to that body of information, and be invited to the table when decisions are being made about the education of their child with a disability. Parents of students suspected of having disabilities must be involved in the deliberations of the team that is making eligibility, placement, and IEP decisions (20 U.S.C. § 1414). Parents must also be involved in disciplinary decisions regarding their child when a disciplinary action could result in a change of placement.

This shift of power from school personnel to parents has resulted in conflict, but one hopes it also results in a better relationship between the school and family on behalf of the child. As Gallagher (2006) has written regarding power and the education of students with disabilities:

> Power is merely a person's ability to achieve what he or she wants and to prevent others from doing what he or she opposes. In that sense, continued power struggles exist within families, between families and schools, between teachers and principals, and between schools and the larger society. The establishment of policy is the tool by which conflicts can be resolved in favor, one hopes, of the child with special needs. (p. 4)

Challenges to Decision Making Through Due Process Provisions

Perhaps one of the most revolutionary changes that occurred with the passage of EHA/IDEA in 1975 was the requirement that school districts provide parents with due process of law during the special education process (20 U.S.C. § 1415). Due process includes the opportunity to challenge school district decisions about the education of their child with a disability. Besides their right to participate in decision making, parents can file complaints with the State Education Agency or the Office of Civil Rights, request mediation, request due process hearings, and ultimately go to court if they and the school district cannot reach an agreement. If the parent prevails in court, the school district may grant the parent attorney's fees.

NCLB, IDEA, and Standardization

Kleinhammer-Tramill, Burrello and Sailor (see Chapter 1) argue that the economically driven theories, policies, and practices that undergird NCLB and current educational thinking stem from an agenda of human capital development that gauges the merit and worth of a person by his or her capacity to contribute to economic productivity. Schools then become instruments of the economy. Since the 1980s when the human capital development/economic discourse began to dominate education, the selfsame theories that have driven the business sector have been adopted by those who are interested in school change, resulting in promoting high standards, continuous assessment, curriculum and assessment alignment, work teams, and the like. Ultimately, business's notion of "the bottom line" took over as a best practice to be used to determine whether schools were performing to standards. Hence, standards-driven curriculum aligned with statewide assessments was born. In addition, business thinking resulted in ideas about what to do with schools that are low-performing, and from that logic came school transformation or reconstitution in which employees were fired, bosses were transferred, new employees were brought onboard, and in some cases, schools were "sold off" to charter school providers much like an underperforming division would be in industry.

Deconstructing the policy narratives in No Child Left Behind (2001) and the Individuals With Disabilities Education Act (2004) reveals their foundations in a human capital agenda that drives schooling. In the human capital agenda, persons are valued for the contributions they make to economic productivity in a society (Postman, 1995; Tyack & Hansot, 1992; Smith & Scoll, 1995). Education then becomes a process of preparing children to take their places in the workforce. An alternative notion, a human capabilities agenda, should replace the current agenda for schooling so that society strengthens as each individual lives out possibilities that he or she values (Kleinhammer-Trammill, Burrello, & Sailor, see Chapter 1). Education becomes an opportunity to explore, nurture, and discover what those possibilities are. Through a human capabilities agenda, the social fabric is woven from the interests of those who value citizenship, economic productivity, personal freedom, individual growth, and community.

The overemphasis on standardized testing and test scores has come about because of concerns that we need a measurable means by which we can determine whether American students will be prepared to compete economically in a global society. Our students' educational performance is constantly compared to that of students in other countries. We as Americans take umbrage at the possibility that we might not be first in the world on a particular measure of student achievement. We extrapolate that concern into threats to our economic stability, leadership, and growth and then further to our prominence in a world that is increasingly more closely connected, more dangerous, and more interdependent (Darling-Hammond, 2010).

No Child Left Behind (2001) is the culmination of the standards-based reform movement and high-stakes accountability. The provisions of NCLB reflect the tenets of human capital theory in that the purpose of education is to develop human resources as capital in order to improve and sustain economic growth. According to this perspective, from economic productivity social opportunities are spurred and social mobility occurs. Under NCLB, those students who struggle academically are expected to respond to higher standards and to the motivation that having to take high-stakes tests provides. Schools are expected to support them by providing test preparation, additional tutoring and supplementary resources, after-school programs, remediation, and retention in grade. From these efforts, "a rising tide raises all ships"—that is, raising the expectations and intensity in the school experience will result in improved student achievement. Particular to NCLB is a target of ensuring that all students were working at grade level (achieving proficiency) in reading and math by 2014.

As a result of the structures and pressures built into NCLB, schools have increasingly become institutions that are focused on standardization and testing. In all schools, the centrality of testing and proficient test scores has resulted in

- narrowing the curriculum;
- intensely focusing attention on remediating reading and math performance;
- creating special programs that allege to improve results;
- packing the school day with those special programs such that other academic and arts programs are forced out of the curriculum;
- adding after-school and Saturday school for students who are in danger of not performing well on tests;
- increasing the numbers of testing occasions so students get the testing routine and so teachers can predict which students are at risk of test failure;
- following pacing guides that ensure teachers will at least minimally cover the content and skills that are included on the test;
- using celebrations, pep rallies, and other carnival-like occasions to motivate students to do well on tests; and
- generally ratcheting up the stress level of students, teachers, administrators, and parents.

The human capital theory that is embedded in NCLB has had a profound influence on the implementation of IDEA. NCLB's provision that students with disabilities are one of 13 subgroups that schools must show as proficient in order to meet the Adequate Yearly Progress (AYP) standard has focused attention on the performance of students with disabilities on standardized tests. Nearly all students with disabilities must participate in statewide assessments of the high-stakes general education curriculum. Special education teachers must be highly qualified to teach content courses.

Some positive outcomes have accrued from the connections between NCLB and IDEA. More students with disabilities are now educated in the general education classroom. Whether they are in the general education classrooms or special education classrooms, they are more likely to have access to the general education curriculum from a teacher who is highly qualified to teach that content. However, the narrowing of the school's work to reading and math as they are measured on standardized tests and the pressure to perform has diminished the education of all students, and especially those who come from families in poverty, which is too often the case with students with disabilities. Students who struggle with reading and writing are not better served when their schoolwork becomes a grind of remedial reading and math. Remedial education as *the* curriculum deflates the student's sense of efficacy, continuously reminds him or her that he or she is deficient, and removes the opportunity to discover other possibilities for learning.

In addition to the economic consequences and concerns about our once unassailable position as a world power, poorly performing schools also remind us that today's youth live in a different world than that of days gone by. They are growing up with more social and cultural instability, less certainty about their economic future, the pressures of consumerism, new technologies that have and will change how we conduct our lives and business, new norms and mores that create tensions between social groups and generations, increasing sociological and interpersonal diversity, and the availability of vast funds of knowledge at a cost rapidly approaching zero. Children have before them tremendous opportunity, tremendous risk, chaotic uncertainty, and continuous rapid change.

As with past generations, we current adults wonder what will become of these children and young people. And they wonder what we expect of them. Many are confident they will work it out—that their educational preparation, good nature, and common sense will see them through. Increasingly, however, many of today's children and youth do not have that confidence. They have experienced an educational system that has neither prepared them for thinking, adapting, and acting on information nor has it given them a solid sense of possibility. The impoverished school curriculum they have experienced has deprived them of their capacity to continue to learn, and the punitive, high-stress, confidence-depleting system of test preparation as curriculum and test results as learning has stripped them of their ability to be curious.

Human Capabilities

Sailor and Burrello (see Chapter 2) suggest that we need a radical overhaul of educational policy and practice that rests on a foundation of human capabilities. There have always been narratives of schooling that competed with the schooling as job training narrative—schooling to create a citizenry, schooling for personal development, schooling as socialization, just to name a few. The current overwhelming dominance of the economic narrative puts the state of our schools and our nation into sharp relief, and it quickly becomes apparent that we need to change our national narrative if we hope to survive into the next century, not only in education but also in our economic, environmental, and social safety net policies as well as our relations with other countries around the world. A human capabilities agenda helps us to do so by emphasizing that our social institutions should support a person's interests, needs, and aspirations as he or she pursues the possibilities of life that he or she values. Our task then as stewards of education who hope to leave a legacy of hope for our children and those who arrive hereafter is to radically and dramatically turn public education on its proverbial ear by looking at its foundational assumptions and its core mission.

A just social policy addresses political, economic, and social structures that value everyone and provides an equitable distribution of social opportunity (Wilson-Cooper, 2009; West, 1999). A just educational policy combines the equity vectors of NCLB with the individual responsiveness and empowerment vectors that are embedded in IDEA to create accessible, high-quality educational opportunities that respond to students' individual differences. A just educational policy encourages educators to craft programs and strategies that fit each child and his or her unique needs and aspirations so the child becomes an adult who can exercise the individual freedom and citizen activism that the Founders envisioned for this country.

Gallagher (2006) asks and then answers:

> So, what is social policy?
>
> Social policy creates the rules and standards by which scarce resources are allocated to meet almost unlimited social needs. An effective social policy should answer the following questions:
> 1. Who shall receive the resources?
> 2. Who shall deliver the resources?
> 3. What are the resources to be delivered?
> 4. What are the conditions under which the resources are delivered? (Gallagher, 1994, p. 337)

Gallagher's (2006) definition brings out a point that is always contentious in policy formation. There are always more demands and needs than there are resources to cover them. This is especially true in those areas, like special education, where the beneficiaries of the policy often are the poor and historically disenfranchised. Although they may be sympathetic to the plight of those policy beneficiaries, the citizenry is also resistant to paying higher taxes to support their needs.

Gallagher (2006) explains his definition further by providing an example of public prekindergarten. Table 3.2 rephrases Gallagher's questions to address the demands and needs that come from special education.

From these questions we come up with three major issues that need policy attention in the reconsideration of NCLB and IDEA: (1) Which students are we concerned about? (2) What is the curriculum? and (3) How will we account for resources and results?

TABLE 3.2. Gallagher's (2006) Example Adapted for Special Education

Who shall receive the resources?	Which students are eligible to receive special education and related services?
Who shall deliver the resources?	Who will teach and provide related services for students with disabilities? What professional development will they need?
What are the resources to be delivered?	What are the curricular, instructional, and assessment resources to be provided to students with disabilities?
What are the conditions under which the resources are delivered?	Where will students with disabilities be educated? What standards will they be expected to achieve? How will we account for resources and results?

Which Students Are We Concerned About?

In Fall 2011, about 6.6 million students aged 3–21 received special education and related services. They were distributed among 13 categories of disability. The largest number (2.4 million) were categorized as having specific learning disabilities; the fewest were categorized as having deaf-blindness (1,515), followed by traumatic brain injury (25,684) and visual impairment (29,117). The 13 categories have been more or less in place since the original passage of the Act in 1975, and they reflect the knowledge tradition in special education (Skrtic, 1991) that values differential diagnosis in the spirit of the medical model, which was the foundation on which much of special education was originally built.

The standardized testing movement and NCLB have shifted thinking about curriculum, instruction, assessment, and placement of students with disabilities. NCLB (2001) and IDEA (2004) require that all students have access to the general education curriculum and participate in the statewide assessment system, although they do make an allowance for those 2%–3% of students with significant disabilities for whom the general education program is not appropriate. The goals then for approximately 97% of all students are learning the general curriculum, performing at proficient levels on statewide assessments, and thereby being eligible to graduate from high school.

If we accept these three goals, students with disabilities can be categorized in three groups. The groups are not exclusive to specific disabilities. They exist for goal-setting purposes for individual students:

1. Students with significant disabilities—those 2%–3% for whom the general education curriculum and statewide assessments are not appropriate and for whom high school graduation is not an appropriate target under the current construction of high school graduation. Examples might include students with significant mental retardation, traumatic brain injury, and multiple disabilities.
2. Students with sensory and mobility impairments—students for whom the general education curriculum and statewide assessments are appropriate with reasonable accommodations and who require an additional curriculum that provides them with access to knowledge, social learning, and their communities. Examples might include students with hearing impairments, visual impairments, and orthopedic impairments.
3. Students with academic disabilities—students for whom the general education curriculum, statewide assessments, and high school graduation are appropriate, if they are provided with reasonable accommodations.

Although the 13 IDEA categories can serve an important diagnostic purpose, particularly for those students who have very complex learning needs, attaching a label to students is a time- and resource-intensive process that can lead to disagreements between parents and schools about what the label should mean. A human capabilities perspective would instead focus the decision-making process on what the short- and long-term goals for the student should be and how instruction should occur to accomplish those goals. In addition, assessment could focus on its formative purposes—providing information about progress and learning characteristics—rather than its current purpose of further categorizing students as proficient or nonproficient.

IDEA introduced requirements for individualization of educational programming and differentiated instruction to American schools. Although our experience with IEPs and thinking differently about teaching and learning have met with resistance and mixed results, individualizing is becoming more widely used. For example, in North Carolina, teachers write Personal Education Plans for students who do not score at proficient levels on the state assessments (North Carolina Department of Public Instruction, 2006). A policy change that required schools to create personalized education plans for each student would be a significant step forward in breaking the cycle of group-centered thinking on which the current system of education is based. While some would bemoan such a system, we must remember that the paperwork burden of IDEA stems from the due process protections for parents of students with disabilities. Such an arrangement would also likely be more successful in shifting power relationships in curricular, instructional, and assessment decision making.

An unfortunate aspect of special education due process provisions is that parents who are poor and historically disenfranchised are not as apt or as able to use their power as advocates for their children. A system of universal personalization would empower more parents with access to resources, knowledge, and political will to challenge the educational decisions made by school personnel. Although this might well be unpopular among school personnel, it would force the issue of whether schools are operating in the interests of children. Creating a system in which labeling of students, including disabilities, giftedness, proficiency, and so on, is deemphasized and personalized planning is the focus would tend to shift power toward the needs and aspirations of all students.

What Is the Curriculum?

NCLB requires states to adopt uniform standards for all school districts. The standards are intended to result in a high-expectations curriculum that challenges students to perform at international levels. Whether these curricula have reached that lofty goal is contentious among educators and curriculum specialists. There are those who believe that the curriculum has actually been watered down in order to enable more students to score at efficiency on the statewide assessments that are used to gauge what students are learning.

In 2009, the National Governors Association and the Council of Chief State School Officers announced a state-led effort to create a high-expectations set of curricular standards that could be adopted by states across the nation. In part, the variations across states in curriculum and assessments were a major impetus for the adoption of the *Common Core*. The common core standards have been adopted by 45 states, and a state's adoption is required for eligibility for Race to the Top funding, which is the Obama administration's strategy for education reform. The Common Core State Standards Initiative (CCSSI, 2011) states:

> The standards are informed by the highest, most effective models from states across the country and countries around the world, and provide teachers and parents the common understanding of what students are expected to learn. Consistent standards will provide appropriate benchmarks for all students, regardless of where they live.

CCSSI states that the standards "are informed by other top performing countries, so that all students are prepared to seek see in our global economy and society." It is apparent then that the common core standards focus on international competition and preparing students for the workforce. They are also intent on standardizing the curriculum in order to address the inequities they perceive to be in place in American schools. However, these "national" standards further remove decision making from the states and diminish state and local control of schools and their curricula.

A human capabilities curriculum would be personalized for each student and reflect his or her needs, aspirations, and experiences. Curriculum standards like the Common Core or the 50 state curricula can be useful to teachers, building administrators, and parents when they look to the standards for ideas or guidance about curriculum content, student development, and authentic assessment practices. However, adopting a standardized curriculum leads to "one-size-fits-all" thinking about student learning. The curriculum for all eight-year-old children becomes the third-grade curriculum, which denies the diversity that exists in any group of 20 to 25 students, even if they come from relatively homogeneous socioeconomic and cultural backgrounds. When we consider the racial, ethnic, gender, religious, language acquisition, ability, socioeconomic, and cultural differences that exist in our schools today, a standardized curriculum makes little sense. Standardization just does not fit the realities of today's public schools and the children who attend them.

While our schools reflect more diversity among and between students, the knowledge, skills, and dispositions that are required for students to be successful in the 21st century are also becoming more diverse. It is often said that we are educating children for a world that we cannot even imagine. If that is so, then the curriculum that is taught and learned in schools should be a curriculum of possibility for all students. In the 21st century, students have access to a wealth of information that expands exponentially every month. The cost of information access is rapidly approaching zero. Therefore, the curriculum available to diverse students should also be diverse. It should not be bounded by standardization, assessments, or lack of imagination.

Bray (2012) and Bray and McClaskey (2012) have described systems for personalizing learning in which they make distinctions between individualizing, differentiating, and personalizing. In personalized learning, "the learner owns the learning" (Bray, 2012, emphasis in original). Planning for learning includes the learner who helps to articulate his or her needs, aspirations, experiences, and interests. The learner also chooses his or her preferences for learning resources and technologies and creates a network of other students, teachers, and other adults to support his or her learning. Assessments are conducted in order to gather information about learning, and the results are used to further guide and support learning. Personalized learning differs from individualization and differentiation because personalization is a student-centered process. Individualizing and differentiating are activities in which teachers engage to provide instruction. Personalization includes individualization and differentiation but extends them by focusing on the learner and learning.

A human capabilities policy would put a personalized learning process into place for all students. Students, parents, and teachers would be collaborators in creating curriculum, experiencing learning, and assessing the student's progress toward goals he or she would be instrumental in setting. Careful attention would be required to ensure that the personalized planning necessary would not become as burdensome as the IEP has become. However, a focus on individualized planning would bring parents, teachers, and others concerned about a child together to discuss the child's needs and what the school would do to address them.

How Will We Account for Resources and Results?

NCLB holds schools and districts accountable by requiring that students be tested using standardized assessments that measure performance on standard curricula and that the aggregate results of those assessments be made public by subgroup. In turn, teachers and principals feel the pressure to ensure that students score at proficiency. Students are taught according to the requirements of the test in order to improve the likelihood that they will score at proficient levels, and low-performing students receive additional tutoring, supplemental education services, and intensive remediation that focuses on basic skills. Subsequently, discussions about such issues as retention in grade and referral for special education center around what teachers can do to improve the performance of these students. Unfortunately, all of these actions take place in a climate that essentializes curriculum and instruction, focuses on student deficits, and demoralizes students and teachers.

IDEA holds schools and districts accountable for compliance with the federal and state regulations that govern special education and related services. When there is a disagreement between parents and the school about the provision of a free appropriate public education for a child with a disability, either party can request a due process hearing in which an impartial hearing officer will make the decisions. Overwhelmingly, parents are the plaintiffs in these cases. Before the due process hearing, the parties can engage in negotiations or mediation, and some states have begun to use a facilitated IEP meeting as a means to coming to an agreement. After a due process hearing, either party can appeal through a state hearing process, and ultimately the case can land in court.

The due process hearing is an expensive, time-consuming process that takes a heavy toll on both parties. The threat of a due process hearing prompts school districts to work more closely with parents. It also accounts for the obsessive concern for correct paperwork and extensive documentation that pervades the administration of special education programs. Due process has caused special education to become a legalistic practice in many ways, resulting in the profession's losing sight of its purpose.

A human capabilities accountability system has its roots in "strong democracy" (Skrtic, 2005). Requiring schools to personalize education would result in more parental involvement in decisions about their children's education. Emphasizing "strong democracy" would mean that school personnel would have to learn how to listen to parents when it comes to students' education. A process for appealing decisions would need to be in place. The civil rights enforcement that is basic to IDEA would be a factor in this proposed process only in those cases where a child's right to an education is jeopardized. Therefore, it would be more likely that the negotiations would focus on educational matters rather than the technical aspects of compliance that have made IDEA so paperwork-heavy and cumbersome.

Skrtic has argued that "strong democracy" as a basis for social discourse "emphasizes democratic equality because it views democratic politics itself as a public good, as a source of reciprocal self-development, and social improvement in which citizens develop and exert their capacities for collective problem solving through reflexive discourse" (p. 415). Strong democracy as a mode of educational accountability brings parents into educational discourse and decision making with the personalized learning of their child at the center. School personnel are professionally obligated to work with parents on behalf of students, which breaks down the silos of the professional bureaucracy by which public schools are organized. Applying this approach to all students means that many more parents will participate, which will push the transformation toward open, democratic, substantive discussions about education forward faster. The due process protections afforded parents with students with disabilities will ensure that these parents will be invited to the table and that their consent will be given before any action occurs. Parents from families in poverty will need additional support participating in this process, and a policy provision requiring that support should be included in any change that is made.

All Students, a Curriculum of Possibilities, Democratic Accountability

An educational policy theory that focuses on human capabilities puts the needs, interests, aspirations, and experiences of students at the center of the school's work. All students, regardless of their characteristics or station in life, should have an equitable opportunity to explore life's possibilities. Rather than being bounded by standards, the school's curriculum would intend to explore knowledge, skills, and understanding so children are literate, active, and lifelong searchers who transform information into individual, communal, social, and economic productivity that serves the values and purposes of local communities and the global society. Democratic governance and democratic accountability are activities that bring people together around issues that are important, and the school is where students learn to participate in the political discourse and power exchanges that are required for a strong democracy to prosper. While their children are learning to be democratically productive, their parents and the community around them are practicing democracy by negotiating educational possibilities, governing schools, and holding one another collaboratively accountable for valued results.

Many questions remain about the possibilities of schools that base their work on developing human capabilities. Schools certainly need to change. Whether their current status represents a "requiem scenario" or not, it is time to think the unthinkable. Schools have been an important part of our history. If we are to meet the challenges of the 21st century, we need new thinking, new technologies, new energy, new activism. And we need investments in all children, expansive curriculum and learning, and collaborative decision making and responsibility. Most of all, to create schools that are good for children, good for communities, good for all of us, we need a change of heart.

References

Bernhardt, V.L. (2003). No schools left behind. *Educational Leadership,* 60(5), 26–30.

Bireda, S., & Miller, R. (2010, March 2). Walking the talk: Closing the comparability requirement in Title I of the Elementary and Secondary Education Act. *Center for American Progress.* Retrieved from http://www.americanprogress.org/issues/2010/03/comparability_brief.html

Bray, B. (2012). *Personalized learning. Rethinking learning.* Retrieved from http://barbarabray.net/personalized-learning/

Bray, B., & McClaskey, K. (2012, January 22). *Personalization vs. differentiation vs. individualization.* Retrieved from http://eepurl.com/fLJZM

Common Core State Standards Initiative. (2011). *Common Core State Standards.* Retrieved from http://www.corestandards.org/about-the-standards

Darling-Hammond. (2010). *The flat world and education: How America's commitment to equity will determine our future.* New York: Teachers College Press.

Education of All Handicapped Children Act of 1975. P.L. 94-142. 20 U.S.C. § 1400 *et seq.* (1975).

Federal Education Budget Project. (2011). *No Child Left Behind funding.* Retrieved from http://febp.newamerica.net/background-analysis/no-child-left-behind-funding

Gallagher, J. (1994). Policy designed for diversity: New initiatives for children with disabilities. In D. M. Bryant & M. A. Graham (Eds.), *Implementing early intervention* (pp. 336–350). New York: Guilford Press.

Gallagher, J. J. (2006). *Driving change in special education.* Baltimore, MD: Paul Brookes.

Hendrik Hudson District Board of Education v. Rowley. 458 U.S. 176 (1982).

Heuer, R., & Stullich, S. (2011). *Comparability of state and local expenditures among schools within districts: A report from the study of school-level expenditures.* U.S. Department of Education, Office of Planning, Evaluation, and Policy Development, Policy and Program Studies Service. Retrieved from http://www2.ed.gov/rschstat/eval/title-i/school-level-expenditures/school-level-expenditures.pdf

Holler, R.A., & Zirkel, P.A. (2008). Section 504 and public schools: A national survey concerning "Section 504-only" students. *NASSP Bulletin, 92,* 19–43.

Individuals With Disabilities Education Act. 20 U.S.C. § 1400 *et seq.* (2004).

Mann, H. (1848). *Horace Mann on education and national welfare. Twelfth Annual Report of Horace Mann as Secretary of Massachusetts State Board of Education.* Retrieved from http://www.tncrimlaw.com/civil_bible/horace_mann.htm

McNell, M. (2011, March). Duncan: 82 percent of schools could be "failing" this year. Politics K-12: Your education roadmap. *Education Week.* Retrieved from http://blogs.edweek.org/edweek/campaign-k-12/2011/03/duncan_82_of_schools_could_be.html

McNell, M. (2011, December). *Duncan's 82% NCLB failure prediction way off base, new data show.* Politics K-12: Your education roadmap. Education Week. Retrieved from http://blogs.edweek.org/edweek/campaign-k-12/2011/12/duncans_82_nclb_failure_predic.html

Miller, R., & Brown, C. (2011, December 2). The persistence of inequality: Newly released data confirms our nation needs educational funding reform. Center for American Progress. Retrieved from http://www.americanprogress.org/issues/2010/03/comparability_brief.html

National Commission on Excellence and Education. (1983). *A nation at risk: The imperative of educational reform.* Retrieved from http://www2.ed.gov/pubs/NatAtRisk/index.html

No Child Left Behind Act of 2001. P.L. 107-110. 20 U.S.C. § 6301 *et seq.* (2001).

North Carolina Department of Public Instruction. (2006). *A vision for literacy in North Carolina.* Raleigh, NC: State Board of Education.

Postman, N. (1995). *The end of education: Redefining the value of school.* New York: Knopf.

Senge, P. Schwarmer, A.O., Jaworski, J., & Flowers, B.S. (2004). *Presence: Human purpose and the field of the future.* New York: Currency Books.

Skrtic, T. (1991). *Behind special education: A critical analysis of professional culture and school organization.* Denver, CO: Love.

Skrtic, T. (2005). A political economy of learning disabilities. *Learning Disabilities Quarterly, 28*(2), 149–155. In Skrtic, T.M., Horn, E.M., & Clark, G.M. (2009). *Taking stock of special education policy and practice.* Denver, CO: Love.

Smith, M. S., & Scoll, B. (1995). The Clinton human capital agenda. *Teachers College Record, 96*(3), 389–404.

Tyack, D., & Hansot, E. (1992). Learning together: A history of coeducation in American public schools. New York: Russell Sage Foundation.

U.S. Department of Education. (2012). *Department of Education budget tables.* Retrieved from http://www2.ed.gov/about/overview/budget/tables.html?src=ct

West, C. (1999). The new cultural politics of difference. In C. West (Ed.), *The Cornel West reader* (pp. 119–139). New York: Basic Civitas Books.

Wilson-Cooper, C. (2009). Performing cultural work in demographically changing schools: Implications for expanding transformational leadership frameworks. *Educational Administration Quarterly, 45,* 694–724.

Yell, M. (2012). The law and special education. New York: Pearson.

4

BUSTING BARRIERS TO FULLY INTEGRATING SYSTEMS OF EDUCATION

Analyzing IDEA and Applying Models of Disability

Shana J. Haines and Rud Turnbull

The central argument in this book—that an integrated system of education will advance the capabilities and outcomes of all students, including those with disabilities—parallels the integration principle of the least restrictive environment (LRE) in the Individuals With Disabilities Education Act (IDEA, 2004). An integrated system can obviate much, if not all, of the separation that LRE presumes is not appropriate for students with disabilities. In other respects, it is quite different. The fundamental conception of education as a single system with no discrete special education component ostensibly eliminates special education as a separate system and puts in its place a single system of supports available to all students. Logically, this integrated system jettisons IDEA's continuum of services and instead creates dynamic supports and services for students in need, universal problem-solving approaches, and combined funding streams.

The argument for an integrated system of education meets some objections, including IDEA itself. In this chapter, we respond to these objections. We begin by describing IDEA's six principles, focusing mostly on the LRE principle. We then connect the relevant IDEA principles to their counterparts in the federal general education law, the Elementary and Secondary Education Act (ESEA, 1965), to demonstrate the statutory opportunities already in place for integrating the presently separate structures of special and general education.

Next, we describe and analyze IDEA's provisions for a continuum of supports and services and how this continuum relates to LRE. We then discuss the Constitutional command that all students be given an equal opportunity for education (*Brown v. Board of Education*, 1954) by describing why "equality" as applied to students with disabilities must be regarded in a different light than equality among others. Thereafter, we argue that a misunderstanding of equality is not the only barrier to an integrated system of education for all. We identify other barriers to integrating systems of education and relate them to the values that underlie the LRE principle and the courts' interpretations of the LRE principle. We then briefly outline three possibilities for policy to decrease barriers to integrating systems of education.

Next, we argue that the models professionals and families use to understand disability profoundly affect the prospects for integrated systems. To illustrate this, we imagine a conference of professionals, parents, and a student with a disability weighing the merits and drawbacks of an integrated system. We conclude by appealing to a sense of justice as articulated by John Rawls (1958) and Martha Nussbaum (2006).

IDEA and ESEA: The Policy Context

The main principles of IDEA and ESEA align with each other in significant ways and thus offer policy reformers an opportunity to integrate the presently separate structures of special and general education. In this section, we outline each law's basic principles and highlight the relevant alignment.

Individuals With Disabilities Education Act: The Special Education Legal Framework

IDEA consists of six principles (Turnbull, Stowe, & Huerta, 2007):

- zero reject (all children have a right to a free appropriate public education);
- nondiscriminatory evaluation (every child must be evaluated according to specified criteria and procedures);
- individualized and appropriate education (education must offer each child an opportunity to benefit);
- least restrictive environment (a presumption that students with disabilities will be educated in the general education environment);
- procedural due process (schools and parents will use methods of mutual accountability); and
- parent participation (shared decision will occur among educators and parents).

The three principles that most promote LRE are nondiscriminatory evaluation, individualized and appropriate education, and, of course, LRE itself. These three principles—representing evaluation, program, and placement—constitute an unbreakable nexus (20 U.S.C. Sec. 1414 (a)–(d)) designed to ensure that a student with a disability is given an authentic opportunity to achieve IDEA's four national outcomes: equal opportunity, independent living, full participation, and economic self-sufficiency (20 U.S.C. Sec. 1400 (c)).

The nondiscriminatory evaluation principle (20 U.S.C. Sec. 1414 (a–c)) has two objectives: to determine whether a student has a disability and, if so, to identify supports necessary for the student to receive an appropriate education and thus benefit from school, including participating in and making progress in the general curriculum. Not only are the evaluation data the foundations of each student's individualized education (20 U.S.C. Sec. 1414 (b)(2)(A)), they also are explicitly required to advance the LRE principle (20 U.S.C. Sec. 1414 (b)(2)(A)).

The appropriate education principle requires, among other things, that the local education agency provide an individualized program (20 U.S.C. Sec. 1414 (d)(1)(A)(i)), necessary related services (20 U.S.C. Sec. 1414 (d)(iv)), and supplementary aids and services to enable education in the LRE (20 U.S.C. Sec. 1414 (d)(v)). An "appropriate education" consists of special education and related services tailored to fit the student's needs (20 U.S.C. Sec. 1401(9)). The Supreme Court, in *Board of Education v. Rowley* (1982), determined that a state provides an appropriate education for a student when "personalized instruction with sufficient support services to permit the child to benefit educationally from that instruction" (III(C)) is provided.

Inasmuch as the evaluation and program decision making are jointly directed at advancing the student's education in the LRE, IDEA defines the general curriculum to include academic, extracurricular, and other school activities (20 U.S.C. Sec. 1414 (d)(1)(A)(iv)(bb)). More important, IDEA holds a legal presumption in favor of the student's placement in each of these domains of the general curriculum, but the presumption is rebuttable if a more integrated placement would not provide an appropriate education (as we discuss below).

For the purposes of considering organizing a single system of education, the LRE principle should drive policy makers and school administrators toward an integrated system. To this extent, the LRE rule is consistent with a reconceptualized special education system—one that is "a temporally bounded instructional support system for any student in the public schools who might need support to achieve his or her full capabilities" (Kleinhammer-Trammill, Burrello, & Sailor, this volume, p. 3) that is embedded in general education. To determine whether that ideal—a system fully embedded in another—is feasible, we turn to the principles of ESEA.

Elementary and Secondary Education Act: The General Education Legal Framework

While IDEA applies to students with diagnosed disabilities, ESEA applies to all students. Like IDEA, ESEA consists of six main principles: accountability, highly qualified teachers, evidence-based interventions (EBI), school safety, local flexibility, and parental participation and choice (Turnbull et al., 2007). Of these six principles, accountability, highly qualified teachers, and EBI support an integrated system of education because each is incorporated by IDEA (Turnbull et al., 2007).

The principle of accountability requires all students to demonstrate proficiency in core academic subjects. The highly qualified teachers principle ensures that teachers have received or are currently receiving adequate education to teach effectively and contribute to students' progress (U.S. Department of Education, 2004). The EBI requirement ensures that the teachers use instructional strategies and techniques proven to be effective in providing students with an appropriate education.

This alignment of IDEA and ESEA makes it legally possible for an integrated system of education to exist. The IDEA provision for a continuum of services, however, presents a barrier to the integrated system. The continuum of services is especially opprobrious because it impedes students with disabilities from being able to "flow in and out of these (universally available and individualized support) services according to their support needs at particular points in time or curricular contexts" (Kleinhammer-Trammill et al., this volume, p. 10).

We agree with the "flow" premise and with the argument favoring an integrated system, and we acknowledge that the continuum is problematic because it is rigid and facilitates out-placements that need not be made. We believe, however, that some students with intense needs will have an appropriate education only if they receive some of their services in more restrictive environments at least some of the time. For example, a student hospitalized for medical purposes should receive her education there, or else IDEA's zero reject principle would not apply. Likewise, a student with a traumatic brain injury may, at one time after the injury, need to receive services separately; that need may dissipate over time and the services should respond to the child's changing need. Having stated a qualification of our support for the "flow" and "integration" principle, we will describe IDEA's provisions related to the continuum and lay out three policy approaches to mitigating the barrier caused by the continuum.

The Continuum of Services

The LRE presumption that a student be educated in the general curriculum (20 U.S.C. Sec. 1414 (a)(5)(A); Turnbull et al., 2007) yields to the reality that disability is a distinction that sometimes makes a difference. Thus, IDEA provides that a student must be educated with students who do not have disabilities to the maximum extent appropriate for the student and that special classes, separate schooling, or other removal of the student from the regular educational environment may occur *only* when the nature or severity of the student's disability is such that education in regular classes with the use of related services and supplementary aids and services cannot be achieved satisfactorily for that student (20 U.S.C. Sec. 1412 (a)(5)(A)). The continuum of alternative placements must include regular classes, special classes, special schools, home instruction, and instruction in hospitals and institutions (34 C.F.R. Sec. 300.115). The word *only* is powerfully limiting and requires educators to consider the severity or nature of the student's disability, nothing more. If they determine the student cannot be educated "satisfactorily" in regular classes even after receiving related services and supplementary aids and services, educators may propose to place the child along the continuum of services.

The LRE doctrine derives from the constitutional principle that, when government has a legitimate reason to infringe the liberty of any citizen, it must do so in the least restrictive or least drastic manner (Turnbull et al., 2007). Thus, the LRE principle presumes people with disabilities have a right to the same liberties and rights people without disabilities have, including the right of an education (*Mills v. District of Columbia Board of Education*, 1972; *PARC v. Commonwealth*, 1971, 1972).

The LRE principle, then, is more than a limiting doctrine; it is a liberating and integrating one. While it limits the government from segregating students, when effectively applied (by highly qualified teachers using evidence-based interventions and supported by related service providers and supplementary aids and services), it also makes it possible for a student to be liberated from segregated special education and integrated into a single system of education.

That is a desired value, if not the most desired value. Martha Nussbaum (2006), in advocating for policies that advance "a life with human dignity" (p. 7), nonetheless recognizes that individuals vary from each other and have varying needs: "so the question of variability cannot be postponed, it is omni-present" (p. 165). Building on Nussbaum's thesis that each person has a right to human dignity, Kleinhammer-Tramill and colleagues (2013) and Lashley (2013) (this volume) adopt a "human development and capacities approach that sees education as fulfilling three roles of liberation, empowerment, and participation" (p. 8). At this point, we address Nussbaum's "variability" and our colleagues' "liberation, empowerment, and participation" goal by considering what equality—that principle that accommodates variability but advances liberation—means in the context of special education and other disability policy.

Equality, the Continuum, and an Integrated School System

Let us return to a point we made above: disability is a distinction that sometimes makes a difference. In particular, it makes a difference in how we think about "equality" and "equal opportunity" to receive a measurable benefit within the right to an education. To address "equality" in the context of an argument for an integrated school system requires us to understand "equality" as it applies to individuals with disabilities.

The meaning of "equality" and "equal opportunity" changes when applied to an individual with a disability (Turnbull et al., 2007). It is useful to think of "equality" as having three tiers. To envision the tier analogy, consider the following three students. One student with a disability may be educated exactly like an individual without a disability and still benefit. For example, a student with a motor disability and no other limitations may still participate in all academic curricula without any adjustments for his sake. Another student has a sensory disability, such as a significant hearing impairment, and needs accommodations, such as interpreters or amplification, in order to benefit from education. A third student has a significant intellectual disability and needs different, more intensive supports in order to benefit.

Purely equal opportunity will benefit the first student; equal opportunity plus accommodations will benefit the second; and unequal treatment, but not invidious or limiting treatment, will benefit the third. Some people with disabilities will fall within the not-purely-equal tiers and may need enabling services and placements to have an equal educational opportunity. This different treatment must be fluid and thus responsive to students' needs. In fact, it is unlikely that the students in tiers two and three will be able to achieve the four national outcomes of disability policy—equal opportunity, independent living, full participation, and economic self-sufficiency—without different treatment.

Notwithstanding this nuanced conceptualization of equality, each of these students (and others like them) can participate in general education. In fact, they are increasingly doing so. The percentage of time that students with all disabilities participate in the general curriculum has increased, and the restrictiveness of placement across disability categories has decreased over time as more students with disabilities participate in general education classrooms for most of their school day and spend less of their time outside the general education classroom (U.S. Department of Education, 2011). In addition, the number of students in self-contained and separate facilities has diminished (U.S. Department of Education, 2011). This trend applies to the overall special education student body, including students of all disabilities, ethnic groups, and geographic locations.

There are several reasons for this trend, including systems and individual-professional capacity building as seen in the more widespread use of response to intervention, universal design for learning, schoolwide positive behavioral support, augmentative and alternative communication, assistive technology, other evidence-based practices, and collaboration between teachers (Turnbull, Turnbull, & Wehmeyer, 2012). It is apparent that, from the perspective of the LRE doctrine and the reconceptualized understanding of "equality," an integrated school system is feasible. But the case for an integrated system is still not closed.

Barriers Beyond LRE and Reconceptualized Equality

Forces that impede integrated systems are the same that impede integration of individuals with disabilities in other domains of life. Fear limits liberty. Some families fear that general education environments and other communities are not safe for their children with disabilities because their children will be stigmatized. Other people fear those with disabilities because they do not understand them and cannot predict their behavior. Others fear difference itself: Segregation allows people without disabilities to put people with disabilities out of their sight and thus out of their minds. Some fear change and are rigidly accustomed to segregation based on ability.

These fears are especially liberty-limiting when held by education professionals. Objectively, it affects their practice; subjectively, it sends their attitudinal message to the students they teach. Foremost, their fear of inadequacy in teaching students with disabilities too often manifests in the presumption that other, more specialized teachers and placements are needed in order to provide an appropriate education for students with disabilities. This attitude affects all students with disabilities but is especially prevalent and insidious when applied to students of historically underserved groups who are disproportionally represented in special education (Artiles, Kozleski, Trent, Osher, & Ortiz, 2010).

In addition to the disproportional representation of non-White students in special education (Artiles et al., 2010; Skiba et al., 2008), these students, once eligible for special education, are placed in more restrictive environments than their White peers across disability categories (Cartledge, Singh, & Gibson, 2008; Fierros & Conroy, 2002; Losen & Welner, 2001; Skiba, Poloni-Staudinger, Gallini, Simmons, & Feggins-Azziz, 2006; Skiba et al., 2008). Ironically, the same law that seeks to protect the civil rights of students with disabilities by guaranteeing them free and appropriate education simultaneously allows their exclusion from the general education classroom through the continuum of services (Ferri & Connor, 2005).

As we have noted, a decision that services need to occur outside the general education classroom can result from a lack of professional capacity. General educators are often ill prepared to work with students with disabilities and therefore lack the confidence to teach these students in their classrooms (Connor & Ferri, 2005; Kozleski & Waitoller, 2010; Matzen, Ryndak, & Nakao, 2010). Professionals often lack the skills and time needed to collaborate to create innovative educational programs (Brownell, Adams, Sindelar, Waldron, & Vanhover, 2006; Matzen et al., 2010), yet the inability of teachers and school administrators to figure out how a student learns and arrange the conditions to facilitate that learning are rarely explored (Ferri, 2009). Intensity of service is often confused with segregation; Taylor (2001) challenges professionals' commonly held belief that more intense aids and services must be provided in more, not less, restricted environments. In fact, students in "cotaught classes received a greater number of related services than students in either resource room or alternate day supports" (Lodato Wilson, Kim, & Michaels, 2011, p. 12).

Although the LRE rule balances the tension between the interests of the student to be in the general education environment and the interests of the schools to educate the student appropriately and in safe conditions, the true nature of "benefit" is often misconstrued, and the most significant impediment to identifying how and where the student benefits most is attitudinal. While the law, research, and much of society support fuller integration, the system hesitates. Perhaps this hesitation stems from a misunderstanding of the values behind LRE.

Values Behind LRE

There are three overlapping values behind the LRE principle: academic benefit, social benefit, and cost containment (Turnbull et al., 2007). These three values are optimally advanced through an integrated, inclusive system of education.

Academic benefit occurs when all students are held to high expectations and offered a genuine opportunity to benefit from the same academic curriculum (Hardman & Dawson, 2008; Lane, Pierson, Stang, & Carter, 2010). Students with disabilities generally experience fewer positive academic outcomes when placed in segregated environments than in more integrated ones (e.g., Hardman & Dawson, 2008). In fact, all students in the general education classes gain academic benefit from the inclusion of students with disabilities in their classes (Cole, Waldron, & Majd, 2004; Salend & Garrick Duhaney, 1999). This benefit is largely due to the services and supports received by students with disabilities (e.g., collaboration between a general education teacher and related services providers) and the expanded teaching skills and styles of their general education teachers (e.g., incorporating the principles of universal design for learning [UDL] in their teaching; Sailor & Roger, 2005).

Social benefit occurs when students with and without disabilities associate with one another, and inclusion makes this association possible by compelling them, and their teachers, to confront not only the fact that some students are more limited than others but also the fact that attitudes and values impede integrated systems of education (Brownell et al., 2006). The essential teaching of the Supreme Court's decision in *Brown v. Board of Education* (1954) and in the Court's decision about parental authority to commit their children to an institution, *Parham v. J.R.* (1979), is that legally compelled confrontation between individuals with different traits is the only socially acceptable method that the courts can take, and that individuals and entities should take, to lessening stigma and increasing tolerance. Attitudinal change, indeed deep cultural change, can happen only when students are in the same space. As with respect to race, so it is with respect to disability: compelled confrontation encourages all students to view difference among themselves as an attribute and decrease intolerance (Salend & Garrick Duhaney, 1999). Minow, Shweder, and Marcus (2008) state:

> Ensuring that subgroups within the general population are able to coexist with each other, revitalizing a framework of ordered liberty, avoiding destructive conflict and intolerance, helping each individual contribute to the well-being of the nation, and promoting the capacities of the next generation to take up the obligations of citizenship—these are the challenges for justice in education. (p. 15)

Positive attribution mitigates stigma and results in increased "acceptance, understanding, and tolerance of individual differences" (Salend & Garrick Duhaney, 1999, p. 120).

Additionally, increasing association boosts students with disabilities' social capital (Bourdieu, 1986)—those networks of people and relationships—secures privilege, status, and power. The outcomes of increased social capital include "supportive friendships [that] buffer against distress and illness, reciprocal relationships [that] create a culture where learning and contribution flourishes, and heightened trust [that] leads to a reduction in crime" (Bates & Davis, 2004, p. 197).

The third value behind LRE, cost containment, occurs when resources are allocated in a dynamic and pragmatic fashion to maximize utility and minimize waste. Educating students with disabilities in the general education classroom can allow more creative scheduling and pooling of resources. Instead of using resources for the student with disabilities in isolation (e.g., in the "resource" room), these resources can be shared more readily in the general education classroom, as discussed elsewhere in this volume. In addition, integrated systems of education allow localities to more creatively structure their budgets (Sailor & Roger, 2005).

The Courts, LRE, Values, and the Continuum

In four overlapping lines of cases, the courts have long recognized the three LRE values in determining whether a more or less integrated education is appropriate for a student with a disability.

The first line of cases (*Roncker v. Walter*, 1983) requires a court to make two determinations:

- Are the segregated special education services more beneficial to the student than the presently available integrated services?
- Can they be recreated in the integrated setting? If so, the LEA must restructure itself, both physically and educationally.

The second line of cases (*Daniel R.R. v. State Board of Education*, 1989) requires two similar determinations:

- Can the child be educated in the general curriculum, including academic and nonacademic activities, appropriately with the use of supplementary aids and services?
- Does the student's education in a segregated academic setting still permit his integration to the maximum extent appropriate for him in other (here, extracurricular) activities? The LEA must consider both academic and non-academic integration, consistent with IDEA's definition of the general curriculum as consisting of academic, extracurricular, and other school activities (20 U.S.C. Sec. 1414 (d)(1)(A)(iv)(bb)).

The third line of cases (*Sacramento City Unified School District Board of Education v. Rachel H (Holland)*, 1994) requires four determinations:

- Are the educational benefits of an education in the general classroom, with supplementary aids and services, comparable to the benefits of an education in a segregated special education classroom?
- What is the nonacademic benefit, to the student with a disability, of associating with nondisabled students?
- Does the student have a negative or learning-impeding effect on the teacher and other students in the general education setting?
- What are the costs of integrating the student with a disability into the general curriculum?

A fourth line of cases began with *Hartmann v. Loudon County Board of Education* (1997), creating a three-part test:

- Will the student with a disability *not* receive an educational benefit from being integrated into a general education class?
- Is the marginal benefit from integrating the student significantly outweighed by benefits that are available *only* in a separate, segregated setting?
- Will the student disrupt the education of other students in the general education classroom?

These four lines of cases are similar in several respects.

- They regard IDEA's LRE provisions as creating a rebuttable presumption in favor of integration.
- They balance the interests of the student with a disability to have an appropriate education with the student's interests in integration. Thus, they construe the LRE provisions as instrumental to and as the means for a student's appropriate education.
- Given the rebuttability of the LRE provisions and their subsumed importance to the principle of an appropriate education, they rely on the concept of a continuum of separate or segregated placements as safety-valves that benefit both the student with a disability and other students and faculty.
- They recognize that the LRE principle advances the student's education; the presumption is that the student will make more academic progress when integrated than when not.
- They acknowledge that the student will make more social progress when integrated than when not. The right of the student to associate with nondisabled peers has the power to destigmatize the student.
- They take into account that integrated education can maximize fiscal and human resources but that maximization does not always result from integration. In some cases, it is disproportionately expensive, considering the benefit to the student and benefits and drawbacks for his peers, to provide an integrated education.

The courts clearly understand the values that underlie the LRE rule. That, however, does not mean that integration is a hard and fast rule. There is nothing in the case law that absolutely impedes an integrated system of education for all. What the cases suggest, instead, is that, where the schools have the will to create an integrated system of education for all, they comply more fully with the values that underlie the LRE rule and blunt the grounds on which it is now permissibly rebutted. Constitutional or statutory rule supports the effective education of all students, not tracking techniques that separate and categorize them.

Where there is a will and administrative and teaching skill, there is a way to create fully integrated schools and erase the lines separating general from special education. Further, IDEA and ESEA align sufficiently for that result to obtain. Courts do not permanently stand in the way; their current interpretation of the LRE presumption-plus-continuum provisions does. To secure more integration, Congress must amend the statute.

Policy Considerations

Congress has several choices if it intends to create a more unified system. First, it can more closely align IDEA and ESEA by insisting that states adopt certification standards that ensure that general education teachers are more competent to teach students with disabilities and that they know and have demonstrated their abilities to use evidence-based instruction. This approach builds on IDEA and ESEA provisions for highly qualified teachers and EBI. It also is consistent with the argument that collaborative teams of educators and related service personnel should design, implement, monitor, and redesign instruction together. In this dynamic system, teams of professionals plan instruction to occur in the setting that makes the most sense for the specific task at hand, but the location where students work is fluid and temporary.

Second, Congress can amend IDEA by setting out criteria that make it more difficult for schools to place students into restrictive environments. It can retain the "only when" limitation on using the continuum, add "related services" to "supplementary aids and services," and clarify "satisfactorily" to mean that the student is absolutely unable to make academic, behavioral, developmental, or functional progress even after highly qualified teachers, other school staff, and related service providers have used evidence-based interventions.

To advance that stricter approach, Congress can create an independent, roving team of inclusion experts, appointed by the state, who would review decisions to place students outside of the general education classroom for a significant amount of time. Each IEP team that proposes services through the continuum would be required to complete a standard questionnaire about the necessity of these services; the alternatives already attempted in the LRE; the race, ethnicity, language, and SES of the student; and the process and timeline for the evaluation process of the placement. This approach would create an additional procedural hurdle (or standard of practice) to placement in the continuum, strengthen the presumption in favor of integration and make it more difficult to rebut, and increase tracking of placement.

Third, Congress can simply abolish the continuum provision and mandate that all students with disabilities be educated exclusively in the general curriculum. Here, Congress would abandon the rebuttable presumption in favor of an absolute presumption. We believe that approach would be unwise; disability often requires different responses, as we discussed when analyzing "equality," and times exist when schools need to provide services outside of the general education classroom.

Taking the statute and case law together, it is reasonable to conclude that the current continuum provisions and the rebuttable presumption do not impede integrated school systems. The obstacles are (a) the unwillingness of school systems and their constituencies to consider the possibilities and benefits of integrated systems that accrue for all students, to stop doing what they are accustomed to doing, and to discontinue the maintenance of a parallel practice; and (b) Congress' and the school system's tolerance of a too-easy-to-use continuum.

Models for Thinking About Disability and Integrated Systems

The statute, cases, and prospective amendments do not reveal the core issue, which is found in this question: How do professionals and families think about disability and how do they act on it, especially when they are confronting the prospects of a fully integrated school system? Do they adhere to the continuum or do they break out of it and advance LRE in the three domains of the general education curriculum? Do they even conceive of and advocate for a fully integrated system of education for all students? The answer depends greatly on how professionals and families perceive the strengths and limitations of both students with disabilities and their educators and educational systems.

There are five models for understanding disability. Each is an umbrella for several submodels, and each submodel holds certain beliefs about disability that may impede or facilitate LRE and an integrated system of education. These beliefs translate into techniques that members of a particular submodel bring to bear in thinking about disability and about disability-related interventions and policies.

The Public Studies Model

The public studies model is primarily concerned about the relationship between the government and its people (Turnbull & Stowe, 2001). This model's submodels include law, political science and philosophy, political economy, demographics, and public administration. Law deals with the rules of a community and balancing the rights and duties of the government and its people. The law submodel views disability as an unalterable trait that requires a positive, or protective, response from government. This submodel holds that a student's right to education must be protected; LRE ensures a student's liberty by limiting the government from segregating the student from her peers. It also champions the student's legal rights and therefore is protective of the student's right to an individualized and appropriate education within the integrated system.

Political science and philosophy studies how governments do or should work and how they can achieve an optimal balance of power between the people and the government. The political science and philosophy submodel is concerned with how LRE is interpreted and implemented. This submodel holds that integrated systems of education can benefit students with and without disabilities, but it acknowledges the possibility that students without disabilities could lose their positive rights without the "protection" of special education.

Political economy focuses on the relationship between politics and economics and is primarily concerned with efficient and effective revenue-raising and spending. Political economy is concerned with LRE's cost and effectiveness. Because political economics also is concerned with the allocation of resources and tax or other fiscal burdens that generate resources, it takes into account the demographics submodel. Demographics is the study of the population. As far as LRE is concerned, demographics focuses primarily on population trends about time spent in and out of the general education classroom. While this submodel encourages combining funding streams through integrated systems, it is concerned with the difficulty of developing and using statistics for administrative purposes (e.g., tracking where students and teachers spend their time).

Public administration is concerned with how government organizations work and how they can optimize collaboration to maximize efficiency and effectiveness. Public administration is particularly concerned with maximizing the benefit from staff collaboration and professional development. This submodel champions integrated systems because one of its purposes is minimizing overlap and maximizing resource allocation and efficiency.

The Human Development Model

The human development model deals with how people develop or acquire capacities. It involves three primary submodels: medical, psychological, and educational. The medical submodel regards people with disabilities as being sick and in need of healing. The medical model supports methods that are scientifically proven to prevent or mitigate the effects of disability and tends to favor interventions that focus on the individual in isolation.

The psychological submodel, on the other hand, regards behavior as learned and focuses on controlling the conditions of person-environment interactions

(Turnbull & Stowe, 2001). The psychological model champions integrated systems as a method for increasing relationships and learning appropriate behavior by creating conditions conducive to that end.

The educational submodel holds that everyone can learn when given an opportunity to engage in a meaningful curriculum. The educational model also champions integrated systems but calls for increased education and collaboration of the school workforce in order to implement curricula that are meaningful for all students and instruction that accommodates human variability. The argument is that, by integrating systems, there will be increased collaboration and shared resources (e.g., technology, professional development, planning time).

The Cultural Model

The cultural model holds that disability is a socially constructed phenomenon. The cultural model's submodels—cultural anthropology, sociology, literature, the performing arts, and history—explain cultures' ideas of disability rather than directly drive policy development. For the sake of policy analysis, the cultural model is concerned with how society perceives people with disabilities. It treats the main role of LRE as dispelling the stigma of disability through ensuring association. Compelled confrontation normalizes disability and increases acceptance of difference, which lessens the cultural construction of disability. Integrating systems further dispels stigma because all students will belong to the same educational system.

The Technology Studies Model

The technology studies model is concerned with the physical world inhabited by people with disabilities (architectural submodel), technology that aids people with disabilities ("hard" technology), and the capacities of professionals to serve people with disabilities ("soft" technology). The technology studies model is concerned with the systems development necessary for students to benefit from LRE within an integrated system. It asks what needs to be done for students to be able to (a) navigate the physical space where education occurs, (b) access the general education curriculum, and (c) benefit from professionals who can facilitate their appropriate education.

The Ethical Model

The ethical model seeks the "right" action. When investigating LRE within an integrated system of education, the ethical model asks if this is the morally defensible action to take. This model recognizes that education is a social learning process that can build social capital of students with disabilities through their interactions with their peers. Students with disabilities need their peer group, and this model finds it unethical to deprive these students of daily opportunities to be taught in the context of their peers.

The Models Applied: A Theatre of Discourse

To see how these models work in action, let's imagine a conference room in a middle school of a hypothetical district that is in the process of merging its educational systems into an integrated system of education. Seated at the conference table, ready for a long discussion, are the various characters in this theatre of discourse.

Dramatis Personae

- Jeffrey Sandoval, a 13-year-old student with Down syndrome who is now in sixth grade, relates well to children and teachers and loves to talk, joke, and create funny stories. His reading skills are not as advanced as his listening comprehension, and he loves to hear phantasmagorical stories read aloud, detail of which he often incorporates into his own stories. Jeffrey speaks Spanish at home with family and English at school. Jeffrey occasionally confuses his languages and he has speech impediments that make understanding his words difficult at times; frustration and fatigue result in occasional outbursts that can escalate to self-injury or aggression against others. Jeffrey calms down quickly when away from his peers and coached one on one. Jeffrey likes his general education teacher, but he only sees him for about 50 minutes each day. He spends the rest of his time in a special education classroom receiving one-on-one or small group instruction. When he completes his work in a timeframe that allows free time, he gets to help the school secretary fill up the soda machine in the teacher's lounge.
- Alex and Lorena Sandoval are Jeffrey's parents. He is an industrial engineer and she is a stay-at-home mom who is involved in the state's parent information and training center. Lorena takes care of her aging parents as well as her three children and is very active in her church.
- Delilia Diaz is a practicing civil rights lawyer from the National Council of La Raza (NCLR), a national civil rights and advocacy organization dedicated to improving the opportunities of Hispanic Americans.
- Paul Gilman, the superintendent of the school system, is a former principal and general educator. He is determined that his school system will demonstrate that it is making more than average annual yearly progress when compared to other school systems in the state.
- Eric Markus is a developmental physician and school psychologist.
- Randy Garret is Jeffrey's sixth-grade general education teacher.
- Jane Walters is a speech-language pathologist who directs the state's assistive technology program.

A Play in One Act

PAUL: (superintendent, who relies on the public studies model): Good afternoon, folks, and thank you for coming in today to discuss how we can ensure that Jeffrey receives an appropriate education in the general curriculum now that the school board has decided we will use a fully integrated approach. So that we all understand what I mean, let me explain it to you.

ALEX: (father, who represents the cultural model): Lorena and I don't really care what kind of school reform you plan. We just want to be sure our son has a genuine opportunity to learn, that he will be with students without disabilities as much as possible. What happens to him now will shape his and his peers' lives as adults.

DELILIA: (civil rights lawyer, who represents the law model): I agree, but I also want to hear about this system! How can we be sure that Jeffrey does not lose his rights to a free and appropriate education in this integrated model? I am here to make sure that Jeffrey benefits, is integrated—that's a matter for him in particular—and that this new model works for him and all other children, too, and I mean all, not just the kids without disabilities or with easier-to-serve disabilities.

PAUL: Good points, and what about you, Jeffrey, what do you want?

JEFFREY: Um, I guess I just want to be able to hang out with my friends.

PAUL: Okay! So, back to defining the school reform approach we will use here! It's one in which we basically will abolish the distinctions between general and special education. No more separate classrooms, no more pull-out or push-in, no more of the old way. . .

JANE: (speech-language pathologist, who represents the human development model, with emphasis on the medical submodel, interrupting Paul): OMG! More of this theoretical stuff! Who has time for this? How in the world will I—and a whole lot of other specialists—ever deliver our services to Jeffrey and other students with disabilities? Specialized interventions must be administered in specialized settings by specialists, and students must be identified in order to receive our limited time and resources. The school board has no idea what they are telling us to do, and the kiddos with disabilities are the ones who will suffer as a result! Are the board members aware that their *theory* may make it likely that students will have less, not more, benefit from school? Have they ever even *been* inside the school?!

RANDY: (general educator, who represents the educational submodel, technology studies model, and ethical model): It's reactions like yours that will hurt the students, not the plan to integrate systems. There are times when we have to change our ways. We have to learn new ways of working together and using the evidence that has accumulated over the years about how to teach everyone more effectively. And beyond this whole matter of building our capacities and adapting, there is something basically right, really right, about opening our systems, and hearts and minds, to the message that we are all in this together—in school, and in life.

JANE: Are you a preacher or teacher?

RANDY: Both! How we treat people in schools has a tremendous impact on how society perceives people. It's a matter of integration. Let me explain. Jeffrey benefits greatly from being in the natural setting of the general education classroom. He has more social opportunities there, and he is challenged by the curriculum. The skills and competencies he learns in the general education classroom transfer more easily to other natural environments. It's also a matter of productivity and contribution. We like to have him in our class, too. He has many friends, and he adds value to the classroom community. Jeffrey has an amazing sense of story and could add vivid detail to our class write-alouds that we do as part of our writing workshop. Unfortunately, he is not usually with us for writing workshop. If I had access to a computer with voice recording, a slant board, and some paper with raised lines, I think he would also write some of his fantastic stories. Jeffrey also helps us with Spanish words sometimes, since he is the only Spanish speaker in our class. Removing him for most of the day causes us to miss out on so much that he has to contribute to our classroom community. It also sends the message to his peers that he is different and less able—maybe even less worthy. It's a matter of dignity. Also, like many 13 year olds, Jeffrey wants to be with his friends. Why should he be denied this choice? It's a matter of self-determination.

ERIC: (psychologist and physician, representing the medical and psychological submodels): OK, OK. Enough. Jeffrey has some real challenges. He's got a fragile psyche, and he's got some health issues, principally around his cardiovascular system. While IDEA calls for him to be educated in the LRE, I am concerned that he will suffer from the chaotic environment of the general education classroom. The interventions we use for students with Down syndrome should be administered one-on-one in separate environments from students without disabilities, just as Jane mentioned. In addition, being with his peers often frustrates Jeffrey and triggers his violent outbursts. It's a matter of individualized appropriate services—do you want him to learn or be agitated?—as well as protecting his peers from harm.

LORENA: Um. . . . I'm sorry to interrupt, but I can't believe that you are making my son into some sort of bully. He is not mean and dangerous! He only gets angry when people do not take the time to listen to him.

DELILIA: Doctor, are you telling us that, since you can't *cure* his disability, we need to segregate him because the general education environment cannot take the time to listen to Jeffrey? Come on, already. Ensuring that Jeffrey and others in his situation benefit from their education is crucial. It is a matter of anti-discrimination. As we learned from *Brown*, separate is inherently not equal. That is why IDEA requires that students benefit from their education. Our duty is to make sure that we provide Jeffrey the reasonable accommodations for him to benefit from education, which means helping him communicate his thoughts and needs within the natural environment. It is also a matter of empowerment and participatory decision making. What are his goals, and which setting will help him achieve these goals?

ALEX: I agree with my wife and Delilia. Why can't you develop environments where my boy can learn his academics while also learning to be with his friends? In my business, we design all sorts of physical environments to suit all sorts of needs of all kinds of people. We call it ergonomics. It's old stuff—a heritage from the early space-shuttle days.

PAUL: Easy does it, everyone. Let's step back a bit and look at this matter—not at Jeffrey in particular but at all students—from my perspective.

RANDY: Oh, here we go again: the old "money talk."

PAUL: Not exactly, but money is a factor in the whole matter of how to adminis-ter an entirely different kind of approach to education—the fully integrated approach, one that doesn't draw lines that separate kids and teachers.

DELILIA: But preserves a benefit for Jeffrey, yes? Let's remember: the goal is an appropriate education, and the means is adherence to the integration rule—LRE.

JANE: OK, if we are talking about administration, we'd better talk about Jeffrey's needs for speech-language therapy. We professionals need to track our time with our students, and we are legally bound to the time we spend with each kiddo. If no lines separate kids and teachers, how can we report our numbers? This is not a simple matter!

LORENA: I don't mean to be abrupt, but, frankly, Alex and I don't want Jeffrey to be the victim of an untried approach and we don't want him put away and labeled a bully.

RANDY: Lorena and Alex, Jeffrey will not be the victim of ideology. Integrating systems is the right educational approach. There are three decades of research that tell us that we can accomplish integration without impairing a stu-dent's right to an appropriate education. And what's more, there will be many more people getting to know Jeffrey when we put two systems together. That's what we learned when our church became open and accepting.

DELILIA: With all due respect, Randy, this is not a religious undertaking. It deals with integration as a matter of constitutional principle and with outcomes as a matter of return on the investment we are making in education for every-one, particularly Jeffrey.

LORENA: Please, Delilia. Of course there are legal issues, testing issues, money issues. But it's just a bit too simple to dismiss the matter of right and wrong. My child has a disability and I will care for him for maybe my whole life. In the long run, school is just a means for Jeffrey to be a full citizen in our soci-ety. His real social security will be his social networks: his family, his friends, his church.

ALEX: Yes! Our family is the foundation of our son's future. We are in this for the long run. You professionals can take the sprint route but we are running a marathon. We are not entirely confident that integration is in his best interest. We don't want him to be stigmatized by his peers, and we worry that being in the general education classroom will undermine his dignity by exposing his differences and instigating his bad behavioral responses. We don't want anyone to think of our sweet boy as a bully or wierdo. We all know that peers can be mean and teachers can get overwhelmed, and we fear the worst. Wearing my engineer's hat, it seems to me that some of the educators and specialists simply don't know the technological innovations that exist, nor do they understand the laws that guarantee an appropriate education for our boy. These educators have the ability to learn the technology and update their knowledge of the law, but what's to ensure that Jeffrey's teachers will have a can-do attitude as well as the time and resources to learn about the best learning technology and the letter and spirit of the law?

LORENA: (a bit teary): Thank you, dear! What we as his family expect is great—that Jeffrey will have an enviable life, one we all want to live ourselves and want him to have. Is that what you all expect? Are we on the same page? Is your culture—your sense of great expectations—the same as ours?

ERIC: (taking a deep breath, speaking deliberately): I agree that we need to work with you to increase everyone's expectations for Jeffrey and all of us. But we need to make sure that the interventions that we implement are evidence-based and administered with fidelity. If an intervention is meant to occur in an isolated setting, we must stay true to the science and use it only in the setting for which it is designed. It's a matter of accountability.

RANDY: It's also a matter of professional capacity-building. We need the skills to work with Jeffrey in the general education classroom if he is to be there. We must use evidence-based instruction or interventions appropriate for the environment in which we implement them. But, Paul, it's also a matter of systems capacity-building. We need to have the technology necessary to offer him appropriate individualized services. We teachers need the skills to work with students of all learning styles and needs. We need to implement universal design for learning for all students, which requires professional development and a different teaching philosophy. And, it's no news to anyone here it's also a matter of coordination and collaboration. We need to make sure that we use our available resources to their maximum potential and eliminate waste in order to maximize efficiency. If Jeffrey benefits from being in the general education classroom, we could use the special education teacher who works with him as another teacher in that classroom. She could be there to support him and also other students who would benefit from her support. In this way, support becomes natural, stigma is decreased, and resources are pooled.

PAUL: Good point, Randy! Increasing collaboration in our schools would certainly help teach all of our students! You general education teachers have a difficult time differentiating instruction because you have to cover so much material to prepare my students for the high-stakes tests. Sharing the classroom would help you implement universal design for learning because it would free up time to be more responsive to all of your students' needs and offer individualized instruction for more students. But you still have a lot to learn about implementing appropriate evidence-based practices, using cutting-edge technology, and universal design for learning, and that's why you need special educators and related service providers, in a fully integrated classroom, which cannot exist except in a fully integrated school system. Of course, Jane's point about the tracking of placement and minutes is valid, but we will change the tracking of these statistics to reflect our new ideals.

PAUL: Here's how I understand what we've all been saying. First, we are concerned that Jeffrey has a right, which we all honor, to receive individualized support—whether it's about his psyche, his behaviors, his health conditions, his speech-language delays, his education and its outcomes—whatever. Second, we agree we must comply with the federal special and general education laws, even though we have not named them. Jeffrey has a right to an appropriate education in the general curriculum, and to benefit from that right he has to be held accountable for learning just as we are held accountable for teaching. Third, our district and this school in particular will undergo some major restructuring, which means building both our system's capacity and our professionals' capacities. Fourth, we want to provide him with—what's that phrase, Lorena—was it "social security?"—and that means making sure that every member of our staff and faculty and all of his classmates understand that they can create a different culture, one that regards him and all of us as worthy. Fifth, there is, as Randy said, an essential ethics to what we do.

ALEX: Well said. Good summary, Paul.

PAUL: Thank you, but we have just now analyzed the challenge we face. The next step is to adduce the research and apply the strategies that make us competent to do what we want to do, which is to bring our perspectives together and do what we know should be done by means that we know work.

ALEX: (turning to Jeffrey): Hey, you've been real quiet in this long meeting. Do you want to say anything?

JEFFREY: Yeah, I like being with my friends. I want to learn and get a job and have friends.

PAUL: That's the best summary of long-winded adults I've heard in a very long time. (Laughter all around!) We'll reconvene next week to talk about the "how"—not the "what" and "why." Meeting adjourned.

It's a Matter of Justice

Several members of Jeffrey's team refer to what is "right" and "just" to do. Their concerns are with the justice of the integrated school movement for one person, but because Jeffrey and his team are proxies for other students, families, and professionals, we should consider the meaning of "justice" of a new system that is designed to benefit all students.

For the purposes of this chapter, we adopt the meaning of "justice" that the most influential American political philosopher of the 20th century, John Rawls, advanced, and the critique that University of Chicago philosopher Martha Nussbaum has made. Rawls argued that justice is fairness—the existence of a "proper balance between competing claims" made by rational and mutually self-interested parties (Rawls, 1958, p. 166). He also argued that a practice is just if it is in accordance with the principle which all who participate in it might reasonably be expected to propose or to acknowledge before one another when they are similarly circumstanced and required to make a firm commitment in advance without knowledge of what will be their peculiar condition, and thus when it meets standards which the parties could accept as fair should occasion arise for them to debate its merits. (Rawls, 1958, pp. 182–183)

Rawls argues that justice consists of fair play among those who are blind to the conditions in which they will want fairness. His argument reconjures the image of Lady Justice, holding scales on which she weighs the competing rights and claims of various parties; she is blind to the parties, just as Rawls insists we who want justice must be.

Returning to the one-act play and the essential issue, Jeffrey's placement in an integrated system of education, the justice question is this: If each of the individuals were to have a child comparable to Jeffrey, and if each were unable to foresee what that child's education would be and where it would occur, then justice is what they, or a majority of them, agree is "fair" to their child.

Special education should be reconceptualized, its delivery reconstructed and relocated, and its benefits spread widely among all students, not just those classified or able to be classified into special education under IDEA. Following Rawls, what is unjust about that? Reconceptualizing special education means regarding special services and supports as fluid and temporary and building an instructional support system accessible to any student who needs support to achieve his or her full capabilities. Nussbaum's argument that justice consists of enhancing the development of capabilities of all students so they may have lives of dignity is central to this reconceptualization. If the will, knowledge, and law exist to reconceptualize and restructure, then universal ascription of dignity may well be the intended consequence. The present law does not bar this integration; it just impedes it to a certain extent and should be amended. Once amended, it can be a vehicle for universal benefit for all students, bringing responsive and individualized education to all students as a matter of right.

References

Artiles, A.J., Kozleski, E.B., Trent, S.C., Osher, D., & Ortiz, A. (2010). Justifying and explaining disproportionality, 1968–2008: A critique of underlying views of culture. *Exceptional Children, 76*(3), 279–299.

Bates, P., & Davis, F.A. (2004). Social capital, social inclusion and services for people with learning disabilities. *Disability & Society, 19*(3), 195–207. doi:10.1080/0968759042000204202

Board of Education v. Rowley, 458 U.S. 176 (1982).

Bourdieu, P. (1986). The forms of capital. In J.G. Richardson (Ed.), *Handbook of theory and research for the sociology of education* (pp. 214–258). New York: Greenwood Press.

Brown v. Board of Education, 347 U.S. 483 (1954).

Brownell, M.T., Adams, A., Sindelar, P., Waldron, N., & Vanhover, S. (2006). Learning from collaboration: The role of teacher qualities. *Exceptional Children, 72*(2), 169–185.

Cartledge, G., Singh, A., & Gibson, L. (2008). Practical behavior-management techniques to close the accessibility gap for students who are culturally and linguistically diverse. *Preventing School Failure, 52*(3), 29–38.

Code of Federal Regulations, 34 C.F.R., §§ 300.115.

Cole, C.M., Waldron, N., & Majd, M. (2004). Academic progress of students across inclusive and traditional settings. *Mental Retardation, 42*(2), 136–144.

Connor, D.J., & Ferri, B.A. (2005). Integration and inclusion: A troubling nexus: Race, disability, and special education. *Journal of African American History, 90*(1/2), 107–127.

Daniel R.R. v. State Board of Education, 874 F.2d 1036 (5th Cir. 1989).

Elementary and Secondary Education Act of 1965 (ESEA), 20 U.S.C. § 7801.

Ferri, B.A. (2009). Doing a (Dis) Service. In W. Ayers, T. Quinn, & D. Stovall (Eds.), *The handbook of social justice in education* (pp. 417–430). New York: Routledge.

Ferri, B.A., & Connor, D.J. (2005). In the shadow of Brown. *Remedial and Special Education, 26*(2), 93.

Fierros, E.G., & Conroy, J.W. (2002). Double jeopardy: An exploration of restrictiveness and race in special education. In D.J. Losen & G. Orsen (Eds.), *Racial inequity in special education* (pp. 39–70). Cambridge, MA: Civil Rights Project, Harvard Education Press.

Gravios, T. A. (2013). Aligned service delivery: Ending the era of triage education. In L.C. Burrello, W. Sailor, & J. Kleinhammer-Tramill (Eds.), *Unifying educational systems: Leadership and policy perspectives* (pp. 109–134). New York: Routledge.

Hardman, M.L., & Dawson, S. (2008). The impact of federal public policy on curriculum and instruction for students with disabilities in the general classroom. *Preventing School Failure, 52*(2), 5–11.

Hartmann v. Loudon County Board of Education, 118 F.3d 996 (4th Cir. 1997), cert. denied, 118 S. Ct. 688 (1998).

Individuals With Disabilities Education Act. 20 U.S.C. §§ 1400 *et seq.* (2009).

Kleinhammer-Tramill, J., Burrello, L.C., & Sailor, W. (2013). Special education: A critical perspective on reframing public policy for students with disabilities. In L.C. Burrello, W. Sailor, & J. Kleinhammer-Tramill (Eds.), *Unifying educational systems: Leadership and policy perspectives* (pp. 3–20). New York: Routledge.

Kozleski, E.B., & Waitoller, F.R. (2010). Teacher learning for inclusive education: Understanding teaching as a cultural and political practice. *International Journal of Inclusive Education, 14*(7), 655–666.

Lane, K.L., Pierson, M.R., Stang, K.K., & Carter, E.W. (2010). Teacher expectations of students. *Remedial and Special Education, 31*(3), 12.

Lashley, C.L. (2013). Toward a human capabilities education policy. In L.C. Burrello, W. Sailor, & J. Kleinhammer-Tramill (Eds.), *Unifying educational systems: Leadership and policy perspectives* (pp. 43–66). New York: Routledge.

Lodato Wilson, G., Kim, S.A., & Michaels, C.A. (2011). Factors associated with where secondary students with disabilities are educated and how they are doing. *Journal of Special Education.* doi:10.1177/0022466911411575

Losen, D.J., & Welner, K.G. (2001). Disabling discrimination in our public schools: Comprehensive legal challenges to inappropriate and inadequate special education services for minority students. *Harvard Civil Rights-Civil Liberties Law Review, 36*(2), 407–460.

Matzen, K., Ryndak, D., & Nakao, T. (2010). Middle school teams increasing access to general education for students with significant disabilities. *Remedial and Special Education, 31*(4), 287–304.

Mills v. District of Columbia Board of Education, 348 F. Supp. 866 (D.D.C. 1972); contempt proceedings, ELHR 551:643 (D.D.C. 1980).

Minow, M., Shweder, R.A., & Marcus, H.R. (2008). Pursuing equal education in societies of difference. In M. Minow, R.A. Shweder, & H.R. Marcus (Eds.), *Just Schools* (pp. 3–20). New York: Russell Sage Foundation.

Nussbaum, M.C. (2006). *Frontiers of justice: Disability, nationality, species membership.* Cambridge, MA: Harvard University Press.

Parham v. J.R., 442 U.S. 584 (1979).

Pennsylvania Association for Retarded Children (PARC) v. Commonwealth, 334 F. Supp. 1257 (E.D. Pa. 1971), 343 F. Supp. 279 (E.D. Pa. 1972).

Rawls, J. (1958). Justice as fairness. *The Philosophical Review, 67*(2), 164–194.

Roncker v. Walter, 700 F.2d 1058 (6th Cir. 1983), cert. denied, 464 U.S. 864 (1983).

Sacramento Unified School District Board of Education v. Rachel H (Holland) (1994).

Sailor, W., & Burrello, L.C. (2013). Shifting perspective to frame disability policy. In L.C. Burrello, W. Sailor, & J. Kleinhammer-Tramill (Eds.), *Unifying educational systems: Leadership and policy perspectives* (pp. 21–40). New York: Routledge.

Sailor, W., & Roger, B. (2005). Rethinking inclusion: Schoolwide applications. *Phi Delta Kappan, 86*(7), 503–509.

Salend, S.J., & Garrick Duhaney, L.M. (1999). The impact of inclusion on students with and without disabilities and their educators. *Remedial and Special Education, 20*(2), 114.

Skiba, R.J., Poloni-Staudinger, L., Gallini, S., Simmons, A.B., & Feggins-Azziz, R. (2006). Disparate access: The disproportionality of African American students with disabilities across educational environments. *Exceptional Children, 72*(4), 411–424.

Skiba, R.J., Simmons, A.B., Ritter, S., Gibb, A.C., Rausch, M.K., Cuadrado, J., & Chung, C.G. (2008). Achieving equity in special education: History, status, and current challenges. *Exceptional Children, 74*(3), 264–288.

Taylor, S.J. (2001). The continuum and current controversies in the USA. *Journal of Intellectual and Developmental Disability, 26*(1), 15–33.

Turnbull, A.P., Turnbull, H.R., & Wehmeyer, M.L. (2012). *Exceptional lives: Special education in today's schools* (7th ed.). Upper Saddle River, NJ: Merrill.

Turnbull, H.R., & Stowe, M.J. (2001). Five models for thinking about disability. *Journal of Disability Policy Studies, 12*(3), 198–205.

Turnbull, H.R., Stowe, M.J., & Huerta, N.E. (2007). *Free appropriate public education: The law and children with disabilities* (7th ed.). Denver, CO: Love.

U.S. Department of Education. (2004). New No Child Left Behind Flexibility: Highly Qualified Teachers fact sheet. Retrieved from http://www2.ed.gov/nclb/methods/teachers/hqtflexibility.html

U.S. Department of Education. (2011). Data accountability center: Individuals With Disabilities Education Act (IDEA) data. Retrieved from https://www.ideadata.org

5

IN SUPPORT OF A SEAMLESS SPECIAL NEEDS STUDENTS SERVICES SYSTEM

A Heuristic Examination of Education Finance Policy, Special Needs Revenue Components, and Flexible Expenditure Possibilities

R. Anthony Rolle, Pakethia Harris, and Leonard C. Burrello

The scope of research defined for this chapter is bounded in this statement: *Provide an informative, comparative investigative report on the structure of education finance systems, their special education components, and their influences on educational quality.* As such, this chapter is designed to answer the following questions:

1. How is education revenue distributed to school districts through state funding formulas?
2. What types of special educational services and personnel revenue components exist within state funding mechanisms?
3. How are different types of special educational revenue structures related to service quality?
4. How can revenues be used to maximize service systems for all students at the district and school levels?

Although the main purpose of this chapter is to address the research questions above, a concomitant purpose is to generate thematic content areas where individual states—and regions—can begin building research capacities that would improve the effectiveness of their special education finance and service delivery at the district and school level. In particular, political events and litigation in Western states illustrate a growing national concern with special education and exceptional students. As such, in lieu of examining all 50 states, this chapter will examine nine Western states (i.e., Arizona, Colorado, Kansas, Nebraska, New Mexico, Oklahoma, Texas, Utah, and Wyoming).

Education Finance Formulas in the Western Region[1]

Making changes—and evaluating the effects of changes—in education funding mechanisms was an issue for all states throughout the decade. Some states had laws that prohibited increases in property taxes (e.g., Nebraska and Colorado), while other states limited other forms of taxation for education. Funding issues led to conflicts over large versus small school districts, resulting in lawsuits. Indeed, at one point, secession was threatened in Kansas. As a result, finding similarities between the nine states of the Western United States was a daunting task, given the wide variation in the types of state-run public school systems present in the nine states themselves. Consider, for a moment, some key markers of school finance in the Western states noted in *Rankings of the States 2010 & Estimates of School Statistics 2011* that illustrate this variation:[2]

- State percentages of education spending ranged from a low of approximately 38% in Texas to New Mexico's 70%.
- Similarly, the number of local education agencies (LEAs) under state jurisdiction ranges from Utah's low of 40 (which has held constant over the last decade) to Texas's approximately 1,200.
- There is wide variation in per-pupil expenditures: Arizona has relatively low expenditures per pupil ($5,900), while Wyoming has relatively high spending ($14,700).

Overall, these figures present a picture of the nine Western states as a diverse aggregation of finance structures and statewide public school systems.

Closer scrutiny, however, yields some key commonalities in challenges, finance structures, and school finance trends among these nine states in the West. For example, Arizona's structure is both equity-based—in that it attempts to equalize spending among districts—and adequacy-based in that it attempts to adjust per-pupil spending based on individual student categories and needs. Additionally, Arizona's plan is equity-based in that it provides a fiscal foundation for all districts, but adequacy-based in its attempts to equalize that foundation based upon district characteristics. It is clear from the Arizona example that many Western states have simply layered school finance policies over each other over time, resulting in a finance system that draws from many strategies.

The nine states examined are caught between a focus on equalization among districts (e.g., reducing disparities between wealthy and poor districts) and movements toward student-based school-funding mechanisms.[3] Some have argued that district-level equalization schemes have greater impact on taxpayer equity than on school equality.[4] However, equalizing expenditures across districts remains an important political issue. The shared challenges, structures, and trends described below all take place within the context of these conflicting priorities within each state's school finance structure itself.

Shared Challenges: Key challenges for school finance in Western states include the following:

- School funding in Western states is lower than in other regions;
- Soaring enrollments in Western states; and
- Growing student diversity in Western states.

Shared Structures: Despite the variation described above, many Western states share commonalities within the structure of their school finance systems.

- Foundation. All nine states claim their school finance structure to be either partly or wholly "foundational" in that they provide a firm floor of funding to prevent school districts from falling into poverty. Many states now supplement this foundation with equalization formulas or strengthen them with guaranteed tax bases (see Table 5.1).
- Weighting. In addition to providing a foundation, all nine states use some sort of weighting factor in order to equalize spending within districts and/or between districts. The three categories most commonly used in weighting formulas are pupil-based, teacher-based, and district-based. Pupil-based weights are applied at the per-pupil level and include special education status, at-risk status, and language status, among others. Teacher weights are based on factors such as education and experience. District weighting factors are most often concerned with a district's size or isolation.
- Equity not Adequacy. Although some of the nine states are on the cutting edge with their school finance structures, most formulas function more with an eye toward equitable spending than toward anticipated outcomes. This equity focus is present in all states save Wyoming, which instead focuses on resources being applied toward student outcomes (see Table 5.1).

TABLE 5.1. Descriptions of State School Finance Structures in the Western Region

Arizona	"Equalized foundation"
Colorado	"Foundation with mandatory local participation"
Kansas	"High-level foundation"
Nebraska	"Foundation and equalization components"
New Mexico	"Foundation program"
Oklahoma	"Two-tiered equalization program"
Texas	"Combined foundation and guaranteed tax base plan"
Utah	"Foundation program"
Wyoming	"Resource block grant model"

Shared Trends: In addition to shared structures, many of the nine Western states are concerned with ensuring that all districts have an equal opportunity to provide a quality education for their students. The following trends highlight efforts across all nine states:

- Equity. By focusing their school finance efforts on equity, all nine states indicate a commitment to equalize educational opportunities for all students. Missing is an explicit link between spending and outcomes.
- Isolated or small district aid. Finally many of the reviewed districts have developed a focus on small/sparse or isolated school districts with an understanding that the operating costs of these districts will be higher than average. This strikes on a particularly Western adaptation within the various school funding formulas.
- Land Use. Many of the nine states also rely upon monies generated by state natural resources to fund public education. Current movements in Arizona illustrate some of the advantages and controversies in such a finance strategy. Although Arizona plans to use land trust funds to supplement its funding for public education, many are concerned if this is an appropriate use of these funds.

No state funding mechanism focuses specifically on the needs of students with special needs. Rather special education financial components are subsumed under or are separate provisions from state mechanisms.[5] States provide additional funding adjustments to districts to defray the cost of educating students with special needs. So long as additional funding is necessary to meet the excess cost of supporting students with exceptionalities, states will have to develop methods to fund special education students and their related services. Supplemental funds are provided through federal monies associated with the Individuals with Disabilities Education Act (IDEA); however, federal involvement is minimal and contributes to approximately 8% of total funding.[6] States are responsible for garnering the means to pay for programs and services as well as the systems of appropriation for those programs and services.

History of Special Education Within the Context of State Finance Formulas in the Western Region

The first established federal grant program for children with disabilities was introduced in 1965 with the passing of the Elementary and Secondary Education Act (ESEA). The Act, however, only provided assistance to state departments of education in their effort to support "particular aspects of education such as the education of the handicapped."[7] It was not until 1966 when an amendment to the Act included Title VI. Title VI of ESEA established grant support to states to assist with the initiation, improvement, and expansion of programs directed to "the education of handicapped children."[8] This initial federal funding allocated resources with the intent to provide a supplement to state and local agencies in their effort to educate youth with disabilities.

The inclusion of special education in education legislation mandated that youths ranging from the ages of 3 through 21 with disabilities were eligible for an education. However, some state and local school districts were reluctant to accept the responsibilities of educating youth with disabilities due to the expenses associated with educating the youth. Often the cost of educating a student with a disability significantly exceeded the cost of a basic expenditure of a nondisabled student.[9] Two well-known landmark cases directed at this issue were *Pennsylvania Association for Retarded Children (PARC) v. Commonwealth of Pennsylvania* and *Mills v. District of Colombia*. The *PARC* case highlighted that a state could not deny services to children with disabilities. Furthermore, the case established the standard of access to a free and appropriate education.[10] The following year *Mills* established that a school district could not deny services to children with disabilities based on budget constraints.[11] The district court ruled a state's capacity to educate children with disabilities was a responsibility that superseded insufficient funding. These prominent cases decided that states were responsible for educating *all* students.

States began advocating for federal legislation to assist in the cost of educating youth with disabilities.[12] Ultimately, congressional hearings in 1975 uncovered millions of children with disabilities were not receiving appropriate education, while others did not have access to schools.[13] As a result, the 1975 Education of the Handicapped Act (EHA) was enacted to provide a free and appropriate education to students with disabilities and to provide a funding mechanism to supplement the additional cost of offering programs to support students in the education system. The Act, also known as Public Law 94-142 (PL 94-142), provided funding based on the state need. The intent was to assist states in their responsibilities of providing services to educate youth with special needs, not to provide full federal funding.

Public Law 94-142 mandated fiscal allotments to states that totaled the number of students with disabilities, ages 3 through 21, who received services, multiplied by 5% to equal the per-average student expenditure granted to states. This total limited the maximum amount of grant monies a state could receive from the federal government. The Act declared the federal government would provide aid for students with disabilities up to 40% of the excess cost of the average per-pupil expenditure. The federal government would gradually increase funding from 5% average per-pupil expenditure in 1978, to 10% in 1979, to 20% in 1980, to 30% in 1981, and to 40% in 1982, placing a limitation that no state would receive less than the amount the state received in the 1977 fiscal year. Further protective measures were added such as limiting the number of children identified with a disability to be included in state counts. States could not exceed 12% of the number of children aged 5 to 17 to count toward grant allocations. The Act attempted to safeguard states from over-identifying students with disabilities to receive more grant funding.

Throughout the years amendments to the Act have added incentives for servicing youth with disabilities from birth to 5 years (Public Law 98-199), increasing funding for preschoolers with disabilities (Public Law 99-457), and expanding discretionary programs for institutions of higher education and transition services (Public Law 101-476).[14] However, significant changes took place with federal funding in special education with the reauthorization of the Individuals With Disabilities Education Act of 1997 (IDEA)—though none of the changes had direct effects on individual state-funding mechanisms.[15] In fact, the allocation of federal grant dollars is a decision made by individual states. Specifically, states have the authority to choose a funding approach to meet the needs of their student population with disabilities. The state-funding mechanisms used to provide services for students with disabilities are intra-mechanism funding formulas. These state special education subformulas are complex and often share characteristics similar to their parent formula.

Parrish and Wolfman (1999) suggest special education funding formulas are usually divided into four broad categories: (a) weighted funding; (b) resource-based funding; (c) percentage reimbursement; and (d) flat funding. Similar to state-funding mechanisms, a *weighted special education funding model* is based on a per-student allocation. Aid is associated with the students' disability category (i.e., learning disability, speech impairment, etc.) or placement (self-contained, resource setting, etc.). Weights are associated with providing student subsidies based on whether it will cost more to educate the student. *Resource-based funding* is based on disability category and placement (e.g., self-contained, pull-out, or general education setting) and creates unit rates for which funding is provided. *Percentage reimbursement* allows districts to recover special education expenditures from the state for expenses associated with the program. Of course, there usually is a cap on the number of students who can be claimed for special education funding. And last, *flat funding* involves dividing the available federal funds into the total number of special education students within the state. The amount is appropriated for each student and is dispersed to the district based on the district's total number of students with disabilities.

A Summary of Special Educational Revenue Components Within Western State Funding Mechanisms[16]

Arizona Basic Support Program: Arizona uses a foundation program, including state funding for maintenance and operation, school transportation, capital outlay, and "soft capital." For maintenance and operation, the state limits expenditures in all districts except for a group of low-enrollment districts. With the exception of the soft capital funds, state funds are considered to be block grants. School districts are not required to spend specific amounts on specific programs, and the monies allocated for capital outlay may be budgeted for maintenance and operations. The foundation formula is weighted to account for special needs and other higher-needs student groups. The state equalization formula provides a base revenue amount per weighted student for maintenance and operation—plus additional funding for school transportation, capital outlay, high school textbooks, and soft capital—from a combination of state, county, and local funds. The state payment is the difference between the district's formula entitlement and the amount raised by the qualifying tax rate from local and county tax sources. There are revenue weights for special needs students in preschool programs through grade 12 for children with cognitive, emotional, or physical disabilities (e.g., including but not limited to hearing impaired; multiple disabilities, autism, and severe/profound intellectual disabilities; and resource and self-contained programs).

Colorado Basic Support Program: Colorado's school funding structure includes a foundation program with mandatory local participation created by the Public School Finance Act of 1994 (Colo. Rev. Stat. § 22–54). Local funding in Colorado comes from property and local vehicle taxes. If a local district's taxes exceed formula amounts without increasing the levy rate, the district must "buy out" the state provisions and fund them on its own. The funding formula allocates all revenue on a per-pupil basis. Each district's per-pupil funding level is determined individually with adjustments to the statewide base to account for size, cost of living, and the proportion of at-risk pupils. The categorical buy-out provisions of the School Finance Act require that certain districts offset or "buy out" state categorical aid with local property tax revenue. Any district that has funded its program cost, less minimum state aid and specific ownership taxes, with a levy less than the prior year's levy or a property tax change less than the sum of inflation plus the percentage change in enrollment must levy additional mills to offset all or part of state categorical support. The categorical programs that are subject to the local buy-out provisions include special education, the English Language Proficiency Act, transportation, and vocational education. Three -and four-year-old special education students and at-risk preschool students also are weighted at 0.5 FTE.

Kansas Basic Support Program: Kansas has a foundation program with a high level of state control. This foundation level is high level, with weighting scheme for programs, low enrollments, and other selected features. Some categorical funds also are described later. In 1992, Kansas passed new legislation, which increased state-level control. The resulting spending equalization plan ensued a large increase in state percentage of funding for its 304 school districts. Kansas uses a uniform local tax rate that is set by legislature. Districts can add up to 25% of base budget with public approval through a local referendum. General State Aid (GSA) is the main funding program for districts' entitlement to state revenue and is based on an enrollment-driven formula. A district's spending power, called State Financial Aid (SFA), is determined by multiplying its adjusted (weighted) full-time equivalent (FTE) enrollment by Base State Aid Per Pupil (BSAPP). Adjusted enrollment includes the full-time regular enrollment of pupils in the district after taking into account a declining enrollment feature and seven other adjustments (weights) that have been added to reflect higher costs associated with serving certain pupil populations, transporting pupils, operating low- or high-enrollment districts, and adding new facilities. Specific weights are for (1) low enrollment, (2) small schools, (3) transportation, (4) vocational education, (5) bilingual education, (6) at-risk pupils, and (7) operation of new facilities. Despite its weighted foundation approach, Kansas still uses a well-defined categorical fund approach for special education funding.

Nebraska Basic Support Program: Nebraska uses a foundation and equalization components in its school finance structure, outlined in the Tax Equity and Educational Opportunities Support Act. The state computes both a "needs" estimate and a "resources" estimate for each school district and equalizes the difference between these two numbers. Nebraska categorizes districts by census data as very sparse, sparse, or standard, and has a set per-pupil amount for each category. For districts within an affiliated school system, the "formula needs" and "formula resources" are aggregated to determine "system needs" and "system resources." Equalization aid is calculated for the system based on the difference between "system needs" and "system resources." School districts are grouped into very sparse, sparse, and standard cost groupings according to census students per square mile in the county where the high school is located, formula students per square mile in the high school system, and distance between high school attendance centers. Estimated general fund operating expenditures per adjusted formula student for each of these groups is calculated. The local system's cost grouping cost per student is then multiplied times the "adjusted formula students" in the system, plus transportation allowance and special education allowance to arrive at "formula need." "Adjusted Formula Students" include the Average Daily Membership (ADM) of the system, resident students the system is contracting out to other systems or service providers, as well as adjustments for demographic factors for poverty, limited English proficiency, and students residing on Native American land. Special needs students are not treated consistently within the funding mechanism.

New Mexico Basic Support Program: The basic structure of New Mexico's 1974 Public School Finance Act still is in place. New Mexico finances public education through a foundation program, which relies on program units. These units are adjusted by special education student count, added together and multiplied by each district's "training-and-experience index" to produce adjusted program units. These units are further modified based on special categories (e.g., students served in nonprofit special education programs, small and rural district status, growing district status, new district status, or at-risk factors status) and save harmless clauses that apply to very small districts. This final figure is used to compute New Mexico's state equalization guarantee. In general, the public school funding formula uses cost differentials to reflect the costs associated with providing educational service to students. The program cost for each school district is determined by multiplying the student full-time equivalency in a particular grade or a program full-time equivalency by the respective cost differential to generate units. Those student full-time equivalencies and program full-time equivalencies are determined by district membership on the 40th day of school and adjusted by the count of special education students on December 1. All of the program units are then added together and multiplied by the district's training and experience index to produce the adjusted program units.

Oklahoma Basic Support Program: Oklahoma uses what is termed a *two-tiered equalization program*. This funding program is based on a foundation formula with transportation supplement and a modified guaranteed yield formula. Oklahoma earmarks school land earnings, motor vehicle collections, gross production taxes, and Rural Electrification Association Cooperative Tax revenues for support of public education. The foundation program for a given local district includes a legislatively determined statewide base support factor multiplied by the district's weighted ADM. The local foundation program income for the district is subtracted from this product. ADM are adjusted for four categories of weights. The first two categories are grade level and special education. For districts that qualify, ADM are additionally provided a small school or isolation weight.

Texas Basic Support Program: Texas relies on a combination foundation and guaranteed tax base plan. The Texas public school funding system is a shared arrangement between the state and local school districts. In order to offset variation in local capacity to fund schools through the property tax, the state provides funding to school districts in inverse relation to district wealth. State and local funds for public education in Texas are allocated through a system of formulas known collectively as the Foundation School Program (FSP). The system consists of two tiers: (a) Tier 1 is a foundation program that includes adjustments and weights designed to distribute funding according to the characteristics of the school district and its students; and (b) Tier 2 is a guaranteed yield program that guarantees school districts equivalent taxable property wealth per weighted student. Tier 1 is the base or "foundation" funding level in the Texas FSP. Calculation of Tier 1 funding begins with the Basic Allotment, which is the base level of funding for each student in average daily attendance (ADA). The formula calls for the Basic Allotment to be multiplied by district adjustments that include the Cost of Education Index (CEI), the Small and Mid-Size District Allotments, and the Sparsity Adjustment. Adjusting the Basic Allotment by all the district adjustments results in the Adjusted Allotment. Instructional program weights are applied to the adjusted allotment, based on the numbers of students enrolled in or served by various special programs. The program weights are applied for special education, compensatory education, bilingual education, career and technology education (i.e., vocational programs), and gifted education. Specifically, for special education and vocational education programs, weights are calculated on a full-time equivalent (FTE) student basis. For other programs, weights are applied to ADA served in the program (or to the school lunch count for compensatory education) on an add-on basis.

Utah Basic Support Program: Utah provides a basic levy amount per-pupil foundation program—called the Minimum School Program—for instruction, maintenance, and operations. These funds are distributed on a per-pupil basis. Special education is weighted in the pupil counts, and districts that experience negative growth are held harmless for one year. Although Utah has implemented a state-mandated tax rate, local districts can tax above it. Funding for Utah's basic support programs is identified in Utah's Minimum School Program as Regular Basic School Programs, which is composed of four sets of services: (1) K-12 Instruction; (2) Necessarily Existent Small Schools; (3) Professional Staff; and (4) Administrative Costs. These services provide for general maintenance and operation functions, which support basic classroom instruction. Funding for these services is based on the Minimum Basic Levy (against local property values) and the state's income tax.

Wyoming Basic Support Program: Wyoming's guaranteed tax base program (with a required minimum levy) is a resource block grant model, based on student attendance and a model school cost-out. The state makes adjustments for smaller districts and regional cost of living. School finance in Wyoming has been driven by the 1995 ruling in *Campbell County v. State*. The Education Resource Block Grant Model (commonly referred to as the MAP Model) provides the Legislature a mechanism to ensure each Wyoming student receives an equal opportunity to receive a proper education (i.e., a legislatively determined basket of education goods and services) by specifying the instructional and operational resources necessary to provide this basket. The model accomplishes this by systematically determining the competitive market costs of educational operating resources and aggregating these costs within each school district. A total revenue amount in the form of a "block grant" is provided to each school district to facilitate provision of the basket. The actual dollar amount of the block grant is a function of an interaction between the model components necessary for implementation of the basket and the characteristics of the schools and students within a particular district. Twenty-five specific cost components necessary to deliver the basket are contained within the prototype for each grade-level grouping. These cost components can be grouped into five major categories, as follows: (1) Personnel; (2) Supplies, Materials, Equipment; (3) Special Services; (4) Special Student Characteristics; and (5) Special School/District/Regional Characteristics. Specifically, the model attempts to avoid segregation of students with special needs by assuming resources for small schools, small class sizes, teaching specialists, and professional development sufficient to enable teachers to deal more effectively with special needs students within the general education classroom setting. The model identifies four categories of special students: Special Education, Gifted Students, Limited English Proficient Students, and Economically Disadvantaged Youth. Importantly, Wyoming replaces 100% of special education costs—this is accounted for in Wyoming's block grant model.

Special Educational Revenue Structures and Student Service Quality

In examining the relationship between the structure of special education school finance systems and educational service quality, the usefulness of any economic or financial analysis rests upon the strength and validity of the assumptions used to define the context of the analysis. This heuristic analysis, therefore, examines the influence of each state's cultural, demographic, and economic contexts on its individual—and regional—educational experiences. Within these refined research objectives, two primary themes form the regional context within which analyses took place:

- There was a shift in the political landscape away from vertically equitable spending on special needs students (i.e., students with different characteristics receiving different amounts of funding in order to create similar educational opportunities) toward a greater demand for more efficient and measurable student, teacher, and school accountability; and,
- There was a shift in education finance policies—and the philosophies that support them—away from ideas of increasing levels of educational expenditure equity among special needs students and toward the investigation—in some cases the development of—educational finance systems based on concepts of educational adequacy (i.e., determining a "base cost" for the provision of educational services that should enable students to attain a prescribed minimum standard).

Given these larger political ideas as background, four themes emerged from this review of the Western states that affected—and will continue to affect—school quality:

- *Changes in Funding Mechanisms.* Across the Western states, court-ordered or legislatively mandated changes to education finance mechanisms marked the beginnings of political change from equity to adequacy in school funding. These changes begin to investigate how much revenue levels, tax rates, access to assessed valuation, and usage of categorical supplements directly influence educational attainment.
- *Major Demographic Changes.* Three significant changes in demographics are notable: (a) General increases in the special needs student population; (b) Increases in the number of special needs students from predominately low-wealth schools and districts; and (c) Increases in the number of ethnic and language-minority special needs students.
- *Erosion of Local Control.* At a fundamental level, due to efforts to link educational outcomes to funding, Western states were forced to consider what equitable educational opportunities actually are for their special needs students. In the midst of these considerations, individual states struggled to maintain local control of schools while developing state-mandated educational standards, assessment instruments, and defend the fairness of their

school finance mechanisms for special needs students. Interestingly, this erosion of local control occurred while the dominant political climate in these states was becoming more conservative. A reversion away from local control should be expected to continue over the next few years.

- *Pressure to Give Local Districts and Schools Revenue Flexibility.* In tight budget times that characterize the last four years in state capitols, as well as the history of inclusive practices suggested by Sailor and Burrello in Chapter Two, school districts and schools want discretions over appropriate administrative, instructional, and policy practices in order to serve all students with special learning needs well. Policy effectiveness should be the driving value here; that is, educational leaders need to ensure resources are utilized in manners that lead to improved educational attainment and postschooling outcomes that are aligned with the goals of federal enabling legislation.

After years of favorable economic conditions—and the consequent growth in state revenues—most Western states ended 2008 struggling over the various ways to reduce expenditures while grappling simultaneously with sharply reduced revenue projections. Given this fact, remember that two specific state actions taken during the "Booming 2000s" may exacerbate the fiscal challenges of the next few (or more) years:

1. State legislatures reduced tax rates. In order to increase rates again, lawmakers will have to take unpopular political action.
2. State legislatures funded new programs. During these austere economic times, new programs such as charters now will compete with long-standing public school services for funding.

With many state budgets being reduced by the current economic slowdown and long-term structural deficits, legislatures are considering a variety of short-term revenue options (e.g., drawing revenues from "rainy day funds"), spending reductions, and tax cuts. The use of certain short-term measures may be appropriate in some cases; however, if the state's budget imbalance primarily reflects structural problems, these measures will only make it harder for states to balance their future budgets. Maintaining funding for wide numbers of existing state services places enormous pressure on state legislatures to continue the proactive strategy of sharply reining in—if not reducing—their appropriations to public education. Being cognizant of these changing economic influences will directly affect the pursuit of any of the recommendations proposed in this research.

Recommendations

In Chapter One, Kleinhammer-Tramill et al. proposed that a hold-harmless provision to funding special education should be instituted to prevent sudden gaps in state/federal support as districts and schools become more effective in serving students inclusively and through to graduation and postschool success. Such an approach might involve providing every school with funds that would normally be available if say 15% of its children had disabilities. The percentage allocated for early intervening services in IDEA would expand from 15% to 100%, with some building-level discretion as to use, based on the assumption that all children would at some point need assistance from problem-solving teams. Special education funding streams would be available only to LEAs and schools that serve all of their students. This proposal is much like what happened to Title 1 in 1994 when funding could become a whole school designation rather than a percentage of targeted students who met preestablished criteria. An example from Finland might be instructive here; Sahlberg (2010) reports that almost half of the 16-year-olds, when they leave comprehensive school, have been engaged in some sort of special education, personalized help, or individual guidance.

In other words, revenue flexibility should facilitate the principle that all resources are to be used for all students. Sailor (2009) argued for schoolwide RtI as an example of how school leaders might use all specialized personnel units in a coordinated and integrated way rather than separately. Or, using a version of the Wyoming resource cost model, one could give districts a block grant using the district's and state's historical commitment to identified students. Say a district is serving 15% of its school population as disabled in a district of 33,500 students. Some 5,000 students historically might have been identified locally. The resource cost model in a state might lead to a budget of $20 million computed using a sliding scale of costs per type of program or personnel unit calculation or individual student foundation, acknowledging the percentage of students being served from mild to significant disabilities. In this merged system model, districts and schools need to identify the total number of students served by subgroup and the range and type of services provided matched with the aggregated achievement of students served on state and local assessments that reflect state and local expectations including four postschool outcomes: independent living, employment, civic engagement, and further education advancement or preparation. Every five years, the districts reporting to the state would have to recalculate their resource needs higher or lower subject to the total number of students served and the results achieved. Due process provisions remain intact to allow parent recourse to school-level decisions that they might contest.

Still, it is important to remember that states practice the science of education inside of political, economic, and social arenas. Educators are asked to perform the difficult tasks of special education finance policy interpretation, implementation, and evaluation. Yet, only recently have these experienced education professionals been asked to *develop* policies that can improve the system of education and educational outcomes. Ironically, state and federal legislators—some with expertise in education, most with none—do develop special education finance policies and organizational goals. Further, even though the responsibility for implementing— and the accountability for achieving—special education finance policy goals are placed on educational professionals, little of their expertise was put to use during the policy development and legislative phases. Therefore, while political influences and mechanisms of legislatures generate education policies—many with conflicting purposes and goals—education professionals are held accountable for attaining positive results from all policies regardless of their original intent. As such, the following five recommendations are offered to the Western states to improve their research and implementation capacities regarding special education finance:

1. *Develop a Common Language Around Specific Education Finance Issues*: When considering aspects of the educational process, most researchers will begin conversations with a discussion of equity components. Until the early 1990s, an examination commenced in this manner was the standard. As we enter a new decade, it now is important to know these concepts as well as those concepts surrounding the idea of adequacy. Principles of equity (e.g., foundation versus minimum attainment definitions) typically focus on the fair distribution of resources while allowing individual student effort to determine outcomes. Principles of adequacy (e.g., professional judgment versus production function models) are an extension of equity ideals and focus on a distribution of resources that ensures desired resources are available to special needs students.

2. *Develop Legislation on Uniform Data Reporting, Collection, Management, and Access*: The complexity of school finance systems require accurate, complete, and timely information to ensure its fair and proper evaluation. Uniform and efficient reporting formats are necessary to enable school districts to generate this level of information as well as to minimize and eliminate the improper classification of expenditure data. Validation of the accuracy of reported information also assumes a greater level of importance under the system because reported information is used by the state in making funding allocation decisions. Specifically, district- and school-level data are needed for categories such as revenues (state, local, federal); expenditures (total, instructional, instructional support services, administration, maintenance and operations, other); gender, race/ethnicity, enrollment, percentage of high school dropouts, class size, number of expulsions-suspensions, number of students taking AP courses, attendance rates, graduation rates, college attendance rates, standardized achievement exams; teacher experience, percentage of teachers with degrees; property tax rates and assessed valuation.

3. *Get Educated on School Finance Mechanisms*: Each state uses some type of formula to distribute tax dollars to school districts. The most popular method is called the "Minimum Foundation Program." In general, the minimum foundation program works like this:

   a) The state determines the minimum amount of money to be spent on each student in all of the districts throughout the state;

   b) The property tax rate to provide this amount in the wealthiest of school districts is calculated;

c)   All districts are required to tax themselves at this rate; and

d)   The state makes up the difference between the dollars raised locally through the mandated tax and the dollars required by the minimum foundation program.

e)   Adjustments are made based on student, school, and district characteristics. About 45 states use some form of the minimum foundation program. The main advantage of this funding program is that it provides a means of equalizing general fund revenues per pupil independent of local property wealth. In addition, the study of the guaranteed tax base funding formula, fiscal recapture, and the anatomies of school finance litigation is encouraged.

4. *Develop Legislation for a Periodic Review of the Efficacy of the State Funding Mechanism*: The Review Committee, in consultation with responsible state and community leaders, needs to determine who should be requested to participate, what information should be collected, how it should be collected, how the results will be compiled, and how the results will be disseminated. At the minimum, a series of annual (or biannual) public meetings should be held to disseminate—and receive—information regarding the K–12 education finance formula, school budgeting processes, and possible reallocation decisions. As such, all participants should receive at least (1) the approved minutes of each meeting, (2) a summary of issues discussed at the meeting, (3) recommendations for proposed actions, and (4) a final meeting report prior to the subsequent legislative session.

5. *Begin Conversations About Changing the Prevailing Education Attainment Paradigm*: The old discussions of dollar inputs and student outcomes no longer are productive. The type, amount, and quality of education services provided to special needs students—as well as how each student uses those services—need to be incorporated into any current discussion of education finance policy and productivity. More specifically, the new educational productivity paradigm should have five stages: (1) Financial and Human Resources Inputs, (2) Educational Services Provisions, (3) Student-Parent-Community Effort, (4) Educational Outcomes, and (5) Postschool Measures of Success after graduation for any student or students with disabilities who might not move to advance through a higher education system or traditional career pathways to determine their level of preparedness for employment and independent living.

In light of these issues—when considering the structure of special education finance systems and school quality—determining how to remove conflicting education legislation, policies, and oversight mechanisms seems to be an appropriate starting point. Increasing the participation of frontline education professionals, practitioners, and researchers in the development of policies and legislation seems to be an appropriate second step. This type of increase in participation and autonomy could be exchanged for increased levels of innovation, parental involvement, and accountability.

Notes

1 This section references material generated originally by a report to the National Education Association titled *A Pilot Study on Education Finance and School Quality in the Western United States* (Rolle, Hessling, & Houck, 2002). This material was updated utilizing Ahearn (2010) and Verstegen (2011).

2 http://www.nea.org/assets/docs/HE/NEA_Rankings_and_Estimates010711.pdf

3 For details on the structure of school finance mechanisms, see Guthrie, Springer, Rolle, and Houck (2007) or Thompson, Crampton, and Wood (2012).

4 Rolle & Houck (2007); Houck, Rolle, & He (2010).

5 Verstegen (2011).

6 Parrish & Wolfman (1999).

7 Public Law 89-10, (1965) Elementary and Secondary Education Act.

8 Public Law 89-750, (1966) Elementary and Secondary Education Act Amendments of 1966.

9 Verstegen (1999).

10 Pennsylvania Association for Retarded Children (PARC) v. Commonwealth of Pennsylvania, 334 F. Supp. 1257 (E.D. PA 1971).

11 Mills v. Board of Education, 348 F. Supp. 866 (1972).

12 Martin, Martin, & Terman (1996).

13 U.S. Congress, Committee on Education and Labor, Select Subcommittee on Education, *Hearings*, 93rd Cong., 1st sess. (1973).

14 Public Law 101-476 (1990) EHA was renamed the Individuals With Disabilities Education Act.

15 Aleman (1997).

16 The National Center of Education Statistics notes that the "link below leads to information on the funding system specific to each state, including information regarding revenue collection, allocation of resources, and other information. The information [reproduced here in this chapter] was provided by finance officials in the state education agencies or other experts with knowledge about the funding systems in their respective states": http://nces.ed.gov/edfin/state_financing.asp.

References

Ahearn, E. (2010). *Financing special education: State funding formulas*. Project Forum, National Association of State Directors of Special Education (NASDSE).

Aleman, S.R. (1997). *Individuals With Disabilities Education Act reauthorization legislation: An overview*. Washington, DC: Library of Congress, Congressional Research Services.

Guthrie, J.W., Springer, M.G., Rolle, R.A., & Houck, E.A. (2007). *Modern education finance and policy*. Boston, MA: Allyn & Bacon.

Houck, E.A., Rolle, R.A., & He, J. (2010). Examining school district efficiency in Georgia. *Journal of Education Finance, 35*(4), 331–357.

Martin, E.W., Martin, R., & Terman, D.L. (1996). The legislative and litigation history of special education. *The Future of Children, 6*(1), 25–39.

Parrish, T., & Wolfman, J. (1999). Funding special education. In T. Parrish, J. Chambers, & C. Guarino (Eds.), *Trends and new developments in special education funding: What states report*. Thousand Oaks, CA: Corwin Press.

Rolle, R.A., Hessling, P., & Houck, E.A. (2002). *A Pilot Study on Education Finance and School Quality in the Western United States, 1991–2001*. A Report for the National

Education Association and NEA Western Regional Offices. Raleigh, NC: Alfonso & Pearl Consulting.

Rolle, R.A., & Houck, E.A. (2007). Curious Georgia studies economics: The tale of a researcher and a superintendent who debate the merits of measuring a school system's level of educational efficiency. *School Administrator, 64*(5), 34–39.

Sahlberg, P. (2010). *Finnish lessons: What can the world learn from educational change in Finland?* New York: Columbia University Press.

Sailor, W. (2009). *Making RtI work.* San Francisco: Jossey-Bass.

Thompson, D.C., Crampton, F.E., & Wood, R.C. (2012). *Money and schools* (5th ed.). Larchmont, NY: Eye on Education.

Verstegen, B. (1999). Funding special education. In T. Parrish, J. Chambers, & C. Guarino (Eds.), *Civil rights and disability policy: A historical perspective.* Thousand Oaks, CA: Corwin Press.

Verstegen, D.A. (2011). Public education finance systems in the United States and funding policies for populations with special educational needs. *Education Policy Analysis Archives, 19*(21), 1–26.

PART III

New Conceptions of Practice

6

ALIGNED SERVICE DELIVERY

Ending the Era of Triage Education

Todd A. Gravois

The current system of special education was developed as a solution to a real problem. It represents a breathtakingly noble undertaking to correct the systematic exclusion and underservice of a group of students. In one broad stroke, special education law ensured legally defined protections, procedures, and processes for students who were historically denied educational opportunities and access to schools. For four decades, many improvements in the education of *all* students have occurred because of this system.

Without doubt, the special education system as we know it has increased the number of professionals who provide quality day-to-day service to students, empowered parents to demand quality education for their children, and prompted researchers to investigate and support the implementation of numerous strategies of instruction and behavior management. This system has directly benefited thousands of students identified for special education services. Over time, the efforts, practices, and research have seeped their way into the functioning of the school as a whole, providing benefit to many more students and teachers than those officially identified as requiring service.

Yet there are clear and known problems with special education as a service (Kober, 2002). The President's Commission on Special Education (2002) noted that "too often, simply qualifying for special education becomes an end-point—not a gateway to more effective instruction and strong intervention. . . . The current system uses an antiquated model that waits for a child to fail, instead of a model based on prevention and intervention." The commissioners recognized that "too little emphasis is put on prevention, early and accurate identification of learning and behavior problems, and aggressive intervention using research-based approaches" (p. 1). This has resulted in delaying support for struggling students.

Since its inception, the original and determining rationale for offering special education services was to serve those students who do not respond to strong and appropriate instruction within the classroom setting. When such services are provided, the focus must be on closing the achievement gap and ensuring that these students are learning and functioning well enough to benefit from and contribute to the larger society.

Today's Problems Come From Yesterday's Solutions

Peter Senge's (2006) statement implies that often our initial effort to address a real problem results not only in success, but also in the creation of new and different problems. Special education as a system is not immune to this implication. As a solution to supporting disabled students, the system of special education has produced its own set of challenges and problems that education-at-large must address. Moving beyond our current status requires an honest assessment of the problems we face and, more important, an understanding that many problems are directly related to our original attempt at special education. Envisioning a new and better solution to effectively educate all students, especially those who have the greatest needs, requires a critical review of the problems that have arisen and the legacy of our nation's first attempt to ensure all students a free and appropriate public education.

Legacy 1: Acceptance of Students as Having Internalized Deficits

A lingering problem created by our current system of special education is the assumption that the etiology of learning difficulties emanated from within the student. Gickling and Gravois (in press) refer to this as the "broken child" assumption where learning difficulties prompt a series of questions largely guided by comparing the student to the larger population of learners to determine the student's need. Of course, there are competing assumptions as to why students don't learn, including ecological variables of family, language, class, race and gender discrimination, and the quality of instruction. Without question, the current version of special education attempts to separate out those students who are impacted by these ecological variables from those whose learning difficulties are internally derived. However, the driving assumption of the special education system is that, for a group of students, the lack of learning is the result of an underlying deficit or defect within the student that must be identified and treated using unique and specialized instruction.

Special education as a system of service is not neutral and greatly influences the entire educational community's view of learners. While there is and continues to be an intellectual debate as to the true underlying cause of the lack of a student's learning, the practical effect of the current special education system is perpetuation of the assumption that a portion of students have an internal deficit that needs to be identified and treated. Rather than spending time focused on increasing the learning of students, the larger educational system spends temporal and financial resources trying to sort and classify, and then defend whether they have made the correct decision.

After nearly 40 years, a presupposition has been created in the minds of *all* educators that influences how they respond when a student does not learn. When educators are faced with a struggling student, this assumption of the deficit child creates a pause to ask: "Is this the one?" The assumption of the deficit child also operates to create a cognitive and emotional dissonance for many educators who struggle with the thought that they might be overlooking a student who requires more than they can provide. It represents a no-win situation for day-to-day practitioners because they are always susceptible to a challenge to prove they have not overlooked a disabled child (aka Type II error).

This is not a small issue and deserves reiteration. The "broken child" assumption permeates the larger educational system, creating constant debates and divisions in the interprofessional relationships within the schools. At the extreme, adversarial relationships are created between parents and schools, between general and special educators, and between educators and eligibility professionals that often affect the entire functioning of a school. This constant push-pull relationship influences professional practices as it relates to all students, not just special education students. Of course, sometimes this results in positive outcomes for all, but at other times it diminishes the educational opportunities. In all instances, resources that could have provided services are redirected toward arguing the fundamental assumption.

The power of the "broken child" assumption influences even the current efforts at reform, such as Response to Intervention (RtI). While there is an outward debate about the value and utility of measuring a student's response to interventions over the traditional discrepancy model in determining a student's eligibility for services, it is most striking that the underlying assumption regarding student difficulties remains largely untouched. For example, it is explicitly stated that an expected percentage of students will not respond and will require intensive services (Batsch et al., 2005). Current efforts have "beefed up" the pre-referral phase requiring measurement of a student's response in a "tiered" model of service, but the end result continues to be a narrow focus on the process of identifying those students who do not respond. As was recently overheard in a school, instead of a student being described as being suspected learning disabled, he was referred to as a "nonresponder." LD is being replaced with NR. Old beliefs are hard to change.

Legacy 2: Acceptance of Educational Triage

Triage is a concept that arose during World War I in treating wounded soldiers and involves sorting and classifying those with most needs to receive services. The process of triaging is geared toward assigning available resources to serve those in need. Since resources are rarely limitless, triage becomes a necessary means by which those with the most need are identified and then offered access to the limited services available.

Special education is a triage system that operates within the larger educational system. While special education cannot take responsibility for introducing the triage system into education, it can, however, be seen as perfecting it. The sorting and classifying process created by special education represents the most powerful force in education today in maintaining triage as the primary means by which services are designed and delivered. More important, the credence that special education gives to the triaging process has influenced every subsequent program of resource that operates in schools today. Whether it be supplemental reading, English for second-language students, interventions for struggling students, tutoring, or programming for poor students, the model of triage that special education perfected is replicated and copied, creating a multitude of "mini-triage" systems within the same school.

Figure 6.1 visually presents the impact of triaging on schools. As shown, schools are challenged to achieve best outcomes for all students with a finite and limited amount of resource. In general, there are three types of resources available in schools. The first and most plentiful is the classroom teacher. Without doubt, the largest budget expenditure is attached to classroom teachers who remain responsible to serve each and every student. The second type of resource found in schools can be generally categorized as ad-hoc services. These resources are largely used and deployed at the discretion of the individual school and will vary school to school. Service providers such as reading specialists, interventionists, school counselors, paraprofessionals, and tutors would be examples of these resources. These resources are considered ad-hoc in that procedures and processes

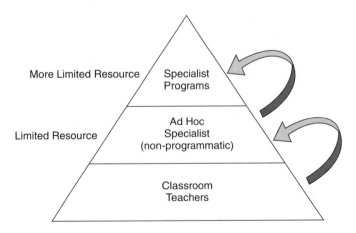

FIGURE 6.1. Triage Education

for distribution and assignment can vary from district to district, from school to school, and from year to year. Variation at this level is also seen in the use of formally developed programs of instruction, and the fidelity by which such services can be deployed. Funding for these resources is rarely tied to external requirements for accountability, but is typically funded by the local budget, allowing for greater flexibility of resource use.

The remaining types of resources available in schools are considered programmatic and highly specialized. These resources exist in all schools, are highly regulated, are rigorous in their entry and exit criteria, and are typically funded externally. Special education is one example in addition to Title services, English Language Learners (ELL), Speech/Language Services, and OT/PT. The use of these resources is highly monitored, and accountability is enforced to ensure they are distributed only for the targeted students.

Combining the triage system with the fundamental assumption that there are subsets of students who are "broken" and therefore must be identified, schools largely have adopted a one-solution model to organize resources and provide services. Schools organize the delivery of resources to allow the triage system to function. While the outward presentation is that the system is to support struggling students, the primary function of the service-delivery model is to manage allocation of the limited resources available. In general, services in today's schools are

- Student-centered;
- Focused so that only those students with the most severe needs access service;
- Characterized by assessments that sort and identify students;
- Fulfilled through a gatekeeper function to determine which students have sufficient need to access limited resources;
- Hierarchical, with specialists seen as better prepared to provide instructional service to students than classroom teachers;
- Designed so that someone other than the classroom teacher typically decides if, how much, and when resources will be provided, and when resources will end;
- One-directional with the flow being away from the classroom (i.e., upward pressure); and
- Accountable for resource management rather than outcomes.

Legacy 3: Acceptance of a Hierarchy of Educator Specialization

As early as 1989, Algozzine and Ysseldyke noted the unintended consequence of special education was that general classroom teachers were led to believe they were incapable of teaching struggling students. This is as true today as then. Slavin and Madden's (1998) early investigation of the triage system, a system designed to separate and segregate struggling students into highly specialized services, found the following:

- Remedial and special education services are too often poorly integrated with the regular education program.
- Such systems burden the most at-risk students with the task of accommodating very different approaches.
- Teacher behaviors associated with outstanding achievement gains in pull-out programs tend to be similar to those found to be effective with all students.
- Effective practices for students at risk tend not to be qualitatively different from best practices of general education.

Despite this and other research (e.g., Kavale & Forness, 1999; Forness, 2001), the prevailing view is that students require specialized, separate instruction provided by highly trained specialists. This view now goes beyond students entitled to special education and permeates all education.

Of course, any student could benefit from better teachers engaging in more effective practices. Likewise, it is not hard to argue against one-on-one instruction as preferred over the increasingly higher teacher/student ratios in the classroom. However, the blanket assumption that more intense, more individualized, and more specialized instruction equates to better outcomes remains largely in question after nearly 40 years (Forness, 2001).

Systems Are People Made

As Lincoln famously stated, "a house divided against itself cannot stand," and education finds itself a system structurally, financially, and philosophically divided as to how to achieve the best possible outcomes for all students. Acknowledgment that people created the current system is an important first step to change. The positive legacy of special education as a system has been to unite around a common consensus that all students deserve, are entitled to, and are protected to receive high-quality education. However, avoiding the mistakes of the past requires directly confronting the inherent flaws and postulating a set of assumptions that can guide the next iteration of service delivery.

For Whom Do Schools Exist?

Sarason (1992) stressed that "schools should exist coequally for the development of students and educational personnel" and that "we have to give up the belief that it is possible to create conditions for productive learning when those conditions do not exist for educational personnel." So, for example, Burrello and colleagues (2013) suggest a fundamental system of education that aims to expand students' capabilities, such as their freedom to promote or achieve what they value doing and being. This is a noble vision and a worthy endeavor. However, one must also address Sarason's view that one cannot create a system of student capabilities when the same is not true for the professionals who serve and support those students. The juxtaposition of these two concepts, the attempt to create a unified system for students against the highly fragmented and isolated system for the teaching staff, is one that must be considered when building a new system.

Capabilities for Adults

The research deemed important for student learning poses an interesting paradox within the current system when considering the adults who serve and support students. A key finding is that learning is increased when addressing real challenges that are embedded in real-world actions (Graesser, Halpern, & Hakel, 2008). As found in the review of the research, learning is enhanced when there are desirable difficulties that cause cognitive disequilibrium. This research has been increasingly incorporated into education practices as it applies to students (e.g., project-based learning and problem-based learning).

Yet, the triage system established for serving struggling students works in opposition to this research when viewing the world of general educators. The current system's singular focus on identifying struggling students and then systematically removing them from the teacher's control actually deprives classroom professionals of the very context required for increasing and improving their own performance. Instead, struggling students are often served by a select group of professionals—specialists. It can be argued that specialists become more and more skilled at serving the most struggling students because they are constantly challenged by the struggles of those students and rewarded professionally by the repeated process of resolving these challenges. Teachers, on the other hand, are deprived of these challenges through the sanctioned system, but are then expected to teach and support these students during the remainder of the school day with little or no support.

A concrete example of the fragmentation of professional functioning and student service was witnessed recently in a school district where classroom teachers were provided in-service training focused on differentiating instruction for the diverse learners in the classroom. Teachers received several hours of discussion about beliefs, a review of evidenced-based strategies, and ideas for using and maximizing curricula material for students who struggled academically. General and special education jointly funded these professional workshops. However, the teachers found upon returning to their school that the system remained unchanged. Each hour a specialist (e.g., Interventionist, Title 1, Reading, Special Education, ESL, etc.) arrived and removed groups of students from the classroom to offer specialized instruction in separate programming—many purported to be evidenced-based. On the surface, while the intended outcome of connecting the most needy students to evidenced-based practices was met, the practical effect was that the classroom teachers' new learning about differentiating instruction was largely negated by the systematic removal of the diverse learners—the challenge was removed. More important, the mixed message was that teachers should differentiate their instruction, except for an identified group of students for which differentiation was insufficient and required specialist intervention.

Further, research results suggest that cognitive flexibility is increased when multiple viewpoints are offered on a problem (Graesser, Halpern, & Hakel, 2008). Again, the current system of triage service delivery continues to segregate professionals rather than promote cooperative action to improve professional functioning of the classroom professional. This harkens back to Burrello and colleagues' original call for special education to be seen as experimental education (Burrello, Tracy, & Schultz, 1973) and more recently promoted as innovative education (Burrello, Sailor, & Kleinhammer-Tramill, 2013). Either term implies that there is a challenge or problem that requires professionals to engage with and seek solutions. However, if the classroom teacher remains segregated and removed from this opportunity by the larger triage system, then only a subset of professionals will acquire and become proficient in the skills required for sustained student learning.

Guiding Principles for a New System

The following guiding principles are offered to directly confront the legacy of our current system and thereby force a new set of practices and skills. These should create discomfort and debate because any reform of practice requires reform of assumptions.

Learning Is an Ecological Construct

Learning occurs because there is a match between the ecological variables controlled by the educator and the student's entry skills. The literature in this area is strong and enduring (see, for example, Bloom, 1976; Dochy, Segers, & Buehl, 1999; Sanders, 1998; Slavin, 2003; Thompson & Gickling, 1992; Wolfe & Brandt, 1998; Vygotsky, 1978), especially our understanding that learning is fostered when the instructional system (teaching, tasks, and curriculum) is effectively matched to the student's entry skills (prior knowledge). As Gickling and Gravois (in press) detail, the ability of educators to accurately assess students' entry skills and then build learning conditions that strategically challenge, but not frustrate, promotes the highest learning outcomes for students (Figure 6.2; Gravois, Gickling, & Rosenfield, 2011).

In this ecological view, investigation of student learning always considers all three components—simultaneously. Understanding and promoting learning requires observation of the student interacting with the curricula tasks and with the delivery of the teacher. It also requires investigation of the effectiveness of the instructor to select and manage the curricula tasks. Efforts to separate these variables for measurement and investigation will provide only a piece of a complex puzzle and rarely result in effective outcomes.

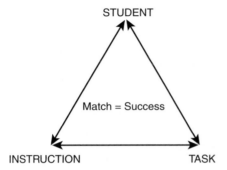

FIGURE 6.2. The Learning Triangle

The assumption is more than the often-batted-about phrase—"All students can learn"—but instead it is a complete recognition that *all students will learn when provided the right conditions*—the match. Adopting this assumption will fundamentally shift practices and skills. No longer will it be acceptable to move students from placement to placement or from tier to tier. Instead of asking whether the student is responding, the question will be what are the instructional conditions to which the student is being asked to respond?

Professional Functioning Improves With Challenge

The lack of student learning should be viewed as a desirable difficulty to embrace rather than avoid. Resources that support professionals' efforts to succeed with struggling learners serve a two-fold purpose. When resources are allocated to supporting the classroom teacher, they directly meet the intention of providing appropriate education for the student because the ultimate outcome of improved professional practice is student achievement. Resourcing the teacher represents embedded professional development for the professional. For too long the intervention support for students has been separated from the professional development of the teachers. This fragmentation is seen in a majority of schools where professionals' development is largely viewed as a separate entity from the resources allocated to support struggling students.

Problem Solving Promotes Deep Reasoning—for Teachers and Students

If the only desire is to identify and allocate services to struggling students, then the current triage structure will suffice. This includes the most recent efforts at RtI where the focus is on using RtI to simply sort and classify the nonresponders.

However, if the ultimate goal is to promote sustained growth and improved academic performance, then schools have to reconceptualize struggling students as the primary vehicle by which professional learning occurs. The ability of individuals to problem solve, assess, take action, and evaluate the impact of that action represents the core of researched learning principles that promote deeper and more meaningful learning. More important, knowledge of, skill in, and practical success with problem solving builds one's capabilities. It provides the foundation for individuals to "promote or achieve what they value doing and being" (Burrello, Sailor, & Kleinhammer-Tramill, 2013, p. 7).

Success Must Be Anchored to the Classroom

Related to the need for problem solving is recognition that learning is deepened and more meaningful when it is anchored to real-world situations. For the classroom teacher, learning is increased when the teacher is integral to the planning and design of instructional delivery for each and every student. Further, if we are going to hold teachers accountable for student learning (e.g., Race to the Top, ARRA PL 111–5, 2009), then they must assume the central role in directing the actions of additional support services that a student receives. To borrow a term from the medical field, the teacher must become the student's *primary care provider*. But this is not a new concept. As stated by the International Reading Association: "IRA believes the classroom teacher, in collaboration with administrators and colleagues should be the central decision maker in determining how instruction is provided, what materials are used, who needs and gets extra services, and how time is allocated" (IRA, 2009).

Resource Management Must Be Considered Within Reform Efforts

Any effort to radically change the direction of special education in the 21st century must recognize a fundamental truth—day-to-day school functioning is largely about resource management. It is important to recognize that this burden goes beyond managing the special education process, special education represents only one type of resource operating in schools. There needs to be a recognition that district and school leaders are constantly challenged to allocate and manage very limited resources with many more identified needs than resources available—hence, the resulting triage system.

While we would like to believe that practices are guided by evidenced-based research, the reality is that most decisions are dictated by availability of resources. Visit any school or district and it is quickly evident that transportation and cafeteria capacity take precedent over evidence-based practices. Further, the challenge of scheduling multiple support services within a highly structured six-hour school day often results in practices that are counterproductive, if not down right bizarre. On more than one occasion schools have scheduled students' supplemental reading services during their scheduled reading class because of limited availability of the reading specialist. The bizarreness comes from the assumption that the students were actually receiving something more, that is supplemental, when in effect they were receiving nothing more than the students remaining in the class. When it comes to serving struggling students, if a school has ample specialized resources available to support struggling students (e.g., tutors, Title 1, reading specialists, interventionists, etc.), then many more students will receive support and it is easier to manage the resource allocation. If there are fewer resources, then fewer students are deemed eligible or eligible students receive less resource time and the triage system prevails.

There is a need to go beyond a mandate to serve struggling students. The need is a coherent system to maximize the resources available and manage the delivery of these resources at the school level. If we do not articulate a clear and accountable system for resource management in our next evolution of special education, then the triage system will prevail and continue to thwart any efforts at real reform.

Envisioning an Aligned System of Teacher and Student Support

Recently enacted legislation and regulations (i.e., IDEA, RtI) require schools to develop a system of service delivery that is coordinated, integrated, and accountable for student success, especially for those students who are experiencing academic and behavioral difficulty. This alignment must also promote enhanced teaching within the classroom setting as opposed to simply removing struggling students and placing them into intervention groups. An aligned system of service delivery should assist school personnel in gathering data to make quality decisions about students' access to resources within the school setting and the effectiveness of those resources in promoting achievement. School-level practitioners need a system that unifies and coordinates the multitude of mandated and available resources in a way that supports their work rather than adds additional burdens.

The development of an aligned service delivery system demands uniformity, consistency, and accountability not just for special education, but also for all resources that are allocated beyond the classroom teacher (e.g., ELL, Title, Supplemental Reading, Behavior Specialists, etc.). A comprehensive system exists when *all* resources are structured and accounted for within the school setting beginning with support of the classroom professional. The use of additional resources for struggling students beyond what is available at the classroom level must be aligned and layered strategically. An aligned system is unified through a common planning process from which all resource providers operate. The system is cohesive by having the classroom teacher remain the central decision maker in developing, assessing, and evaluating the effectiveness of resulting plans. Resource providers work under the single plan and remain accountable to achieving the goals established by the classroom teacher.

The Crux of the Problem

The major barrier in designing an evolved system to allocate resources for struggling students continues to be our ability to distinguish professional needs (i.e., instructional support) from child-centered needs (i.e., disabilities). For a new system to be sustainable, this distinction must be parceled out as part of an integrated planning process and well before resources are allocated to students. Past efforts that solely focus on differentiating eligible from noneligible students through increasingly complex psycho-educational measurement techniques have largely failed to make the distinction between professional and student needs. These efforts can also be seen as continuing the concept of "broken child" because the assumption remains that a subset of students are fundamentally not achieving due to some internalizing deficit.

The failure to ensure the delivery of effective classroom instruction results in fragmentation of services for students, diffused ownership of student goals, and inefficient use of scarce resources. This narrow focus on identifying struggling students (i.e., low scores on a measure) and allocating resources is overly simplistic and perpetuates the triage system. The failure of this practice results in predictable scenarios that are ineffective in helping students achieve and inefficient in yielding the best outcomes with the resources available:

- *Scenario 1*: Resources are allocated to students who score low on a measure; however, the classroom teacher can adequately meet the needs of these students without additional resources (inefficient).
- *Scenario 2*: Resources are allocated to students who score low on a measure; however, no change occurs in the ongoing classroom instruction (ineffective/inefficient).
- *Scenario 3*: Resources are allocated to students who score low on a measure; however, the resource provider develops goals separate from the teachers' goals (ineffective/inefficient).
- *Scenario 4*: Resources are not allocated because the student does not score low enough; however, the classroom teacher remains uncertain about instructional delivery (ineffective/inefficient).

Even current efforts at reform (e.g., RtI) provide little examination of the instructional delivery occurring within the classroom setting and instead resort to high-inference techniques to infer whether instructional quality is present or not (e.g., if 80% of the students score well, then the core instruction is considered appropriate; Batsche et. al., 2005). Without differentiating student and professional needs, resources are allocated based on identification criteria that are largely arbitrary and more related to how many resources are available rather than the actual number of students who could benefit. Furthermore, the classroom teacher is involved neither in determining the problem nor the measurable goals that will be achieved for students who receive resources, and he or she is involved to a lesser degree in the strategies to be implemented.

Expanded Model of Resource Service Delivery

Specialists in schools currently deliver their services using what is considered to be a direct service model (Gutkin & Curtis, 1999), where they work directly with identified student(s). In this model, any interaction with the classroom teacher is at best considered a coordinated exchange between equal service providers (Figure 6.3) and at worst two separate instructional programs for the student(s) in question. The primary focus of direct service is to deliver prescribed instruction to the student(s) by a specialist with little consideration of the ongoing classroom instruction. Unfortunately, this service delivery model promotes continued fragmentation and diffused ownership for student achievement and creates a false professional hierarchy where a specialist is perceived to have substantially different and enhanced knowledge not held by the classroom teacher.

Reforming special education and other resource roles requires reconceptualizing the service model that has existed in schools for nearly four decades. Instead of narrowly viewing resource services as relegated to the time of direct work with an identified student, service is focused on the entire context (ecology) in which the student receives instruction, including the instruction delivered by the classroom teacher.

The role, purpose, and expectations of special educators and other resource personnel need to be redefined as being supportive to both teachers and students. This will require incorporating skills and structures of indirect service delivery (Gravois, Groff, & Rosenfield, 2009; Frank & Kratochwill, 2008). As shown in Figure 6.4, indirect service delivery seeks to effectively support students by

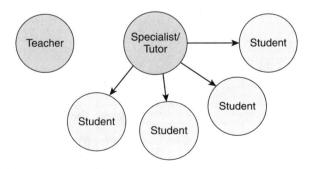

FIGURE 6.3. Direct Service Delivery

supporting the classroom context in which they spend most of their instructional day. The teacher retains primary instructional leadership for each and every student, and the resource provider works to support the teacher in planning and delivering instruction within the classroom.

There are both short-term and long-term benefits of indirect service delivery. The immediate outcome is to create, align, and maximize resource effectiveness for the student(s). However, the long-term impact is to treat the experience of problem solving and planning as embedded professional development so that the classroom teacher enhances his or her skills and knowledge for future students. This reformed system of resource delivery then

- Remains student- *and* teacher-centered;
- Starts with supporting teachers in assessing, planning, and delivering quality instruction within the classroom;
- Recognizes the teachers' role to establish the measurable goals that drive instruction and resource use;
- Allocates additional resources beyond the classroom according to the plan and goals established by the teacher;
- Utilizes student data to monitor student achievement and to measure effectiveness and efficiency of use of resources; and
- Holds resources equally accountable for impact of services on student outcomes as measured by the goals established by the teacher.

An indirect service model aligns resources around a single goal that is established by the classroom teacher and ensures the delivery of effective and quality

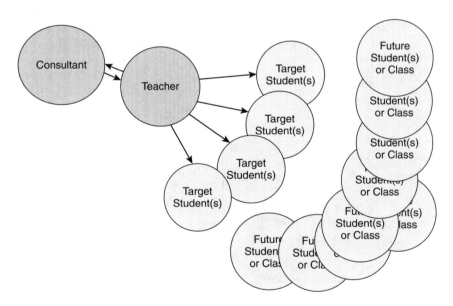

FIGURE 6.4. Indirect Service Delivery

instruction within the general education classroom as initiation of the support process. Once effective instruction is ensured, then additional layers of support and resource can be systematically accessed and their effectiveness adequately assessed.

Instructional Consultation Teams: A Model of Aligned Service Delivery

The Instructional Consultation Team model (Gravois, Gickling, & Rosenfield, 2011; Rosenfeld & Gravois, 1996) has evolved over 25 years as a complex innovation bundle that incorporates structured, data-based consultation with teachers (Instructional Consultation; Rosenfield, 1987, 2008; Rosenfield, Silva & Gravois, 2008); direct assessment of students' performance in existing classroom curricula (Instructional Assessment; Gickling & Havertape, 1981; Gickling & Gravois, in press); and delivery through a highly structured, accountable, coordinated team (IC Teams; Rosenfield & Gravois, 1996).

The core of the system is ensuring all resources, including classroom teachers, principals, special educators, Title 1, ESL, and so on, are equally trained in and adhere to a common process of collaborative, data-based problem solving as the primary service delivery process. Once trained, these team members operate in a Case Manager role, partnering with teachers to facilitate interactions that are consistent, uniform, and accountable (Figure 6.5).

Uniformity is achieved because team members adhere to the structured process of problem solving articulated by Rosenfeld's (1987, 2008) model of Instructional Consultation and engage in Instructional Assessment as presented by Gickling (Gickling & Havertape, 1981; Gickling & Gravois, in press; Gravois & Gickling, 2008). Regardless of a team member's professional role or the content of concern presented by the teacher, consistency is ensured through a process that assesses student performance within the classroom, specifies baseline performance, and establishes measurable goals in collaboration with the teacher directly related to the curriculum.

Each resource professional brings the unique skill and knowledge of his or her respective profession and yet is held accountable by using a single process of evaluation. The goal established by and with the teacher becomes the measure of student growth and achievement regardless of the number or role of professionals who provide service for that student. This shifts accountability from simply reviewing a student's response to a strategy to evaluating the effectiveness of resource allocation in achieving measurable goals. The teacher is central in the process, but each resource provider also has "skin in the game."

The IC Team case management structure is guided by the principles described earlier. IC Team case managers assume dual responsibility for supporting the classroom teacher in evaluating current instructional practices (*anchored learning*) and for co-developing a clear and measurable plan for individuals or groups or classes of students (*multiple viewpoints promote cognitive flexibility*). Through this dual role, the case manager seeks to improve, enhance, and increase student

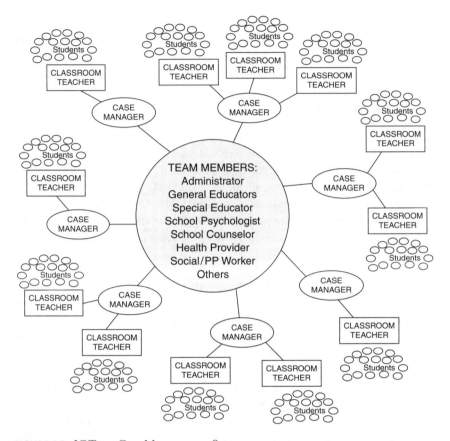

FIGURE 6.5. IC Team Case Management Structure

achievement through improving, enhancing, and increasing the teacher's capacity to plan and effectively address a student's growth (*professional functioning improves with challenge*).

Process of Instructional Consultation and Assessment

The IC Team model explicitly adheres to an ecological assumption that quality instruction and behavior management, matched to a student's assessed entry skills, increases student success, reduces behavioral difficulties, and supports an alignment of resource allocation. An essential characteristic of the IC Team model is the focus on instructional context and the importance of supporting teachers in creating optimal learning conditions as the foundation of the service delivery system. Case managers and teachers engage in specific steps to evaluate the instructional triangle (Figure 6.2) by (a) examining the student's prior knowledge, level of skill development, and learning rate; (b) use of instructional time, classroom management procedures, instructional delivery, and assessment, in conjunction with the teacher's expectations for the student; and (c) the task demands presented to the student.

The IC Team staged-based problem-solving process serves as an accountability structure to promote uniformity of service delivery among the many resource providers in their role as case managers. It also promotes reflection about the problem at hand and ultimately an internalized heuristic that teachers retain to apply to future similar problems. The process includes the following:

Identifying and Analyzing the Needs of Students and Teachers

Identifying students who demonstrate an academic or behavioral need is relatively easy. Analyzing whether the student's need is a result of mismatched instruction or an indication of need for additional support, however, remains challenging. The first step in the IC Team service system is a structured consultation (Rosenfeld, 1987, 2002) with the classroom teacher that assesses the appropriateness of the classroom instruction. Specifically, teachers are partnered with an IC Team case manager who collaborates with the teacher and conducts Instructional Assessments (Gickling & Gravois, in press; Gravois & Gickling, 2008). The Instructional Assessment is conducted within the classroom curricula by the case manager, allowing the teacher to observe and participate.

This process engages the classroom teacher in an analysis of the current instructional delivery and allows professional reflection on how current instructional practices either support or hinder effective learning for the student(s). Most important, this process of assessment provides required verification as to whether current instruction is appropriate for the student.

Specifying a Plan That Includes Baseline and Short-Term, Measurable Goals

Results of the consultation and assessment between teacher and case manager allow for prioritizing of concerns and then collection of data related to the student's current performance—the baseline. Targeted, measurable goals result from the systematic, problem-solving activities. Goals are established for 4–6 weeks and are measured relative to the classroom curriculum. The teacher establishes the instructional goals in collaboration with an IC Team member so that continuity of services and resources will be achieved.

Formulating Classroom Instructional Practices

The primary purpose of the structured consultation and assessment is to specify strategies that are to be incorporated into the classroom instruction or management of classroom behavior by the classroom teacher. The decision to access and allocate additional resources represents a secondary decision and does not deter from this primary purpose, to revise and adjust existing instruction to support the student's need. The fundamental realization within the IC Team process is that classroom instruction cannot remain unchanged.

Implementing Classroom Instructional Practices

Fidelity and accuracy in implementing designed classroom strategies is a known weak point in the entire problem-solving process. Efforts to support teachers on a frequent and ongoing basis during the implementation of a newly designed strategy remain critical (Noell et al., 2005). The IC Team case manager remains a committed resource, engaging with the teacher to ensure that necessary support is available to actually implement the instructional plan with fidelity. This includes providing demonstrations of new or varied strategies, offering opportunities for the teacher to observe others using the selected strategies, and problem solving unforeseen issues preventing effective implementation of the agreed-upon strategies.

Accessing and Aligning Additional Resources

Additional resources, concurrent with implementing classroom practices, may be accessed when the previous steps have been achieved. Upon assessing current instructional practices and establishing measurable goals, resources can be accessed and layered onto the instructional practices occurring in the classroom. Additional resources are aligned with the plan established by the teacher in collaboration with the IC Team case manager and are guided by the goals established as part of the structured problem-solving process that has occurred.

Evaluating Student Progress

The classroom teacher and IC Team case manager remain responsible to measure and monitor student progress on a weekly basis. The teacher and case manager measure progress toward the goal, even if a resource provider is involved in directly providing services to the student beyond what is provided in the classroom. Success in meeting the goals results in the discontinuing of resources and establishing the next level of short-term goals. Lack of progress is analyzed to determine the effectiveness of strategies and the effectiveness of resources allocation for the targeted student(s).

Evaluating Resource Effectiveness

Beyond the progress of the student(s), schools must be supported to evaluate whether resource allocation is effectively producing the desired outcomes.

Unfortunately, resource effectiveness is rarely monitored relative to student progress. For example, schools rarely ask whether using a resource for a student actually made an impact on instructionally relevant goals. Instead, schools reason in the opposite direction—a lack of impact from receiving a resource is used to justify the need for *more* resources.

Throughout the evaluation, the classroom teacher remains the central determiner of the goals of student(s) as part of a structured, accountable process. This allows an evaluation of resource effectiveness relative to a common metric—the progress of student(s) in achieving goals directly related to the context of the classroom curricula. By monitoring achievement using centrally established teacher goals, school professionals can begin assessing which resources make the greatest impact. It also forces resource professionals to expand their focus beyond their venue of direct service and assume responsibility for effective classroom instruction even when the student is not within their direct control. A summary of the process of instructional consultation and assessment is depicted in Figure 6.6.

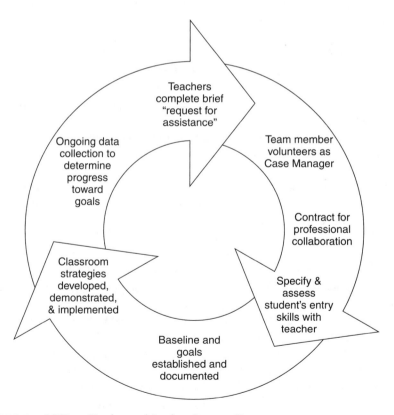

FIGURE 6.6. IC Team Teacher and Student Support Process

Case Example of Resource Alignment Using IC Teams

As of this writing there are more than 500 schools implementing the aligned process of IC Teams. Some are supported through state-level initiatives (e.g., Nevada) and others work in collaborative consortia developed among district leaders who share a common vision of recreating service delivery options for their teachers and students (e.g., Michigan). Still others work individually at the school level influencing those variables and resources within their purview. Regardless of the larger context, each school grapples with transitioning from a system of using resources directly with struggling students (i.e., triage) to expanding to include and use resources indirectly as a support to the larger context of the classroom in which students function.

One such school is Millennium Elementary, a school of nearly 600 students. Millennium Elementary is a predominantly upper-middle-class community and by any measure would not be considered a school requiring extraordinary attention. However, prior to implementing IC Teams resource allocation was very much the triage system. That is, assessments were conducted, struggling students were identified, and then these students were systematically assigned to the various resources available. Those with reading concerns were served by the reading specialist, those who had limited English proficiency were served by the English as Second Language Teacher, articulation and language problems were assigned to the Speech Pathologist, and the disabled to the Special Educator. The school was especially proud of its inclusion of disabled students within the general education classroom. To achieve this, the school would group special education students strategically into select teachers' classrooms and then have the special educator co-teach within those classrooms for portions of the school day. From the outside looking in, the school appeared to run as a well-oiled machine and typical of most schools.

However, the triage system both worked and did not work. As long as there were enough direct service resources to cover the list of identified students, the school could effectively claim to serve the needs of its most struggling students. Regardless, a subgroup of students that teachers "wished" could receive some extra assistance always remained in the classroom. This tension of not enough direct resources was ultimately tested when the school did not achieve AYP—the subgroups of identified ELL and Special Education students did not demonstrate expected adequate yearly progress.

As would be expected with most schools, the initial reaction was to discuss how to give these now twice-identified students more direct service. (Twice-identified alluding to the fact that students were first identified as needing specialized service and now were being identified as needing even more service.) However, real dissonance was evident when the principal observed, "These students are receiving every available resource we have, and we don't have anymore. We have to change what we do for these and all students throughout the instructional day, not just when a service is provided." Being identified as an underperforming school understandably demoralized the staff and created additional pressure on the resource providers to do more than ever. However, the principal saw the opportunity to confront the larger system issues and to plan for sustainable growth both for students and teachers.

The IC Team concept had been used within the building for several years, but had not been fully embraced largely because the existing competing triage system promoted focusing on the deficits of students rather than the ecological context of the classroom. The school not making AYP created the opportunity to reintroduce the IC Team as a support to classroom instruction and fundamentally changed the entire service model practiced in the school by all resources, not just special education.

The case of Mrs. Jones represents the shift in service delivery. Mrs. Jones had several students who had been seen daily by the Reading Specialist and the Special Educator the previous year, some of the very same students who were part of the group that did not meet the AYP standards. These students were assessed at the beginning of the current year using a universal screening measure, continued to perform below expectations, and according to the triage model would automatically qualify to be directly served by the Reading Specialist or Special Educator. However, instead of simply sending the students to these resources, Mrs. Jones was partnered with an IC Team member (e.g., the school psychologist, Ms. Thomlin) who would work as case manager.

As Mrs. Jones and Ms. Thomlin followed the problem identification and analysis process, it became evident that Mrs. Jones was struggling not only to help these identified students, but also to help all of her students improve their comprehension skills. Instead of focusing narrowly on the subgroup of students identified through the universal screening, the teacher and case manager conducted individual and classwide assessments, having the students work in the text material that fifth graders were expected to read and respond to throughout the day. This process resulted in a class goal established to improve specific, measurable areas of comprehension directly related to the district and state curricula standards.

After collecting baseline data on the class performance, Mrs. Jones and Ms. Thomlin collaboratively planned specific instructional strategies that would be introduced and delivered as part of classroom instruction. Using evidenced-based practices, the teacher began teaching students metacognitive strategies for improving comprehension and then allowing them to work in cooperative groups to practice and receive feedback on the use of the strategies. Mrs. Jones and Ms. Thomlin then measured and charted the class performance on a weekly basis.

As the teacher and case manager reviewed weekly data, they noted that a few students might benefit from additional repetition and practice of the strategies being introduced. They shared their case at the team meeting and described the need. At this point the Reading Specialist, also a member of the team, indicated that she could provide some targeted repetition using the same strategy, if needed. The case manager and teacher decided to incorporate 15 minutes of repetition and feedback into the strategy to be delivered by the reading specialist. After two additional weeks, the data being collected by the case manager and the teacher indicated the goals were being achieved and the case was closed, including the extra support being provided by the reading specialist.

In this case, the reading specialist still retained a direct service role; however, her work was guided by the plan developed by the teacher. More critical, the service that the reading specialist provided was aligned with the strategies being used in the classroom by the teacher. Finally, the teacher and case manager maintained the role of collecting and analyzing data to determine the students' progress and to also determine whether having the reading specialist involved actually added value in achieving the goals established. This process allowed the school to become more active in managing its resource allocation. In the triage model, resources would have been assigned to the student(s) having an identified need; in IC Teams, resources are best seen as being attached to the process of establishing and achieving goals. When the goals are met, then resources are available to be reallocated and redeployed.

The example of Millennium Elementary is useful for better understanding that aligning resources should not be confused with eliminating resources. Instead, the case demonstrates how important it is to first allocate resources to help the teacher assess, plan, and alter her delivery of classroom instruction. The school psychologist represented an indirect support to the teacher and provided an objective support of the teacher's planning process. Alignment does not dilute the need for a school psychologist; instead it reallocates this important service toward impacting both students and teachers. Aligning resource deployment serves to build skills and knowledge of the classroom professional for current and future students.

Aligning Services for Students With Significant Needs

The concept of alignment is especially important when considering those students who have significant needs—students identified under categories of service such as autism, physical impairment, emotional disability, visual impairment, hearing impairment, and so on. Ensuring access to the general educational setting is important in planning for these students. However, one of the major criticisms of current inclusive practices is that high-needs students are often included in general classroom settings with little or no support for the teacher. More troublesome is the convoluted allocation of resources to first identify these students as requiring more intense services, and then ultimately including the student into the very same classroom deemed incapable of meeting his or her needs initially (Zigmond, Kloo, & Volonino, 2009).

A guiding principle of aligning services is that success should be anchored to the classroom setting for both students and teachers. The system of aligning services begins with supporting the teacher in assessing the student's performance, establishing clear goals, and then assisting in the design and delivery of quality matched instruction. This does not change because a student has been identified as having significant needs. Indeed, for those students with more intense needs, it would be expected that more services will be involved, and at times these services will be delivered through a direct service model. The more services involved, the more important alignment becomes. The critical difference is that the process starts and ends with the classroom teacher. Alignment is created when all professionals, classroom or resource, remain responsible to achieve the goals that have been established in collaboration with the teacher, regardless of if, when, or where additional services are provided. As stated before, it also forces resource professionals to expand their focus beyond their venue of direct service and assume responsibility for effective classroom instruction even when the student is not within their direct control.

Key Considerations in an Aligned Service Delivery System

Alignment requires federal, state, and district administration commitment to reconceptualize policy, funding, and staffing responsibilities. Without the involvement of all, school-based practices will continue to follow the most pressing mandate or accountability directive. Aligning services and resources involves ensuring that appropriate personnel are included and adequately skilled to deliver a variety of support services, that time is allocated to key problem-solving actions, that accountability exists for resource use and outcomes and for explicit efforts to align philosophical perspectives. The following five areas will be important to consider:

- *Personnel Alignment.* All nonclassroom service providers will be integrated into an aligned service system. Resource professionals become part of a coordinated team structure and are expected to align their professional service to include collaborative consultation with classroom professionals. A concerted effort to redirect, refocus, and reallocate these resources toward a primary function of supporting student achievement within the general education classroom will require involvement at the highest levels of policy and administration.
- *Skill Alignment.* Sustaining an aligned system of resource delivery requires that various resource providers within each school become skilled in both direct and indirect service delivery models. The extant research indicates that preservice and in-service training in indirect service delivery is often superficial or nonexistent (Anton-LaHart & Rosenfeld, 2004). It will be a mistake to assume that individuals enter their professional roles ready for such expanded roles. Instead, there needs to be dedicated time and professional development activities to develop resource professionals' capacity to serve in consultative roles with the classroom teacher.

- *Time Alignment.* Schools currently allocate time to direct student service, and little time is available for joint problem solving between professionals. Shifting to an aligned service delivery model will mean managing time to allow resource providers and teachers to collaboratively conduct critical aspects of the problem-solving process. The first challenge will be to elevate the value of having the classroom teacher available during the problem-solving and assessment process. This is often perceived as "taking time away from students" and not seen as meaningful, especially in the current triage system. However, the principles of student and professional growth dictate that the classroom teacher have time to co-conduct a thorough problem identification, including an instructional assessment of the student(s) performance within the classroom material.
- *Accountability Alignment.* For a service delivery model to become a service delivery *system* there must be a unifying structure of accountability that allows schools to evaluate the effectiveness and efficiency of resources through a common perspective. An aligned service delivery system measures effectiveness of resource providers (e.g., Title, ELL, Counselors, Psychologists, Truancy Workers, Specialists, etc.) by their success in assisting the classroom teacher to establish instructionally relevant goals through a structured problem-solving process, implementing practices, and achieving the established goals for student academic and behavioral success.
- *Philosophical Alignment.* Creating a vision for aligned service delivery requires leadership at the district and school level to articulate the expectation that the delivery of quality classroom instruction is the responsibility of all professionals, not just classroom teachers. Professional performance is judged on how well it supports the ecological variables that influence learning and actions taken to ensure alignment of student services with classroom goals. Such a philosophy of service delivery ensures that the classroom teacher remains involved in establishing the goals that will guide both classroom instruction and supplemental services provided to students.

Summary

We have a unique opportunity to transform schools by reforming the services that operate within them. A major challenge in this reform is the ability to reframe our guiding principles and underlying assumptions about struggling learners. Confronting the triage system of resource management that has evolved within special education and all other supplemental programs offers a chance to expand service delivery as a support to students and the professionals who serve them. While this chapter has promoted the concept of aligning services into a single system of school support, it also offers an illustration of a current model of team-based services—IC Teams—that serves as a comprehensive approach to reform schools. When confronted by those who questioned whether we can indeed create an integrated system that supports professional and student growth, one IC Team

Principal replied, "This is not doable, it is 'done able'." The question, then, for policy makers and educational leaders is not whether we have the means to align services; rather, it is whether we have the will to do so.

References

Algozzine, B., & Ysseldyke, J.E. (1983). Learning disabilities as a subset of school failure: The oversophistication of a concept. *Exceptional Children, 50,* 242–246.

American Recovery and Reinvestment Act of 2009 (ARRA). (2009). Section 14005-6, Title XIV, (Public Law 111-5).

Anton-LaHart, J., & Rosenfeld, S. (2004). A survey of preservice consultation training in school psychology programs. *Journal of Educational & Psychological Consultation, 15,* 41–62.

Batsch, G., Elliott, J., Graden, J., Grimes, J., Kovaleski, J., Prasse, D., ... Tilly, D. (2005). *Response to intervention: Policy considerations and implementation.* Alexandria, VA: National Association of State Directors of Special Education.

Bloom, B.S. (1976). *Human characteristics and school learning.* New York: McGraw Hill.

Burrello, L.C., Sailor, W., & Kleinhammer-Tramill, J. (2013). *Unifying educational systems: Leadership and policy perspectives.* New York: Routledge.

Burrello, L.C., Tracy, M.L., & Schultz, E.W. (1973). Special education as experimental education: A new conceptualization. *Exceptional Children, 40*(1), 29–31.

Dochy, F., Segers, M., & Buehl, M.M. (1999). The relationship between assessment practices and outcomes of studies. *Review of Educational Research, 69*(2), 145–186.

Forness, S.R. (2001). Special education and related services: What have we learned from meta-analysis? *Exceptionality, 9,* 185–197.

Frank, J. L., & Kratochwill, T. R. (2008). School-based problem-solving consultation: Plotting a new course for evidence-based research and practice in consultation. In W.P. Erchul & S.M. Sheridan (Eds.), *Handbook of research in school consultation* (pp. 13–30). New York: Lawrence Erlbaum Associates.

Gickling, E.E., & Gravois, T.A. (in press). *Instructional assessment: The path to effective reading instruction.* Baltimore, MD: ICAT.

Gickling, E.E., & Havertape, J.R. (1981). Curriculum-based assessment. In J.A. Tucker (Ed.), *Non-test based assessment.* Minneapolis: National School Psychology Inservice Training Network, University of Minnesota.

Graesser, A., Halpern, D., & Hakel, M. (2008). *25 principles of learning.* Task Force on Lifelong Learning at Work and at Home. Retrieved from www.psych.memphis.edu/learning/whatweknow/index.shtml

Gravois, T., & Gickling, E. (2008). Best practices in instructional assessment. In A. Thomas & J. Grimes (Eds.), *Best practices in school psychology: Vol. 5* (pp. 503–518). Washington, DC: National Association of School Psychologists.

Gravois, T.A., Gickling, E., & Rosenfield, S. (2011). ICAT: *Training in instructional consultation, assessment and teaming.* Baltimore, MD: ICAT Publishing.

Gravois, T.A., Groff, S., & Rosenfield, S. (2009). Teams as value-added consultation services. In T. Gutkin & C. Reynolds (Eds.), *Handbook of School Psychology* (4th ed., pp. 808–820). New York: John Wiley & Sons.

Gutkin, T., & Curtis, M. (1999). School-based consultation theory and practice: The art and science of indirect service delivery. In C. Reynolds & T. Gutkin (Eds.), *Handbook of School Psychology* (3rd ed, pp. 598–637). New York: John Wiley & Sons.

International Reading Association. (2009). IRA offers policy recommendation to U.S. President-elect Barack Obama. *Reading Today, 26*(3), 1, 4, 5.

Kavale, K.A., & Forness, S.R. (1999). *Efficacy of special education and related services.* Washington, DC: American Association of Mental Retardation.

Kober, N. (2002). *Twenty-five years of educating children with disabilities: The good news and the work ahead.* Washington, DC: American Youth Policy Forum.

Noell, G.H., Witt, J.C., Slider, N.J., Connell, J.E., Gatti, S.L., Williams, K.L., et al. (2005). Treatment implementation following behavioral consultation in schools: A comparison of three follow-up strategies. *School Psychology Review, 34,* 87–106.

President's Commission on Excellence in Special Education. (2002). *A new era: Revitalizing special education for children and their families.* Washington, DC: U.S. Department of Education.

Rosenfeld, S. (2008). Best practices in instructional consultation and instructional consultation teams. In A. Thomas & J. Grimes (Eds.), *Best practices in school psychology: Vol. 5* (pp. 1645–1660). Washington, DC: National Association of School Psychologists.

Rosenfeld, S.A. (1987). *Instructional consultation.* Hillsdale, NJ: Lawrence Earlbaum Associates.

Rosenfield, S.A., & Gravois, T.A. (1996). *Instructional consultation teams: Collaborating for change.* New York: Guilford Press.

Rosenfield, S., Silva, A., & Gravois, T. (2008). Bringing instructional consultation to scale: Research and development of IC and IC teams. In W. Erchul & S. Sheridon (Eds.), *Handbook of research in school consultation: Empirical foundations for the field* (pp. 203–224). Mahwah, NJ: Lawrence Erlbaum Associates.

Sanders, W. (1998). Value-added assessment. *The School Administrator, 11*(3), 24–27.

Sarason, S. (1992). *The predictable failure of educational reform: Can we change course before it's too late?* San Francisco: Jossey-Bass.

Senge, P. (2006). *The fifth discipline: The art and practice of the learning organization.* New York: Crown Business.

Slavin, R.E. (2003). *Educational psychology: Theory and practice.* New York: Pearson Education.

Slavin, R., & Madden, N. (1998). What works for students at risk: A research synthesis. *Educational Leadership, 46,* 4–13.

Thompson, V.P., & Gickling, E.E. (1992). A personal view of curriculum-based assessment: A response to "critical reflections…" *Exceptional Children, 58*(5), 468–471.

Vygotsky, L. (1978). *Mind in society: The development of higher psychological processes.* Cambridge, MA: Harvard University Press.

Wolfe, P., & Brandt, R. (1998). What we do know from brain research. *Educational Leadership, 56,* 8–13.

Zigmond, N., Kloo, A., & Volonino, V. (2009). What, where, and how? Special education in the climate of full inclusion. *Exceptionality, 17,* 189–204.

7

SERVING STUDENTS WITH EXTENSIVE SUPPORT NEEDS IN GENERAL EDUCATION CONTEXTS IN A RECONCEPTUALIZED SYSTEM OF EDUCATION

Diane Lea Ryndak, Ann-Marie Orlando, and Debra Duran

At various points in their educational experience, any student might require different types of supports and services to be successful (Kirkpatrick, 1994). For students whose life experiences are extremely challenging (e.g., students who are homeless, live in poverty, are migrant, are linguistically or racially diverse, or have significant cognitive disabilities), those supports and services might be considered to be extensive; that is, more specialized, or needed more broadly across content areas and contexts, when compared with the majority of students. In Chapter One, Kleinhammer-Tramill, Burrello, and Sailor (2013) reconceptualize special and general education within one system in which all students achieve their capabilities together in the same classes within their neighborhood schools. They describe "special education" as a "temporally bounded instructional support system for any student in the public schools who might need support to achieve his or her full capabilities" (p. 3). Using this support system, teachers would blend academic, social, and behavioral interventions into a rich and engaging curriculum that enables all students to learn at high levels and prepares them for postschool life (p. 23). Thus, the needs of students with extensive support needs would be met within instructional activities and classes provided for all students of the same age.

The purpose of this chapter is to describe one approach a problem-solving team could use to identify, provide, and evaluate the effectiveness of supports for any student with extensive support needs within this reconceptualized education system. The chapter uses one group of students with extensive support needs (i.e., significant disabilities) to provide an example for all students with extensive support needs. The chapter first provides conceptual underpinnings for serving students with significant disabilities in general education classes; second, it provides information on current educational outcomes and evidence-based practices for students with significant disabilities; third, it describes how a problem-solving team might meet the needs of a student with significant disabilities at one period of time; and fourth, it presents suggestions for preparing personnel to participate on problem-solving teams.

Conceptual Underpinnings

Several conceptual underpinnings lay the foundation for supporting students with significant disabilities in general education classes with age peers. These underpinnings relate to how students are perceived, how decisions about curriculum and instruction are made, and how these shape educational services for students with significant disabilities in contexts with their age peers. While not an exhaustive list, five such concepts are discussed below.

Purpose of Education and Desired Long-Term Outcomes Drive Educational Services

Broadening the purpose of education to ensure that all students acquire and apply both academic and alternate content in their current and future lives in society emphasizes postschool outcomes (e.g., employment, relationships, natural support networks, community participation). For students with significant disabilities, the purpose of education historically has been described as assisting each individual to participate as independently as possible in current and future environments (Brown et al., 1979) in the manner and contexts of their choosing (Agran & Hughes, 2005). Such discussions about the purpose of education facilitate articulation of desired long-term outcomes and, thus, short-term outcomes for measuring meaningful progress toward those long-term outcomes.

Least Dangerous Assumption and Presumed Competence Shift Inadequacy to Instruction

The criterion of least dangerous assumption "asserts that in the absence of conclusive data, educational decisions should be based on assumptions which, if incorrect, will have the least dangerous effect on the student" (Donnellan, 1984, p. 142). Donnellan argues that if a student is not successful in a context (e.g., a general education class), instead of perceiving a deficit inherent to the student that is negatively impacting the student's ability to learn, the instruction should be interpreted as inadequate for meeting the student's learning needs. Jorgensen (2005) extends this assertion and argues that collaborative problem-solving teams must presume that every student, regardless of appearance or first impression, is competent and able to learn. This presumption of competence encourages the use of universal design for learning (UDL) principles and assistive technology (see Toson & Frattura, this volume, Chapter Ten).

Access to General Education Includes Content, Context, and Accountability

Federal initiatives and legislation require that all students have access to general education and to participate in the general education accountability systems. If the desired outcome for students with significant disabilities is their participation in activities that naturally occur in general education and other contexts, it is critical that access comprises all components of general education (e.g., common core content, instructional and noninstructional activities, content specialists, age- and grade-level peers). Collaborative problem-solving teams then can ensure instructional content derived from common core standards, taught with evidence-based instructional practices in naturally occurring contexts, and assessed with activity-based strategies to determine the impact on each student's life.

For a student with significant disabilities, assessment of progress must reflect the use of knowledge and skills in meaningful activities across general education and natural contexts. In addition, assessment of their progress must include performance on grade-level core curriculum content, alternate content for participation in current and future general education and natural contexts, foundational skills (e.g., communication, social behaviors, on-task behaviors), and meaningful measures of quality of life. To be effective, assessments for students with significant disabilities must be frequent, include both informal and formal processes, and address the learning needs of each student with significant disabilities.

Desired Outcomes, Context, Content, Instruction, and Assessment Are Interrelated

Logically, the content on which students are assessed must be consistent with the content on which they receive instruction. Presumably, assessment content reflects the knowledge and skills believed to be most relevant for individuals to participate meaningfully in society, both as children and adults. If this is the case, then content of their assessment and instruction should be driven by the contexts in which they are expected to participate, and those contexts determined by the desired educational outcomes.

If it is accepted that the desired educational outcomes for all students include the acquisition and use of academic and alternate content in their communities, then the contexts in which a student with significant disabilities participates must be used to determine the (a) knowledge and skills that are most relevant for their acquisition and use, and (b) contexts in which instruction and assessment on that content occurs. Thus, instruction and assessment must be conducted within the same activities that naturally occur across general education and other natural contexts and must address both grade-level and alternate content required for participation.

Collaborative Partnerships on Problem-Solving Teams Positively Impact Outcomes

Meeting the needs of all students in the same contexts requires the formation and smooth functioning of collaborative partnerships among school personnel, families, students, and community members. For students with significant disabilities, collaborative partners jointly provide instruction and assessment across activities in general education and natural contexts, through the use of individualized accommodations/modifications that extend those already in place based on UDL principles.

Outcomes and Evidence-Based Practices for Students With Significant Disabilities

This section describes the current outcomes of educational services, and evidence-based practices, for students with significant disabilities. This information will be reflected in the ensuing example of a problem-solving team meeting the needs of a student with significant disabilities in the reconceptualized education system.

Outcomes

Kleinhammer-Tramill et al. (2013) argue that the U.S. construct of disability locates educational problems solely within students, leading to "an unjust and unfair parallel system of programs and services that results in less efficacious outcomes than those realized by students in the general education system" (p. 9). This particularly is true for students with significant disabilities who frequently are segregated in "special" classes and schools, and whose academic and social outcomes are extremely poor. For instance, the U.S. Department of Education (2008) reports that during the 2005–2006 school year more than 6 million of the students enrolled in public schools (13.2%) were reported as having disabilities and receiving special education services. Of these students, only 33.0% left school with a regular diploma, while 24.3% either left with a certificate of completion or dropped out. The National Longitudinal Transition Study-2 (NLTS2) indicates that more than 75% of students with disabilities scored below the mean across subsets of standardized achievement tests, and 22–38% scored more than six standard deviations below the mean in functional measures (Wagner, Newman, Cameto, Levine, & Garza, 2006).

Approximately 2% of the total student population could be considered to have significant disabilities (i.e., intellectual disabilities, multiple disabilities, deaf-blindness, autism spectrum disorders [ASD]). While this 2% of students tends to remain in school through age 21, data from the NLTS2 (Wagner et al., 2006) suggest that during the 2005–2006 school year (a) an average of 34.6% left school with a certificate of completion instead of a high school diploma; and (b) an average of 14.6% dropped out of school. After leaving school, more than 66% of these students scored six or more standard deviations below the mean on overall independence, and an average of 41.6% had trouble communicating with others.

When determining outcomes related to employment, rights, service planning, community inclusion, choice, and health and safety reflected in adult lives for individuals with disabilities, public developmental disabilities agencies across 27 participating states use standard measures (i.e., National Core Indicators http://nationalcoreindicators.org). These data for 2009–2010 indicate that: (a) only 14% of respondents were employed in either competitive or supported positions in the community, while an additional 45% wanted such employment; (b) 53% of those employed in the community earned between $1.00 and $7.25 per hour, and only 22% received employment benefits; (c) 73% of those in a sheltered workshop earned between $1.00 and $2.50 per hour, and 16% earned between $2.51 and $5.00 per hour; and (d) only 19% of respondents chose their own home, and only 25% chose their own roommate.

Such outcomes are dismal, demonstrating the lack of positive outcomes for adults with significant disabilities. There also is a lack of data to inform service providers of either (a) the types of services that result in different types of outcomes, (b) outcomes related to components of general education content acquired during the school years, or (c) measures related to the quality of life experienced by adults with significant disabilities. To determine the effectiveness of educational services, indicators of evidence-based practices in inclusive education (Barnitt et al., 2007) could be used to collect annual data on the location in which the adult received services, the type and quality of supports and services provided, and how access was provided to general education contexts, content, and accountability systems. The proposed shift to a human capabilities approach to conceptualizing education could lead to evaluation of academic, functional, and quality of life outcomes; how those relate to employment, independence, self-determination, and other outcomes that an individual adult has reason to value; and the supports and services that led to better outcomes.

Evidence-Based Practices

Two groups of evidence-based practices are discussed in the following sections. The first group focuses on instructional strategies implemented with students who have significant disabilities and the curriculum content taught with those strategies over time. The second group focuses on the context in which instruction on that content occurs.

Instructional Strategies and Curriculum Content

Following the passage of P.L. 94-142, research was initiated on the education of students with significant disabilities. It was found that students who previously had been segregated from society through placement in institutions and self-contained schools demonstrated specific learning characteristics (e.g., difficulty generalizing the use of acquired knowledge or skills across contexts) (see Stokes & Baer, 1977) and, when these learning characteristics were purposefully addressed during instruction, the students' learning was positively impacted (Ryndak, Morrison, & Sommerstein, 1999). Thus, the field began to identify evidence-based instructional strategies that are effective for meeting the needs of students with significant disabilities (Wolery, Ault, & Doyle, 1992). Initially, however, the content on which these students received instruction was limited by beliefs in the developmental sequence and importance of prerequisite skills (Brown et al., 1979).

Research efforts then turned to the acquisition of alternate content (e.g., functional activities; foundational skills) that would facilitate the participation of students with significant disabilities in natural contexts at school, at home, and in the community (see Gee, Graham, Sailor, & Goetz, 1995; Nietupski, Hamre-Nietupski, Curtin, & Shrikanth, 1997). This body of research supports the use of instructional strategies for acquisition of alternate content to facilitate the participation across contexts with grade-level peers who do not have disabilities.

More recently, research has determined that these same evidence-based instructional strategies are effective when teaching age- and grade-level general education content to students with significant disabilities (see Browder et al., 2007) when embedded in general education academic classes (McDonnell et al., 2006). Studies also have demonstrated that instruction for students with significant disabilities on a combination of both age- and grade-level general education content, and alternate content, is effective (a) when provided during instruction with peers across general education and other natural contexts (Ryndak et al., 1999), and (b) when embedding evidence-based instructional strategies within activities across general education and other natural contexts (Riesen, McDonnell, Johnson, Polychronis, & Jameson, 2003).

Context

Jackson, Ryndak, and Wehmeyer (2009) discuss the essential role of context in the provision of effective services for individuals with significant disabilities, embedding this discussion in general-education learning theories. Their discussion is supported by the sets of studies discussed above in relation to instruction and content. Findings from these sets of studies indicate that, for students with significant disabilities, increased access to contexts in which age- and grade-level peers who do not have disabilities are receiving instruction on general education content has led to their increased acquisition of general education content and use of alternate content in meaningful activities across natural contexts (see, for example, Ryndak, Ward, Alper, Storch, & Montgomery, 2010). Ryndak and Billingsley (2004) describe this as access to general education, including "every component of the general education experience" (p. 35). The general education experiences of all students per grade include their explicit and implicit curriculum content, school and class settings with which the students interact, instructional and noninstructional activities in which the students participate, materials used across activities and settings, and the use of previously acquired skills that allow students to participate across settings. It can be argued, however, that the context also consists of the: (a) instructional personnel who interact with all the students, including their knowledge base and expertise; and (b) type and quality of services provided for all students.

Finally, research efforts have begun to focus on the long-term impact of access over time to general education content and contexts configured based on the incidence of students with and without disabilities in the general population. Fisher and Frey (2010) suggest that the general education classroom should consist of no more than 1% students with significant disabilities, 12% students with mild to moderate disabilities, and 87% students without disabilities. This set of studies indicates that such access has led to a positive impact on the quality of life both during and after exiting school for individuals with significant disabilities (Ryndak, Ward, Alper, Montgomery, & Storch, 2010; Ryndak et al., 2010).

Instructional Configurations

While not studying, per se, the impact of various instructional configurations, the previously discussed sets of studies utilize various instructional configurations during the interventions, including various (a) group sizes (Volonino & Zigmond, 2007), (b) students constituting groups (Dymond, Renzaglia, & Rosenstein, 2006), and (c) instructors (Logan & Malone, 1998). These studies suggest that the needs of students with significant disabilities can be met across various combinations of group size, students in groups, and instructors. Three specific findings are of particular importance. First, in a series of studies Giangreco and his colleagues found that the use of adults, instead of classmates, as instructional supports for students with significant disabilities inhibits the students' participation with their classmates who do not have disabilities (Giangreco, Halvorsen, Doyle, & Broer, 2004; Giangreco, Suter, & Doyle, 2010). Second, Carter, Sisco, Melekoglu, and Kurkowski (2007) found that when peers provided instructional support to students with significant disabilities in general education classes, the peers' engagement in academics did not decline. Finally, Logan and Malone (1998) found that the time that students with significant disabilities were in instruction and on-task was greater in general education contexts than in self-contained contexts.

Assessment

It is logical that for all students a connection should exist between content that is being taught and being assessed. This logic is even more compelling when considering the difficulties that students with significant disabilities frequently demonstrate with generalizing knowledge and skills (Brown, Nietupski, & Hamre-Nietupski, 1976; Stokes & Baer, 1977). Initiatives for the use of standardized assessments for all students on common core standards fail to be reconciled with the original special education concept of "individualized goals" developed for a student's IEP. This failure is particularly troublesome for students with significant disabilities, for whom the context and format of assessment are crucial for obtaining accurate and meaningful information about progress. Historically, therefore, authentic assessment strategies across exemplars (e.g., settings, activities) have been used, resulting in individualized assessment portfolios. While national efforts have been focused on standardizing alternate assessments (Tindal et al., 2003), to date these efforts have not succeeded in capturing meaningful data that accurately and adequately describe the progress made by students with significant disabilities. It is imperative, therefore, that research continues on assessment strategies that consider students' performance in instructional contexts in school and community settings. In addition to assessment strategies, further research is needed on the content of assessment for students with significant disabilities. For instance, research is needed on gathering detailed meaningful data on the acquisition, use, and maintenance of knowledge and skills related to (a) grade-level common core standards, (b) other general education content not specifically linked to the common core standards, (c) previously taught general education content, (d) content for participating with peers who do not have disabilities across general education and other natural contexts, (e) foundational/critical skills (e.g., communication, social interactions), (f) quality-of-life variables (e.g., community access and participation), and (g) development and use of a natural support network. Finally, research is needed on evaluating the impact of various supports and services on the short- and long-term progress demonstrated by students with significant disabilities.

Collaborative Partnerships

Research on educational services for students with significant disabilities is replete with support for the use of collaborative partners to determine instructional content, instructional strategies and adaptations, and progress evaluation practices focused on the student's ecology. This research supports partnerships among the student with disabilities, his or her family members, general education classmates and natural support network members, and relevant school personnel (Dymond et al., 2006). In addition this research supports the partners' use of collaborative processes to identify: (a) relevant and challenging instructional content that provides access to grade-level content, addresses the student's and family's preferences, and is applicable in the student's natural environments (Giangreco, Cloninger, & Iverson, 1998; Ryndak & Alper, 2003); (b) appropriate and effective adaptations to the general education instruction and materials (Lee, Wehmeyer, Soukup, & Palmer, 2010); (c) appropriate and effective multitiered systems of support (e.g.,

PBS, RTI) (Fisher & Frey, 2010); and (d) problem-solving strategies (Giangreco et al., 2004; Hunt, Soto, Maire, & Doering, 2003).

Collaborative partners demonstrate a shared vision, shared goal, and shared desire to maximize outcomes for all students, including students with significant disabilities. Through role release, each partner instructs other partners on specialized expertise, as well as learns expertise from the other partners, for use during a student's instruction across contexts (Ryndak & Alper, 2003). This practice leads to partners addressing the student's learning characteristics (e.g., generalization) by identifying and providing instruction with high-quality accommodations and modifications of instructional activities, materials, and support for the student within general education and natural contexts. In turn, this facilitates the student's: (a) access to general education content and contexts, while addressing his or her alternate learning needs for participating in those contexts; and (b) acquisition and use of grade-level academic and alternate content within activities across general education and other natural contexts.

Meeting the Needs of Students With Significant Disabilities: One Example

One of the paradoxes mentioned in Chapter One of this text states that, "The field of special education continues to espouse the ideal of LRE while maintaining rigid adherence to the concept of a continuum of services. This means, ipso facto, that some children must be placed at various stages of the continuum, and away from general education, for the continuum to exist" (p. 4). This paradox holds true when LRE is interpreted as a continuum of *locations*. However, when LRE is interpreted as a continuum of *services*, the restrictiveness of an environment is determined by the student's access to effective supports and services within that environment, rather than the environment itself. Regardless of the supports and services necessary to benefit, a student can move along a continuum of *services* and never leave general education classes. In fact, a student might move along the continuum of *services* in general education classes across the school day, depending on the instructional objectives, tasks, materials, and activities encountered.

With new policies focused on systemwide strategies that are embedded within NCLB and IDEA (2004), supports and services are provided for students through the use of multitiered systems of support. For example, one schoolwide multitiered system of support, the response to intervention (RtI) process, was signed into law as part of the IDEA (2004). It replaces the IQ-achievement discrepancy model previously used to identify children with learning disabilities, and it mandates early intervention to all children at risk of academic failure (IDEA, 2004). The RtI process is intended to assess how all students, regardless of their instructional needs, respond to instructional strategies in academic contexts (Gresham et al., 2005). This process: (a) uses a continuum of assessing, evaluating, and defining specific supports; (b) embeds those supports within evidenced-based instructional practices and interventions; and (c) engages in continuing evaluation of the effectiveness of those supports, instructional practices, and interventions. This process is meant to be multidirectional and fluid, with students moving from one set of support to another set of support based on their learning needs at any given moment, in any instructional context. The RtI process is intended to focus on the strengths and weaknesses of the instruction provided for each student, as opposed to focusing on each student's deficits and limitations (Downing, 2010).

RtI is an approach to problem solving that could be used by collaborative teams with all students, as they collectively (a) assess students' progress, (b) determine students' learning needs, (c) identify additional supports or services that would facilitate each student's success during instruction, (d) provide those supports, and (e) collect formative assessment data to evaluate whether the supports and services were effective at meeting each student's learning needs in general education contexts. In this way, RtI and other schoolwide initiatives incorporate the learning needs of all students, including those with significant disabilities, allowing them to learn both general education and alternate content during activities that naturally occur in general education contexts.

The implementation of schoolwide, multitiered systems of support often results in the categorizing or grouping of students by the supports and services they require to progress in the general curriculum. This can result in students being excluded from supports and services that are less extensive and provided in general education contexts. For instance, if a student receives extensive supports and services outside of general education classes, then that student would be excluded from the instruction, instructional content, activities, and access to personnel that other students are receiving. This is the case for students with significant disabilities who are placed in self-contained classes or schools. The reconceptualization of education presented in this book promotes a view of the student as an individual with capabilities that might change based on the instructional objectives, tasks, materials, and activities presented. When students are not given access to the same contexts as their age- and grade-level peers, there is a risk of assuming that students' capabilities are static and unaffected by instructional objectives, tasks, activities, and materials.

For schools to view all students, including those with significant disabilities, as learners who should be included in schoolwide, multitiered systems of support, schools must reflect certain qualities. Janney and Snell (2004) suggest that these qualities include providing environments that welcome and make accommodations for all students, valuing diversity, supporting collaboration, and developing a sense of community within the school. Other qualities that might contribute to viewing all students as learners include: (a) educating all students in the school they would attend if they did not have a disability to facilitate the development of natural support networks; (b) supporting teachers considered to be highly qualified in academic content areas and specialized pedagogy,

TABLE 7.1. Steps for Developing a Lesson Plan for All Students

1. Identify the curriculum unit that will be taught to all students over a 6- to 9-week period.
2. Identify state standards and benchmarks (e.g., main concepts from the unit) that will be taught to all students.

Apply UDL principles to:

3. Identify instructional activities that will address the main concepts addressed in the unit.
4. Write a lesson goal that reflects UDL principles.
5. Consider other general education and functional content embedded within the activity relevant to all students.

Apply UDL principles and information from students' education plans to:

6. Identify additional supports and services needed (i.e., instruction, materials, human) for specific students to achieve the lesson goal as written.
   - a) Instruction   b) Materials   c) Human
7. Identify alternate content (i.e., academic, functional) that could be embedded within the activity for specific students.
8. Identify supports and services (i.e., instruction, materials, human) needed for specific students to achieve an alternate goal.
   - a) Instruction   b) Materials   c) Human
9. Identify both summative and formative data that will be collected to determine each student's progress toward the lesson goal and individual academic and functional goals.

to ensure that general and special educators are knowledgeable of the content they are teaching and provide students access to high-quality instruction; and (c) implementing schoolwide, multitiered systems of support for all students across all school personnel.

This section provides an example of a lesson plan designed to meet the needs of all students, including those with extensive support needs, in the same environment. To accomplish this, the example will focus on steps a collaborative team could use when developing a lesson plan to meet the needs of all students in the classroom (see Table 7.1).

Step 1: Start With the Grade-Level General Education Curriculum for All Students

Step 1 simply ensures that a collaborative team begins with the grade-level general education curriculum and the related course curricula designed to meet the learning objectives for a content area. Course curricula comprise several units, each addressing a set of standards and benchmarks to be achieved within a given time frame. The team first identifies the unit that will be presented to all students during the given time frame.

Step 2: Identify Common Core Standards and Benchmarks

For the second step, the team determines the main concepts embedded in the unit to be taught to all students and how those main concepts are linked to national or state common core standards, benchmarks, and assessments. For example, in a 7th-grade reading curriculum with a focus on literature, a unit might address the following common core standards (http://www.corestandards.org/the-standards/english-language-arts-standards/reading-literature-6–12/grade-7/):

- RL.7.1. Cite several pieces of textual evidence to support analysis of what the text says explicitly, as well as inferences drawn from the text.
- RL.7.2. Determine a theme or central idea of a text and analyze its development over the course of the text; provide an objective summary of the text.
- RL.7.3. Analyze how particular elements of a story or drama interact (e.g., how setting shapes the characters or plot).

Step 3: Apply UDL Principles and Identify Instructional Activities

Team members use principles of UDL to develop a lesson plan based on the main concepts of the curriculum. Rose and Meyer (2002) state that "Barriers to learning are not, in fact, inherent in the capacities of learners, but instead arise in learners' interactions with inflexible educational goals, materials, methods, and assessments" (p. vi). To address these inflexible variables, the principles of UDL require that lesson plans are written with options for multiple means of (a) representation of the information to students, (b) students' expression of information, and (c) students' being engaged (CAST, 2011). In the third step, the team applies these principles as they determine instructional activities for teaching the main concepts. When the team selects activities that are accessible to learners with a wide range of learning needs, they minimize the need for additional adaptations (Rose & Meyer, 2002). The team then selects instructional activities for each class period.

Step 4: Write the Goal of the Instructional Activity

Writing the goal of the lesson is central to creating a lesson plan that meets the needs of all students. Often the method of achieving the lesson goal is embedded within the goal. For example, if a lesson's goal states that students will read a text and write a list of the text's main ideas, then students with physical or visual impairments might not be able to meet the goal as it is written. As discussed by Rose and Meyer (2002), some students might be limited in their ability to meet the goal because the method to demonstrate achievement of the goal is predetermined, fixed, and inflexible. However, when the team writes a lesson's goal such that the intent is disentangled from the method for demonstrating goal achievement, then multiple methods for demonstrating goal achievement can emerge, and the goal becomes attainable to a wider range of learners. For example, in Table 7.2, the lesson's goal states that students will review the text and generate main ideas. This goal is not constrained by a method of demonstrating achievement, thus students might demonstrate goal achievement by using multiple methods (e.g., report verbally, generate a list with the use of a computer). Most students could demonstrate goal achievement by using technologies readily available in the class (e.g., digital text readers, adapted keyboards, speech-to-text applications) as part of UDL, while some students might require additional assistive technologies.

TABLE 7.2. Sample Lesson Plan

1. Identify the curriculum unit that will be taught to all students over a 6- to 9-week period.
   Ex. Focusing on multiple texts, students will address common core state standards.
2. Identify state standards and benchmarks (e.g., main concepts from the unit) that will be taught to all students.
   Ex. Florida Common Core Standards:
   - RL.7.1. Cite several pieces of textual evidence to support analysis of what the text says explicitly as well as inferences drawn from the text.
   - RL.7.2. Determine a theme or central idea of a text and analyze its development over the course of the text; provide an objective summary of the text.
   - RL.7.3. Analyze how particular elements of a story or drama interact (e.g., how setting shapes the characters or plot) (http://www.corestandards.org/the-standards/english-language-arts-standards/reading-literature-6-12/grade-7/)

Apply UDL principles (i.e., multiple means of representation, engagement, and expression) to:

3. Identify instructional activities that will address the main concepts addressed in the unit.
   Ex. Instructional activity: Review teacher-selected text and identify main ideas.
4. Write a lesson goal for the instructional activity that will address the main concepts.
   Ex. Lesson goal: (a) Generate questions about the main idea; (b) Work with peers to select the main ideas for the text; (c) Work with peers to generate questions about the main ideas; and (d) Respond to questions about the text. (Adapted from http://www.readwritethink.org/classroom-resources/lesson-plans/active-reading-through-self-30702.html?tab=4#tabs)
   Multiple means of representation, engagement, and expression can be provided through digital text readers, abridged versions of the text, or abridged versions of the text with graphics. Students can review a text through various forms of the text and generate ideas using traditional orthography, photos, and icons.
5. Consider other general education and functional content embedded within the activity relevant to all students.
   Ex. Students will engage in reciprocal communication and collaborate with peers.

Apply UDL principles and information from students' education plans to:

6. Identify additional services needed (i.e., instruction, materials, human) for specific students to achieve the lesson goal as written.

Instruction—Use of prompting strategies.	Materials— Access to digital text.	Human—Support from peer to set up laptop for reading.

7. Identify alternate content (i.e., academic, functional) that could be embedded within the activity for specific students.
   Ex. Student will engage, communicate ideas with peers using speech-generating device.
8. Identify services needed for specific students to achieve an alternate goal.
   Ex. Identifying characters in the text.

Instruction—Use of system of least prompts.	Materials—Abridged version of book with graphics.	Human—Paraprofessional will support student to identify characters using a system of least prompts.

9. Identify both summative and formative data that will be collected to determine each student's progress toward the lesson goal and individual academic and functional goals.
   Ex. Identify characters in a text.
   Ex. Engage in 4 reciprocal exchanges with peers during a 20-min group activity.

Step 5: Consider Other Goals Embedded Within the Activity

After the lesson's goal is written, the team considers other goals for all students that might be embedded within the instructional activity. For example, when an activity involves peers interacting with one another, goals such as working with others and problem solving become part of the activity, although they are not the primary goal. In addition, the team considers goals that were previously taught either during the current school year or in prior years, which could be reviewed and reinforced within the activity. For example, in the goal stating that students will review the text and generate main ideas, the previously taught skill of writing sentences with subject–verb agreement is embedded within the current goal because the current instructional activity provides a naturally occurring opportunity to practice this skill.

Step 6: Apply Information From Section 504 Plans and IEPs

After applying UDL principles to the class lesson plan, the team addresses the additional supports and services necessary for specific students to achieve the lesson's goal, as it is written. These supports and services are determined by the problem-solving team and delineated in each student's plan (i.e., Section 504 Plan or IEP). In general, these supports and services alter the instructional materials or method, or provide human support so a student can access the general curriculum. For some students, it might be necessary to use assistive technologies (e.g., word prediction software) to access the written materials provided and to achieve the lesson's goal as it is written. Other alterations to the instructional materials could include additional time with the materials to complete the activity, or limited focus on a portion of the materials.

A second type of alteration is the use of student-specific instructional methods that are delineated in an IEP. Problem-solving team members can plan alternate evidence-based instructional strategies (i.e., prompting, constant-time delay) for teaching the lesson's goal to a specific student, instructional approaches such as differentiated instruction (Tomlinson, 1999), or flexible instructional configurations, without altering the lesson's goal.

A third type of alteration is the provision of support from a peer or an adult during instruction. In the example provided, peer collaboration is part of the instructional activity. This form of peer support might assist some students in achieving the lesson's goal, as it is written. When embedded in the lesson plan, there is no change in the curriculum content that the students learn, and such supports are available to all students participating in multitiered systems of support (Fisher & Frey, 2010). Though peer supports are preferable, adults (e.g., teachers, paraprofessionals, volunteers) also could provide supports when needed.

Step 7: Identify Alternate and Functional Goals From the IEP Embedded in the Activity

As noted previously in this chapter, students can move along the continuum of services within general education classes depending on the task, activity, and materials. If a student's IEP includes alternate academic goals linked to the general curriculum (Janney & Snell, 2004) or functional goals, then embedding instruction on these is another option for the team to consider. When using this option, the team identifies the alternate academic or functional goals from a student's IEP that can be embedded within the instructional activity in which all students participate. In the example provided, a student with significant disabilities could participate in the same instructional activity by (a) listening to an abridged audio version of the text, (b) listening to an audio version of the text and looking at related graphics, (c) identifying key concepts contained in the text, or (d) participating in shared reading with peers. However, the lesson's goal would be different for this student; it would address the alternate academic or functional content included on the student's IEP, such as identifying the principal character in the text, or sequence of events in the text. Because the students work with classmates to generate questions about the main idea, the instructional activity also creates a naturally occurring opportunity to address a student's functional goals (e.g., reciprocal communication with classmates).

Step 8: Identify Additional Supports and Services Needed to Achieve Alternate Goals

When developing an IEP for a student, the problem-solving team delineates the instructional methods, materials, or human supports necessary for the student to meet the goals of instruction on grade-level standards, and on alternate academic or functional curriculum. In the example provided, an IEP alternate goal is for the student to identify five key words contained in the text. In this step, the team identifies the supports and services needed for the student to achieve that alternate goal and embeds those in the full class instructional activity, such as the use of (a) an additional evidence-based instructional strategy, (b) adapted materials (i.e., abridged version of the book), and (c) human support (i.e., peer support).

Step 9: Identify Methods for Evaluating Students' Progress Toward Goals

Finally, the problem-solving team determines methods for evaluating a student's progress toward the lesson's goal, as it is written, toward alternate academic goals, and toward alternate functional goals. To accomplish this, the team considers how all the students will demonstrate learning of the lesson's goal and how this might be different for a student who requires additional supports and services. In addition, the team considers the quantity and quality of work that will be sufficient to determine whether each student has achieved both the lesson's goal and his or her alternate academic and functional goals.

The use of summative and formative assessments for all students is important for documenting student learning; however, this is particularly the case for students with significant disabilities. Because students with significant disabilities might not demonstrate their knowledge on summative assessments due to their learning characteristics, authentic assessments are critical to determine their progress toward achieving the lesson's goals and their alternate goals. Authentic assessments provide multiple opportunities to assess a student's progress across a variety of contexts and with familiar materials (Nilsen, 2009).

Personnel Development

To meet the needs of students with significant disabilities in general education contexts with their grade-level peers who do not have disabilities, the manner in which personnel are prepared must emphasize their active participation on collaborative problem-solving teams. Because disposition is key to both problem solving and collaboration, all educational personnel must demonstrate knowledge and understanding of the evidence base that supports providing all students excellent and equitable access to general education content and contexts (Jackson et al., 2009) and evidence-based practices for meeting the needs of all students together.

All instructional personnel also need to be specialists in at least three additional areas. First, they need to have demonstrated expertise in the design and development of contexts and instructional activities that reflect UDL principles for all students. Second, they need to have demonstrated expertise in the implementation and evaluation of instruction for variously sized heterogeneous groups of students. Third, they need to have demonstrated expertise in collaboration and problem solving to facilitate their participation with team members who have other varying areas of expertise.

Finally, each problem-solving team member needs to bring a specialized set of expertise to the collaborative process. For example, general education teachers need to bring specialized expertise related to content that reflects the common core standards for one or more subject areas, depending on the grade level(s) they teach. Special education teachers and related services personnel need to bring specialized expertise related to determining the specific needs of each student and strategies for meeting those needs with accommodations or modifications to the instructional content, activities, strategies, or materials. Such expertise must incorporate the embedding of assistive technology, peer or adult support, and specialized instructional strategies (e.g., time delay) within grade-appropriate general education contexts.

In addition, all educational personnel, paraprofessionals, and other school support staff need skills to meet the more global needs of students with significant disabilities, although these skills might be determined based on the specific students with whom they interact. For instance, they might need skills that facilitate a student's interaction with grade-level peers, participation in instructional activities with those peers, or completion of tasks on which they might be receiving instruction.

To participate on effective problem-solving teams, all licensed personnel need both formal preparation and practical experiences on such teams. Effective teaching entails more than knowledge of content; it entails instructional activities that are interesting, motivating, and authentic, while targeting goals on alternate content for each student. It entails instructional strategies that support each student's use of content already mastered, and their guided acquisition and use of new content. It entails the collection and use of meaningful formative and summative assessment data to determine each student's current level of acquisition and mastery of content, and his or her use of that content in meaningful activities that occur in general education and other natural contexts. Such preparation must be structured, tiered, and monitored by individuals who, themselves, demonstrate expertise in current evidence-based practices and the preparation of personnel.

Conclusion

At various points in his or her educational experiences any student could face challenging issues that might require additional supports or services in school. For several sets of students (e.g., students who live in poverty, are homeless, are culturally diverse, have significant disabilities), these challenges might require extensive supports, possibly across subject areas or contexts. In a reconceptualized education system, Kleinhammer et al. (2013) argue for all students achieving their capabilities together in general education classes in their neighborhood schools. They further argue that reconceptualized special education services would consist of temporally bounded instructional support for any student demonstrating a need for additional supports, which would be provided through a collaborative problem-solving team within general education classes.

To realize this envisioned-system, academics, researchers, teacher preparation faculty, district and school administrators, teachers and other school personnel, and parents collectively need to adopt this vision and demonstrate a systemic understanding of the issues faced across all students. Without this common vision and understanding, the status quo will be maintained, including the belief that: (a) homogeneity of curriculum content, homogeneity of short- and long-term instructional support needs, and homogeneity of assessment strategies is good for all students; and (b) responsibility for lack of response to services lies with students, not with the services. These beliefs result in students being removed from services provided for "all" and being placed in other services, frequently in contexts that segregate them from their age- and grade-level peers.

The intent of this chapter was to describe one approach problem-solving team members could use as they identify, provide, and evaluate the effectiveness of supports and services for any student with extensive support needs within this reconceptualized system of education. To meet this intent, the chapter provided an example for one type of student with extensive support needs—a student with significant disabilities. To set the stage for that example, information was provided on the poor outcomes reported for adults with significant disabilities, and some research-based practices that address the needs of students with significant disabilities.

To describe the educational culture in which the example would occur, conceptual underpinnings were discussed. One federal initiative (i.e., response to intervention) was used to demonstrate how the needs of a student with significant disabilities could be met within the reconceptualized education system. Finally, the expertise needed to provide educational services within this reconceptualized system was discussed.

With the emphasis on both excellence and equity of educational opportunities for all students, and a human capabilities agenda that drives the purpose of education for all students, collaborative problem-solving teams within this reconceptualized system focus on meeting the needs of each student by embedding additional supports within the same contexts, on the same general education content and alternate content, within the same instructional activities provided for all grade-level peers. The focus is on identifying what the educators could do differently to meet the needs of each of their students together, rather than on establishing a different context for some students, in which different curriculum and instructional practices are used to address learning issues perceived inherent to those students. Educators are charged with changing their behaviors to meet each student's needs, rather than changing something inherent in the student or the context to meet the adults' needs. In this manner, meeting the needs of "all" students through schoolwide initiatives like RtI really does mean meeting the needs of *all* students together in the same contexts, with evidence-based practices embedded in general education instruction, materials, and strategies across general education contexts (see Tables 7.1 and 7.2).

References

Agran, M., & Hughes, C. (2005). Introduction to special issue: Self-determination reexamined—Are people with severe disabilities any more self-determined? How far have we come? *Research and Practice for Persons With Severe Disabilities, 30*(3), 105–107.

Barnitt, V., Benner, S., Hayes, E., Weser, S., Ryndak, D.L., & Reardon, R. (2007). *Best practices in inclusive education: An assessment and planning tool for systemic change.* Tallahassee: Florida Department of Education.

Browder, D.M., Wakeman, S.Y., Flowers, C., Rickelman, R.J., Pugalee, D., & Karvonen, M. (2007). Creating access to the general curriculum with links to grade-level content for students with significant cognitive disabilities: An explication of the concept. *Journal of Special Education, 41,* 2–16.

Brown, L., Branston, M.B., Hamre-Nietupski, S., Pumpian, I., Certo, N., & Gruenewald, L. (1979). A strategy for developing chronological-age-appropriate and functional curricular content for severely handicapped adolescents and young adults. *Journal of Special Education, 13*(1), 81–90.

Brown, L., Nietupski, J., & Hamre-Nietupski, S. (1976). Criterion of ultimate functioning. In M.A. Thomas (Ed.), *Hey, don't forget about me! Education's investment in the severely, profoundly, and multiply handicapped* (pp. 2–15). Reston, VA: Council for Exceptional Children.

Carter, E.W., Sisco, L.G., Melekoglu, M.A., & Kurkowski, C. (2007). Peer supports as an alternative to individually assigned paraprofessionals in inclusive high school classrooms. *Research and Practice for Persons With Severe Disabilities, 32*(4), 213–227.

CAST (Center for Applied Technology). (2011). *Universal Design for Learning Guidelines version 2.0.* Wakefield, MA: Author.

Donnellan, A. (1984). The criterion of the least dangerous assumption. *Behavioral Disorders, 9,* 141–150.

Downing, J., (2010). *Academic instruction for students with moderate and severe intellectual disabilities in inclusive classrooms.* Thousand Oaks, CA: Corwin Press.

Dymond, S.K., Renzaglia, A., & Rosenstein, A. (2006). Using a participatory action research approach to create a universally designed inclusive high school science course: A case study. *Research and Practice for Persons With Severe Disabilities, 31*(4), 293–308.

Fisher, D., & Frey, N. (2010). *Enhancing RTI: How to ensure success with effective classroom instruction and intervention.* Alexandria, VA: Association for Supervision and Curriculum Development.

Gee, K., Graham, N., Sailor, W., & Goetz, L. (1995). Use of integrated, general education, and community settings as primary contexts for skill instruction for students with severe, multiple disabilities. *Behavior Modification, 19,* 33–58.

Giangreco, M.F., Cloninger, C.J., & Iverson, V.S. (1998). *Choosing outcomes and accommodations for children (COACH): A guide to educational planning for students with disabilities.* Baltimore, MD: Paul H. Brookes.

Giangreco, M.F., Halvorsen, A.T., Doyle, M.B., & Broer, S.M. (2004). Alternatives to over-reliance on paraprofessionals in inclusive schools. *Journal of Special Education Leadership, 17*(2), 82–90.

Giangreco, M.F., Suter, J.C., & Doyle, M.B. (2010). Paraprofessionals in inclusive schools: A review of recent research. *Journal of Educational and Psychological Consultation, 20,* 41–57.

Gresham, F. M., Reschly, D. J., Tilly, W. D., Fletcher, J., Burns, M., Prasse, D., et al. (2005). A response to intervention perspective. *The School Psychologist, 59*(1), 26–33.

Hunt, P., Soto, G., Maire, J., & Doering, K. (2003). Collaborative teaming to support students at risk and students with severe disabilities in general education classrooms. *Exceptional Children, 69,* 315–332.

Individuals With Disabilities Education Improvement Act of 2004, 20 U.S.C. § 1400 *et seq.* (2004).

Jackson, L.B., Ryndak, D.L., & Wehmeyer, M.L. (2009). The dynamic relationship between context, curriculum, and student learning: A case for inclusive education as a research-based practice. *Research and Practice for Persons With Severe Disabilities, 33*(4)/*34*(1), 175–195.

Janney, R., & Snell, M. (2004). *Modifying schoolwork* (2nd ed.). Baltimore: Brookes.

Jorgensen, C. (2005). The least dangerous assumption: A challenge to create a new paradigm. *Disability Solutions, 6*(3), 1, 5–9, 15.

Kirkpatrick, P. (1994). Triple jeopardy: Disability, race, and poverty in America. *Poverty and Race, 3*(3), 1–8.

Kleinhammer-Tramill, J., Burrello, L.C., & Sailor, W. (2013). Special education: A critical perspective on reframing public policy for students with disabilities. In L.C. Burrello, W. Sailor, & J. Kleinhammer-Tramill (Eds.), *Unifying educational systems: Leadership and policy perspectives* (pp. 3–20). New York: Routledge.

Lee, S., Wehmeyer, M.L., Soukup, J.H., & Palmer, S.B. (2010). Impact of curriculum modifications on access to the general education curriculum for students with disabilities. *Exceptional Children, 76*(2), 213–234.

Logan, K.R., & Malone, M. (1998). Comparing instructional contexts of students with and without severe disabilities. *Exceptional Children, 64*(3), 343–359.

McDonnell, J., Johnson, J.W., Polychronis, S., Riesen, T., Jameson, M., & Kercher, K. (2006). Comparison of one-to-one embedded instruction in general education classes with small group instruction in special education classes. *Education and Training in Developmental Disabilities, 41*(2), 125–138.

Nietupski, J., Hamre-Nietupski, S., Curtin, S., & Shrikanth, K. (1997). A review of curricular research in severe disabilities from 1976 to 1995 in six selected journals. *Journal of Special Education, 31,* 36–55.

Nilsen, B.A. (2009). *Week by week: Plans for documenting children's development* (4th rev. ed.). Clifton Park, NY: Delmar Cengage Learning.

Riesen, T., McDonnell, J., Johnson, J.W., Polychronis, S., & Jameson, M. (2003). A comparison of constant time delay and simultaneous prompting within embedded instruction in general education classes with students with moderate to severe disabilities. *Journal of Behavioral Education, 12*(4), 241–259.

Rose, D.H., & Meyer, A. (2002). *Teaching every student in the digital age: Universal Design for Learning.* Alexandria, VA: Association for Supervision and Curriculum Development.

Ryndak, D.L., & Alper, S. (2003). *Curriculum and instruction for students with significant disabilities in inclusive settings* (2nd ed.). Boston, MA: Allyn & Bacon.

Ryndak, D.L., & Billingsley, F. (2004). Access to the general education curriculum. In C.H. Kennedy & E.M. Horn (Eds.), *Including students with severe disabilities* (pp. 33–53). Boston: Pearson.

Ryndak, D.L., Morrison, A., & Sommerstein, L. (1999). Literacy prior to and after inclusion in general education settings. *Journal of the Association for Persons With Severe Handicaps, 24*(1), 5–22.

Ryndak, D.L., Ward, T., Alper, S., Montgomery, J., & Storch, J.F. (2010). Long-term outcomes of services for two persons with significant disabilities with differing educational experiences: A qualitative consideration of the impact of educational experiences. *Education and Training in Autism and Developmental Disabilities, 45*(3), 323–338.

Ryndak, D.L., Ward, T., Alper, S., Storch, J.F., & Montgomery, J. (2010). Long-term outcomes of services in inclusive and self-contained settings in a one-building school district for brothers with comparable diagnoses. *Education and Training in Autism and Developmental Disabilities, 45*(1), 38–53.

Stokes, T.F., & Baer, D.M. (1977). An implicit technology of generalization. *Journal of Applied Behavioral Analysis, 10*(2), 349–367.

Tindal, G., McDonald, M., Tedesco, M., Glasgow, A., Almond, P., Crawford, L., & Hollenbeck, K. (2003). Alternate assessments in reading and math: Development and validation for students with significant disabilities. *Exceptional Children, 69*(4), 481–496.

Tomlinson, C. (1999). *The differentiated classroom: Responding to the needs of all learners.* Alexandria, VA: Association for Supervision and Curriculum Development.

U.S. Department of Education. (2008). Office of Special Education Programs, Thirtieth Annual Report to Congress on the Implementation of the Individuals With Disabilities Education Act, Parts B and C. Retrieved from http://www2.ed.gov/about/reports/annual/osep/2008/parts-b-c/index.html

Volonino, V., & Zigmond, N. (2007). Promoting research-based practices through inclusion? *Theory into Practice, 46*(4), 291–300.

Wagner, M., Newman, L., Cameto, R., Levine, P., & Garza, N. (2006). Executive summary: The academic achievement and functional performance of youth with disabilities. A report from the National Longitudinal Transition Study-2 (NLTS2). (NCSER 2006–3000). Menlo Park, CA: SRI International.

Wolery, M., Ault, M.J., & Doyle, P.M. (1992). *Teaching students with moderate to severe disabilities: Use of response prompting strategies.* New York: Longman.

8

ACCOUNTABILITY FOR WHAT MATTERS: USING POSTSCHOOL OUTCOMES TO BUILD SCHOOL AND COMMUNITY RENEWAL

Mary E. Morningstar, Gregory Knollman, Sarah Semon, and Jeannie Kleinhammer-Tramill

Two themes in Chapter One of this book pose important considerations for school to postschool linkages. These are, first, moving from a closed system of accountability that is bounded by students' K–12 school achievement to an open system that uses adult outcomes as an indicator of school improvement and school success, and, second, moving from a human capital agenda for education to a human capabilities agenda. As discussed in this chapter, these two themes are intertwined in that employment is a primary indicator for both postschool outcomes for students with disabilities and for achieving the human capital agenda, as explicated by Smith and Scoll (2005). This chapter describes the policy shift from school processes to student outcomes that characterized the No Child Left Behind Act (NCLB) of 2002 and the Individuals With Disabilities Education Act (IDEA) amendments of 2004 and reviews what we currently know about postschool outcomes for students with disabilities. Our discussion of NCLB and IDEA as well as postschool outcomes for students with disabilities suggests that, while policy mechanisms for examining postschool outcomes exist for all students, they have largely been neglected as a source of information that schools might use to improve their work. Likewise, while studies of postschool outcomes specific to students with disabilities have provided a rich source of information, they have led to little progress in improving the lifestyle, employment, engagement, and full community participation that would characterize the full range of human capabilities for persons with disabilities. In the final section of the chapter, we provide an overview of an emerging policy framework that holds promise for providing accountability for the success of all students in achieving positive postschool outcomes. States' recent adoption of the *College and Career Readiness Standards*, or *Common Core State Standards*, has been accompanied by federal investments in state systems for collecting longitudinal data, including postschool outcomes, for all students. We use these emergent policy trends together with what we know from existing studies of postschool outcomes for students with disabilities to provide recommendations for the types and uses of data needed to ensure rich and meaningful accountability for the success of all within the preK–12 system and beyond.

NCLB and IDEA: Addressing Postschool Outcomes

Prior to the 2002 reauthorization of the Elementary and Secondary Education Act (ESEA), now referred to as NCLB, federal funding and support for public education came with different contingencies for schools based on inputs and processes rather than outcomes. Schools that received funding through the ESEA were held accountable for demonstrating that compensatory education services were provided rather than for the outcomes they produced. A common strategy schools used to provide services as well as to demonstrate that they were meeting the ESEA mandate was to provide separate, pull-out services for students who were entitled to them because of poverty indicators. Accountability for implementation of the Education of All Handicapped Children Act of 1975 that grew out of Title VI of the ESEA likewise focused on inputs and processes. With the reauthorization of IDEA in 2004, the bar of compliance and accountability was raised for states' programs serving students with disabilities. Despite the increased focus on achievement and accountability, we assert that, in general, both laws have reinforced a myopic focus on "the now" of accountability for student's academic achievement.

Both laws reference postschool outcomes. For NCLB, this remains, as it has historically been, a requirement only for state programs and services for special populations of students. Under IDEA 2004 and preceding authorizations, states began tracking educational and transition service provisions that potentially link with postschool outcomes in the areas of living, learning, and working. In this section, we explore the policy foundation for postschool accountability within current education laws. We contend that future legislation should build on this foundation and adopt an expanded view of what it means to measure student outcomes and student success.

Accountability Under NCLB

The purpose of NCLB is to "ensure fair, equal and significant opportunity to obtain a high-quality education and reach, at minimum, proficiency on challenging State academic achievement standards and state academic assessments" (Sec. 1001. Statement of Purpose. 20 U.S.C. 6301). The Act mandated that states implement single statewide accountability systems based on high standards and aligned assessments to improve overall academic achievement of students in grades K–12. Further, the Act required states to set targets for what they considered Adequate

Yearly Progress (AYP) toward proficiency for all students and to publicly report results. Progress toward proficiency was to be accomplished by ensuring alignment between state academic standards and "high-quality academic assessments, accountability systems, teacher preparation and training, curriculum, and instructional materials" (Sec. 1001. Statement of Purpose. 20 U.S.C. 6301). Further, states were directed to improve low-performing schools and provide alternatives for students who attend such schools.

The NCLB accountability measures were tightly focused on state academic standards and assessment performance for all students, including subgroups such as students with disabilities, who are typically left out of states' assessment initiatives. States, local education agencies, and schools were also to be accountable for increases in English proficiency and academic achievement for LEP students. While the law required states to assess themselves, it also stipulated independent external evaluations of legislation itself, specifically, the NCLB standards and performance assessment of national literacy, dropout, graduation, grade retention for children who participate in HeadStart, EvenStart, English Language Learners (ELL), migratory programs, or programs for disadvantaged children (neglected, delinquent, at-risk, incarcerated, homeless).

NCLB requires school districts and states to report on longitudinal outcomes for a few special populations of high-need or disadvantaged students. For example, while authorized through other statutes, HeadStart and ELL programs are directed to examine programmatic outcomes for improving academic, vocational, and technical skills of the enrolled children. Likewise, when states implement behavioral and drug prevention or intervention programs, they must report on the effort, outcomes, and effectiveness of such programs on a biannual basis. This report must be made public and should include data on incidence, prevalence, age of onset, perception of health risk, and perception of social disapproval of drug use and violence among youth, schools, and communities. The law also stipulates assessment requirements for programs and activities designed for Native American and homeless children and youth funded through set-aside funds or the Native American Education Act. Aside from these special populations, accountability for school success currently ends at grade 12 or with graduation, not with how youths use their education beyond school completion.

State Accountability and Performance in IDEA

Historically, IDEA (2004) has allowed and later mandated effective educational services from birth to age 21 for children and youth with disabilities. The 2004 reauthorization of the law went beyond implicit connections between successful outcomes for students with disabilities and the provision of access to general education curriculum, individualized instruction, behavioral supports, and parental participation. It now asserts that educational and transition services for students with disabilities can and should be linked to graduation and dropout rates as well as postschool outcomes. Specifically, IDEA (2004) mandates that states set measurable goals, publicly report annual data, and ensure the individualized educational planning and delivery of education, social health, mental health, and transition services to support students with disabilities. Alongside this, states must report the percentages of students (by disability, ethnicity, gender, age) who are employed, enrolled in higher education, or other postsecondary educational settings. As the law recognizes the difficulties of providing challenging educational and transition services for students with various levels of need, it calls on states to provide for professional development for general and special educators, paraeducators, and administrators. It also calls for innovative instructional configurations and collaboration or consultation models to facilitate service coordination and ensure successful postsecondary transitions.

Student Outcomes and Assessment in IDEA

While IDEA (2004) requires that students with disabilities have access to, and be held accountable for, the same statewide academic or alternate achievement standards as mandated by NCLB, it also promotes a longer view where schools and teachers are asked to facilitate the students' success beyond high school through transition services. Transition services are defined as an outcome-oriented process involving assessment, instructional programming, and service provision linked to student-developed postsecondary goals in the areas of living, learning, and working. The law also stipulates that if a school or services provider fails to provide transition services as outlined in the child's Individualized Education Plan (IEP), the IEP team must meet and develop alternative strategies to ensure provision of service to meet the student's objectives. Upon graduation or termination of specialized services for students with disabilities, a Summary of Performance document must be developed. This document, provided to the student and/or legal guardian, summarizes academic and functional performance and provides recommendations for support to assist the student in meeting his or her postsecondary goals. The legislation also contains provisions to support technical assistance, research, demonstration models, specialized personnel and leadership preparation, and dissemination of information to sustain innovation and reform to improve outcomes for students with disabilities.

NCLB and IDEA: Falling Short of Longitudinal Accountability

There is a postschool emphasis in IDEA 2004 that contrasts with the K-12 academic accountability mandated in NCLB. IDEA requires states to track between one and three years of postschool outcomes such as employment, independent living, and further education for students with disabilities, while NCLB attends to annual growth in academic achievement for all students during the K-12 years. We recommend an expansion of accountability measures, starting with a blending of both approaches, where states use extant data sources to assess the impact of educational opportunity, access, and service provision with student outcomes. This comprehensive approach will be a richer indicator of the quality of educational outcomes and need for improvement than students' academic achievement progress alone. These are important measures of accountability with many potential benefits for all students. As discussed later in this chapter, states already have access to a number of longitudinal data systems that will assist with such efforts.

Longitudinal Accountability: Beyond K-12

As described by Haines and Turnbull in Chapter Four, NCLB and IDEA took historic steps in increasing attention toward focusing attention on accountability for all students, including those in general education as well as those with identified disabilities. When examining the impact that increased accountability and universal standards might have on student outcomes one can consider the IDEA requirements regarding transition for students who are preparing to exit secondary settings to see how increased emphasis on accountability might positively or negatively impact students with disabilities. Transition includes more than planning for postschool outcomes. It also includes an identification of the necessary supports to assist students who are preparing to move from school to postsecondary education, employment, and possibly independent living environments. Kochhar-Bryant, Shaw, and Izzo (2007) summarize changes to the transition initiatives in the 2004 reauthorization of IDEA. Some of the key changes included a change in transition age from age 14 to age 16, a shift in emphasis from outcomes to results in order to improve academic and functional achievement, revision of interagency responsibilities to emphasize the importance of collaboration, and an emphasis on how transition fits within a standards-based education system.

The National Longitudinal Transition Study (NLTS) was first developed and implemented in the early 1980s with the aim of identifying postsecondary outcomes of a nationally representative sample of students with disabilities across the United States. The initial study was funded under the 1983 Amendments to the Education of Handicapped Children Act (P.L. 98-199) and was one of the first federal initiatives on transition bringing attention to the needs of secondary students with disabilities (Flexer, Simmons, Luft, & Baer, 2007). NLTS was noteworthy because it provided a picture of outcomes from a nationally representative sample and advanced the Office of Special Education and Rehabilitation Services' (OSERS) goal of investigating the outcome-oriented process (Will, 1983).

The results from the first NLTS indicated that employment rates and postsecondary education enrollment for youth with disabilities lagged behind those of same-age peers without identified disabilities. Using a comparison group of youth without disabilities, created from the United States Department of Labor National Longitudinal Study of Youth, Blackorby and Wagner (1996) reported that nearly 1 in 5 youths with disabilities were unemployed 3 to 5 years after exiting school. When looking at the postsecondary outcomes of youth within the 11 disability categories, only 17% of students with multiple disabilities were employed 3 to 5 years after high school, compared with 65% of youth with learning disabilities and 69% of individuals without disabilities. Postsecondary enrollment rates were also very low for individuals with disabilities as compared to other students. Two years after exiting high school an average of 14% of youth with disabilities reported that they attended some form of postsecondary education compared with 53% of the general population without disabilities. While after 3 to 5 years, the percentage increased to 27%, the rate of youth without disabilities enrolling in postsecondary education was 47% higher. When looking at specific disability categories, the gap in enrollment was even larger. When specifically looking at youth with multiple disabilities, only 9% had enrolled in postsecondary education within 3 to 5 years after high school. When comparing the rates of enrollment 2 years after high school and 3 to 5 years after high school, the postsecondary enrollment of students who were identified with a serious emotional disability, intellectual disability, or multiple disabilities showed no significant increase. While the initial findings from Blackorby and Wagner (1996) were calculated as weighted averages and thus only estimates of postsecondary outcomes for youth with disabilities, the findings from the first NLTS indicated that there were fewer positive postsecondary outcomes for youth with disabilities.

Shortly after the reports concluded for NLTS, a second national longitudinal study was designed and funded. The second National Longitudinal Transition Study (NLTS2) was designed to continue the work of the NLTS. This second study, funded by the Office of Special Education (OSEP) in 2000 and 2001, also followed a nationally representative sample of students, this time for a longer period of time and at more intervals between 2000 and 2009 (Wagner, Kutash, Duchnowski, & Epstein, 2005). The repeated measures as described by Wagner et al. (2005) "Permit tracking aggregate changes in important status variables over time" (p. 30). Several studies have reported on findings from one or more waves of NLTS2 since its inception. The results continue to highlight the lower rates of postschool goal attainment among individuals with disabilities especially for those with autism and intellectual disabilities.

Katsiyannis, Zhang, Woodruff, and Dixon (2005) indicate that young adults and youth with disabilities continue to experience high school failure and dropout, lower employment, and lower participation in postsecondary education. Through an analysis of Wave 1 data from NLTS2, Katsiyannis et al. found that students with intellectual disabilities had lower rates of participation in general education, were less involved in the postsecondary goal planning, and had a higher likelihood of making little to no progress toward their transition goals when compared with respondents with learning disabilities and those with emotional or behavioral disabilities. When looking specifically at postschool planning, vocational training, transportation, and postsecondary education supports were identified as areas where students had the greatest needs across all disability categories among Wave 1 participants (Shogren & Plotner, 2012). Students with intellectual disabilities and students with autism were more likely to need transportation support, whereas students with disabilities other than intellectual disabilities or autism were more likely to need postsecondary education accommodations and supports.

Bouck (2012) examined Waves 1 through 4 of NLTS2 while focusing on the curriculum offered to students with moderate and severe intellectual disabilities. Results of the analysis indicated that the majority (70.6%) of respondents received instruction that was defined as a functional curriculum in school. Among the respondents, 78% received instruction within a special education setting, indicating a smaller rate of inclusion within a general education setting. Upon exit from school, 97% of students with moderate or significant disabilities lived dependently and 93.4% had not pursued postsecondary education. Furthermore, 69.2% of the respondents were not employed at the time of the NLTS interviews and 56.6% had never worked in paid jobs. When examining whether the curriculum that the students with moderate or significant disabilities received impacted their postschool outcomes, there were not statistically significant differences between the frequencies of outcomes for students who had received a functional versus an academic curriculum. The curriculum was not determined to be a predictor of postschool outcomes related to independent living, postsecondary education, or employment (Bouck, 2012).

A secondary data analysis of Wave 4 Parent and Youth responses likewise indicated that students with intellectual disabilities had significantly less positive postsecondary education and employment outcomes as compared to students without intellectual disabilities (Grigal, Hart, & Migliore, 2011). For students who had postsecondary education and employment goals, 46% of students with intellectual disabilities were employed after exiting high school as compared to 74% of students without intellectual disabilities. In addition to lower rates of employment, students with intellectual disabilities were also less likely to attend postsecondary education (30%) when compared to individuals without intellectual disabilities (56%). Furthermore, when examining whether post–high school transition goals were a significant predictor of employment, the only goal that was a predictor of employment was attending a two- or four-year college (Grigal et al., 2011).

The results of both NLTS and NLTS2 offer a nationally representative description of postschool outcomes for individuals with varying exceptionalities. A third national longitudinal study commenced in 2012 and will once again collect information from a sample of 15,000 participants aged 13 to 21 across 400 school districts in 2012 and again in 2014. The purpose and methods are closely linked to the previous longitudinal studies so that researchers can continue to investigate the challenges that students face as they transition from school to postschool education, employment, and independent living.

Aside from NLTS and NLTS2 data, other large-scale studies indicate that individuals with disabilities do not reach postschool outcomes. Using the March supplement to the monthly Current Population Survey (CPS) produced by the U.S. Bureau of the Census from 1993 to 1996, Yelin and Trupin (2000) found that persons with disabilities were 30% as likely to be employed at any time compared to persons without disabilities. Furthermore, among the 93,000 individuals aged 18 through 64 who participated in the survey, persons with disabilities were less likely to be employed, and, if unemployed, less likely to enter employment and much less likely to maintain jobs than persons without disabilities. Neither age nor educational level had a strong impact on the probability of whether the individual with a disability would maintain a job once employed. Use of census data, however, is debated as to the quality and ability to estimate employment rates for people with disabilities, given the broad definitions used to categorize those with disabilities (Burkhauser & Stapleton, 2004).

Recent efforts to develop correlational studies related to transition include the development of epidemiologic causal models that predict postschool outcomes. Using a record review, student exit interview, and 1-year follow-up phone interview with questions derived from NLTS surveys, Flexer, Daviso, Baer, McMahan Queen, and Meindl (2011) examined the effect of inclusion, participation in career and technical education, and work-study on postsecondary employment for students with disabilities within the state of Ohio. The results indicated a significant positive correlation between inclusion and career and technical education on postsecondary employment; however, the positive correlation was based on several factors, including gender, race, and whether the participant was identified with an intellectual or developmental disability. Students with intellectual disabilities were the least likely to be included in general education settings or participate in career and technical education. Whereas inclusion and participation in career and technical education or work-study correlated with higher rates of postsecondary employment, significance levels also varied widely for individuals with intellectual and developmental disabilities.

The processes of moving from adolescence to adulthood and what constitutes successful and complete transitions from school have changed dramatically (Osgood, Foster, Flanagan, & Ruth, 2005). Federal laws including NCLB have focused greater attention on accountability and standards, but the postschool outcomes of individuals with disabilities remain highly varied as evidenced by multiple large-scale studies. Though federal legislation emphasizes the need for postsecondary planning and collaborative goal setting, the participation rate of individuals with autism and those with intellectual disabilities in the planning process is low as is the attainment of planned postsecondary outcomes.

Accountability Measures for All

Reconceptualizing accountability to include postschool outcomes for all students is a critical step toward school improvement. Such a shift moves accountability from a "closed system" focusing only on standards and academics ending with the diploma to extending outcome data collection for all students exiting high school (Burrello, Sailor, & Kleinhammer-Tramill, 2013). A focus of public education that has always been implied is to prepare students for participation in our democratic society. Most recently, federal policy has framed this as "college and career readiness." Advocates for educational reform have responded to ongoing concerns regarding insufficient preparation of students in secondary schools for future college and careers. Concerns raised by such groups as the National Association of Secondary School Principals (NASSP), National Governors Association (NGA), and the Chief State School Officers (CSSO) have produced educational policies and initiatives that take the long view of education by creating a systematic approach to education, from preschool to postsecondary outcomes.

As reviewed by Morningstar, Bassett, Kochhar-Bryant, Cashman, and Wehmeyer (in press), the late 1990s focused significant attention on critical reform efforts with the publication of *Breaking Ranks: Changing an American Institution* (1997) and *Breaking Ranks II* (2004). These policy documents outlined three core areas critical for reform: (a) providing collaborative leadership, professional development, and strategic use of data; (b) personalizing the school environment; and (c) making learning personal: curriculum, instruction, and assessment (NASSP, 2004). The NASSP recommendations aligned with IDEA's focus on shared responsibility, youth empowerment, and academic and functional performance. As a follow-up, *Breaking Ranks II* (2004) offered specific strategies to improve student performance. These strategies included (a) advancement of core knowledge, (b) interactions and connections with students, (c) a comprehensive advisory program for students, (d) use of a variety of instructional strategies and assessments, (e) flexible use of scheduled time, (f) structural leadership changes, and (g) continuous professional development for educational professionals.

By 2005, many states were establishing policies and procedures with a comprehensive focus on education, beginning in preschool and culminating with a college degree or a career credential (Education Commission of the States [ESC], 2010). Commonly known as P-16 initiatives, these efforts are championed by national and state educational stakeholder groups (e.g., National Conference of State Legislatures, National Governors Association). Today, 32 states have active P-16 initiatives (ECS, 2010). P-16 reform initiatives have focused on models connecting stakeholders from across educational and workforce systems to support children and youth as they move through the school years into higher education and full employment.

Most recently, the Council of Chief State School Officers (CCSSO) launched an initiative to develop continuity across state standards and align goals regarding the performance of American students. The *Common Core State Standards*, known as *College and Career Readiness Standards* (*CCSS*), were finalized in June 2010 and are being adopted by a majority of states (NGA, 2010). As defined by the Common Core State Standards Initiative (2010), the standards:

Define the knowledge and skills students should have within their K-12 education careers so that they will graduate high school able to succeed in entry-level, credit-bearing academic college courses and in workforce training programs. The standards:

- Are aligned with college and work expectations;
- Are clear, understandable and consistent;
- Include rigorous content and application of knowledge through high-order skills;
- Build upon strengths and lessons of current state standards;
- Are informed by other top-performing countries, so that all students are prepared to succeed in our global economy and society; and
- Are evidence-based. (p. 1)

The U.S. Department of Education articulated clear and compelling arguments for the importance of preparing students to be college and career ready in the policy document, *A Blueprint for Reform: The Reauthorization of the Elementary and Secondary Education Act*: "Raising standards for all students. We will set a clear goal: Every student should graduate from high school ready for college and a career, regardless of their income, race, ethnic or language background, or disability status" (U.S. Department of Education, 2010, p. 3). Furthermore, the *Blueprint for Reform* articulated critical support for developing a new generation of measures to better determine if students have acquired the skills needed to matriculate into postsecondary education and future careers.

All but a handful of states have adopted the *Common Core State Standards* (CCSS) that build toward college- and career-readiness and are aligned with the national efforts to design assessments aligned with these standards (http://www.corestandards.org/in-the-states). The focus of the CCSS is to ensure that all students are learning what they need to succeed, and therefore, standards are based on evidence regarding what students must know and be able to do at each grade level to be on track to graduate from high school college- and career-ready (U.S. Department of Education, 2010). Furthermore, the standards can provide families and communities information to determine whether students are on track to college- and career-readiness and to evaluate school effectiveness.

A glaring omission among all current efforts to improve secondary education, however, is the understanding of the role of post–high school outcomes data as a critical component to evaluate whether schools are successful in preparing students to be college and career ready. We would argue that educational reform will not be able to sufficiently ensure achievement of these critical standards without attention to and use of outcomes measures for improvement. Similar to the accountability measures established more than two decades ago for students with disabilities, the programmatic impact of the college and career readiness standards can only be fully evaluated by collecting postschool outcomes data for all students. Currently, one initiative supported by the U.S. Department of Education could set the stage for postschool accountability for all students. The Statewide Longitudinal Data Systems (SLDS) Grant Program supports the successful design, development, implementation, and expansion of K-12 and P-20W (preschool through workforce) longitudinal data systems. These systems are intended to enhance the ability of states to efficiently and accurately manage and use education data, including individual student records. Using longitudinal data systems, states, districts, schools, educators, and other stakeholders will be able to make data-based decisions to improve student learning and outcomes, as well as to facilitate research to increase student achievement and close achievement gaps.

State Longitudinal Data Systems to Support Postschool Outcomes

Authorized by Title II of the Educational Technical Assistance Act of 2002, the SLDS Grant Program has awarded grants to all but seven states since 2005 (http://nces.ed.gov/programs/slds/stateinfo.asp). Longitudinal data systems are defined as an educational data system "that collects and maintains detailed, high quality, student- and staff-level data that are linked across entities and over time, providing a complete academic and performance history for each student; and makes these data accessible through reporting and analysis tools" (National Forum on Education Statistics (NFES), 2010, p. 7). A critical element of these systems is that data on an individual student can be connected across years (Smith, 2008). Traditionally, data systems used by school districts consisted of summary statistics (e.g., numbers of students receiving special education services or free- or reduced-price lunch, the percentage of students passing a statewide exam). However, states can only use summary data to develop aggregate "snapshots" of school performance. While this may be valuable to educators and policy makers, it does not provide the information necessary to sufficiently evaluate program impacts or outcomes, such as the relationship between course taking and college readiness, or the impact of dropout prevention programs on at-risk youth (NFES, 2010). In fact, only a set of data on the characteristics and experiences of each student across his or her school years as well as across campuses that then connects student data with outcome data (course completion, college enrollment, workforce entrance) will offer states the ability to thoroughly investigate and analyze relationships between factors affecting student achievement and long-term success.

To ensure that students make the successful transition from high school to postsecondary education and career experiences, as it applies to students with and without disabilities, the longitudinal data system should collect four levels of data: (a) performance on college admissions, placement, and readiness tests; (b) tracking students who do not take college tests to match those records to separate enrollment and program participation databases; (c) student transcripts,

TABLE 8.1. Student-Level Secondary School Data Linked to Postschool Outcomes

Student level data	What will be known
College and Career Readiness Test Scores	• How participation rates and scores on SAT, ACT, AP exams change over time for all students, and particularly, low-income and minority students; • Percentage of students who meet the proficiency standards on state middle school year assessments who go on to take AP or IB courses in high school; • Percentage of low-income students who meet the proficiency standard on the state high school test who take the SAT and ACT exams and score at college readiness benchmark levels on those exams.
Information From Students Not Participating in College Readiness Test	• Which students were not tested by grade and subject and why; • Trends over time in the number and percentage of untested students from each student group (English language learners, special education students, different ethnic groups, etc.); • Whether or not particular schools and districts have excessive absences on test day or questionable patterns of absences and exemptions across years; • Whether the same students are excluded from testing over time, and why.
Student Transcripts	• Number and percentage of students who are enrolling in, and completing, rigorous courses in high school, disaggregated by ethnicity and income status; • The middle schools that are doing the best job of preparing students for rigorous courses in high school; • Whether or not students in more rigorous courses in high school have been more successful in college or in the workplace; and • Whether or not there is evidence of grade inflation (e.g., students with the same test scores receive dramatically higher grades in the same course in certain schools or districts).
Graduation and Dropout Data	• When and why students leave the state's public education system; • The percentage of first-time ninth graders in a given year who graduate from high school within four, five, or six years; • The schools and school systems that are doing the best job reducing the dropout rate; and • The characteristics of high school dropouts and whether or not there are early warning signs that schools can look for in elementary and middle school.

Source: Adapted from *The 10 Essential Elements in Detail for 2008–09*, by Data Quality Campaign, 2009. Retrieved from http://www.dataqualitycampaign.org/survey/elements

as well as other more detailed course-taking and outcome information; and (d) graduation and dropout rates (Data Quality Campaign (DQC), 2009). Table 8.1 offers further details.

The scope of a longitudinal data system is not limited to the K–12 grade levels. Indeed, the value of longitudinal data is even greater when it spans beyond these years into early childhood and postsecondary education, and the workforce.

Systems that span these years are commonly referred to as *P–20* systems. Given the intense federal and state focus on college- and career-readiness standards, it stands to reason that aligning student performance on the *Common Core State Standards* with postschool outcomes (enrollment in postsecondary education, workforce participation) should be an essential requirement of states. With a connection between education and workforce data, researchers and policy makers will be able to answer questions about whether schools, colleges, and universities are preparing students for long-term success in the workplace (DQC, 2007). Given the support and resources offered through the state longitudinal data system grants, the ability for states to implement postschool outcomes data collection for all students is not far away.

Conclusions

Important steps in the evolution of educational policies toward accountability for the success of all students seem to be occurring. The standards-based reform framework reflected in NCLB and the 2004 authorization of IDEA provided important groundwork for developing accountability for schools' progress in helping their students achieve to high standards and in providing assessment data for use in continuous improvement of K-12 curriculum and instruction and aligned professional development. However, as pointed out by the authors, the accountability perspective provided by NCLB now seems a bit myopic in that it neglected the longer-term outcomes of education—an educated citizenry who can successfully participate in society.

Under the auspices of IDEA, the field of special education has been somewhat more attentive to how students with disabilities fare when they leave school. States are now asked to report data on processes such as transition planning as well as results using postsecondary enrollment and employment as primary markers. The availability of these data has allowed for useful research to identify the correlates of positive postschool outcomes. Two interrelated findings from these studies that have direct implications for practice are low rates of postschool participation for students with significant disabilities and improved rates of participation for those students with significant disabilities who are educated with their peers who do not have disabilities. As discussed in Chapter Seven by Ryndak, Orlando, and Duran (2013) and as argued in the initial chapter (Kleinhammer-Tramill, Burrello, & Sailor, Chapter One), reframing of special education policy would, of necessity, promote high levels of engagement of all students with their peers who do not have disabilities.

Recent reports such as widespread adoption of the *College and Career Ready Standards*, or *Common Core Standards*, and the *Blueprint for Reauthorization of the Elementary and Secondary Education Act* are highly promising steps toward achieving an open, longitudinal system of accountability for all enrolled in preK-12 education and beyond. These initiatives, together with practical steps to enhance data systems and increase the feasibility of their use, offer much promise for building linkages between K-12 education and postschool results as well as providing opportunities to examine K-12 practices in terms of how well they prepare adults for the workforce.

We would suggest that the next step will be to determine whether K-12 students are prepared, socialized, and have opportunities to achieve the full range of human capabilities. That is, are children and youth prepared to live in, enjoy, and fully participate as adults in leisure activities, relationships, and the political and social life of our communities? This question will necessitate new approaches to school/community partnerships. Indeed, this is the crucial step for promoting full membership for all in school and beyond the classroom doors.

References

Blackorby, J., & Wagner, M. (1996). Longitudinal post-school outcomes of youth with disabilities: Findings from the National Longitudinal Transition Study. *Exceptional Children, 62,* 399–413.

Bouck, E.C. (2012). Secondary students with moderate/severe intellectual disability: Considerations of curriculum and post-school outcomes from the National Longitudinal Transition Study-2. *Journal of Intellectual Disability Research, 56,* 1–12.

Burkhauser, R.V., & Stapleton, D.C. (2004). The decline in the employment rate for people with disabilities: Bad data, bad health, or bad policy? *Journal of Vocational Rehabilitation, 20,* 185–201.

Burrello, L.C., Sailor, W., & Kleinhammer-Tramill, J. (Eds.). (2013). *Unifying educational systems: Leadership and policy perspectives.* New York: Routledge.

Data Quality Campaign. (2007). *Measuring what matters: Creating a longitudinal data system to improve student achievement, 2*(5), 1–4. Washington, DC: Author.

Data Quality Campaign. (2009). *The 10 essential elements of a statewide longitudinal data system.* Retrieved from http://www.dataqualitycampaign.org/survey/elements

Education Commission of the States. (2010). *P-16 What states are doing.* Retrieved from http://www.ecs.org/html/issue.asp?issueid=76

Flexer, R.W., Daviso III, A.W., Baer, R.M., McMahan Queen, R., & Meindl, R.S. (2011). An epidemiological model of transition and post-school outcomes. *Career Development for Exceptional Individuals, 34,* 83–94.

Flexer, R.W., Simmons, T.J., Luft, P., & Baer, R.M. (Eds.). (2007). *Transition planning for secondary students with disabilities.* Upper Saddle River, NJ: Prentice Hall.

Grigal, M., Hart, D., & Migliore, A. (2011). Comparing the transition planning, postsecondary education, and employment outcomes of students with intellectual and other disabilities. *Career Development for Exceptional Individuals, 34,* 4–17.

Individuals With Disabilities Education Improvement Act of 2004, Pub. L. No. 108–446.

Katsiyannis, A., Zhang, D., Woodruff, N., & Dixon, A. (2005). Transition supports to students with mental retardation: An examination of data from the National Longitudinal Transition Study 2. *Education and Training in Developmental Disabilities, 40,* 109–116.

Kleinhammer-Tramill, J., Burrello, L.C., & Sailor, W. (2013). Special education: A critical perspective on reframing public policy for students with disabilities. In L.C. Burrello, W. Sailor, & J. Kleinhammer-Tramill (Eds.), *Unifying educational systems: Leadership and policy perspectives* (pp. 3–20). New York: Routledge.

Kochhar-Bryant, C.A., Shaw, S., & Izzo, M. (2007). *What every teacher should know about transition and IDEA 2004.* Boston: Pearson.

Morningstar, M.E., Bassett, D.S., Kochhar-Bryant, C., Cashman, J., & Wehmeyer, M.L. (in press). Aligning transition services with secondary education reform: A position statement of the Division on Career Development and Transition. *Career Development and Transition for Exceptional Individuals.*

National Association of Secondary School Principals. (1997). *Breaking ranks: Changing an American institution.* Reston, VA: Author.

National Association of Secondary School Principals. (2004). *Breaking ranks II: Strategies for leading high school reform.* Reston, VA: Author.

National Forum on Education Statistics. (2010). *Traveling through time: The Forum Guide to Longitudinal Data Systems. Book One of Four: What is an LDS?* (NFES 2010–805). Washington, DC: National Center for Education Statistics, Institute of Education Sciences, U.S. Department of Education. Retrieved from http://nces.ed.gov/pubsearch/pubsinfo.asp?pubid=2010805

National Governors Association Center for Best Practices, Council of Chief State School Officers (2010). *Common Core State Standards (Introduction).* Washington, DC: Author. Retrieved from http://www.corestandards.org/the-standards

No Child Left Behind (NCLB) Act of 2001, Pub. L. No. 107–110.

Osgood, D.W., Foster, E.M., Flanagan, C., & Ruth, G.R. (2005). Introduction: Why focus on the transition to adulthood for vulnerable populations? In D.W. Osgood, E.M. Foster, C. Flanagan, & G.R. Ruth (Eds.), *On your own without a net: The transition to adulthood for vulnerable populations* (pp. 1–26). Chicago: University of Chicago Press.

Ryndak, D.L., Orlando, A.-M., & Duran, D. (2013). Serving students with extensive support needs in general education contexts in a reconceptualized system of education. In L.C. Burrello, W. Sailor, & J. Kleinhammer-Tramill (Eds.), *Unifying educational systems: Leadership and policy perspectives* (pp. 135–155). New York: Routledge.

Shogren, K.A., & Plotner, A.J. (2012). Transition planning for students with intellectual disability, autism, or other disabilities: Data from the National Longitudinal Transition Study-2. *Intellectual and Developmental Disabilities, 50,* 16–30.

Smith, N. (2008). Putting the "L" in LDS. *DQC Newsletter, 3*(3). Washington, DC: Data Quality Campaign (DQC). Retrieved from http://www.dataqualitycampaign.org/

U.S. Department of Education. (2010). *A blueprint for reform: The reauthorization of the Elementary and Secondary Education Act.* Washington, DC: Author.

Wagner, M., Kutash, K., Duchnowski, A.J., & Epstein, M.H. (2005). The Special Education Elementary Longitudinal Study and the National Longitudinal Transition Study: Study designs and implications for children and youth with emotional disturbance. *Journal of Emotional and Behavioral Disorders, 13,* 25–41.

Will, M. (1983). *OSERS programming for the transition of youth with disabilities: Bridges from school to working life.* Washington, DC: Office of Special Education and Rehabilitation Services. (ERIC Document Reproduction Service No. ED 256 132).

Yelin, E., & Trupin, L. (2000). Successful labor market transitions for persons with disabilities: Factors affecting the probability of entering and maintaining employment. In B.M. Altman & S.N. Barnartt (Eds.), *Expanding the scope of social science research on disability* (pp. 105–129). Stamford, CT: JAI Press.

PART IV

Leading Diversity in a Unified System

9

WORTH, BURDEN, AND CONTROL

The Rejection of Personhood and the Most Dangerous Assumption

Julia M. White

In 1986, 11 years after the passage of the Education for All Handicapped Children Act (PL 94-142), Madeline Will, Assistant Secretary for the Office of Special Education and Rehabilitative Services (OSERS), in a report to the Department of Education, envisioned a system of education that blends "the intrinsic strengths" of both special and general education (p. 12). Will's report, recognized as the framework of the Regular Education Initiative (REI), made recommendations for educational reform that do not do away with special education; instead, Will affirms that schools should "deliver the resources and provide the personalized [individualized] instruction each child must have to achieve to his or her greatest potential" (p. 23). Instead of using special education as a "panacea" to which frustrated general education teachers refer needy students, Will advocated for a collaborative, unified system of shared responsibility and accountability that would "bring the program to the child rather than one that brings the child to the program" (p. 23). The major reason Will cited as the impetus for REI is outcome measurements—postschool graduation and employment rates for individuals involved in special education programs. While Will's report was directed at the education of students with high-incidence disabilities, she does leave open the possibility, "as we improve our knowledge," of REI's applying to "those with more severe disabilities" (p. 1). Advocates of students with significant disabilities took up that challenge and continued their work and research. This report, and the advocacy work around the inclusion of students with significant disabilities, sparked a firestorm of controversy around "the radicalization of special education reform" (Fuchs & Fuchs, 1994) and "inclusion versus full inclusion" (Fuchs & Fuchs, 1998) that rages still.

In 2012, on the cusp of the reauthorization of the Elementary and Secondary Education Act (ESEA) and the passage of the Keeping All Students Safe Act, there continue to be tensions around blending the recognized strengths of general and special education. Kleinhammer-Tramill, Burrello, and Sailor (2013) rightly consider this cusp to be "the occasion and opportunity for a critical reconceptualization of special education policy and practice," the necessity of which arises from "the identity crisis of special education" (p. 5) based in large part on the current system and whether it serves "to improve the lives and learning of children or to buttress the existing system" (p. 4). In this chapter, I will explore this identity crisis through three distinct, yet connected discussions. I begin with a critical examination of issues around worth, burden, and control in the context of recent news reports about individuals with significant disabilities and how these representations impact public assumptions about them; next, I provide an overview of the legislative and policy contexts of accountability and students with significant disabilities, including the reauthorization of ESEA, as constructed in representational contexts and the competing ideologies of the field; and I conclude with a discussion of the proposed Keeping All Students Safe Act and the reauthorizations of ESEA and the Individuals With Disabilities Education Improvement Act (IDEIA) in the context of slippery slopes and their impact on school membership of students with significant disabilities.

Coming to Understand Worldviews About Ability and Disability

Media "reflects and affects our social worldview" (Pavlides, 2005, p. 52). News media "has the power to change perceptions and . . . reinforce stereotypes" (Luther, Lepre, & Clark, 2012, p. 268). Clogson (1994) finds that general news around disability is portrayed in a traditional manner—reinforcing medial and social stereotypes and viewing individuals with disabilities as "dysfunctioning in a medical or economic way" (p. 46). These beliefs take on political meanings and can influence how teachers, administrators, and lawmakers understand and determine the status of students with significant disabilities in schools.

In early 2012, there were news reports around four stories related to significant disability: (1) Amelia Rivera, who has Wolf-Hirschhorn syndrome, was denied a kidney transplant; (2) Ariel and Deborah Levy won a $2.9 million wrongful birth lawsuit because their daughter was born with Down syndrome; (3) the UK's *The Guardian* reported on the proliferation of the Ashley treatment; and (4) a Boston television station released video of a teenager being restrained and administered electric shocks that was presented as evidence in a trial against doctors from the Judge Rotenberg Center. These four stories were reported at around the same time that two bills were being introduced in Congress: the Keeping All Students Safe Act, on restraints and seclusion in schools; and the Student Success Act, on the reauthorization of ESEA. The news reports illustrate ideas around cultural representations and perceptions of significant disability: human worth, or the rejection of personhood of individuals with significant disabilities, and significant disability as a burden and something that has to be controlled. Similarly, the legislation currently before Congress intends to codify the worth of individuals labeled as disabled in the educational system and the ways that these individuals, who are perceived to be burdens to school "success," can be controlled in schools.

Worth

Chrissy Rivera has been occasionally blogging (20 posts in two years) about her daughter Amelia (Mia), at www.wolfhirschorn.org since March 17, 2010, shortly after Mia, who has Wolf-Hirschhorn syndrome, turned two. Shortly after Mia was born, her parents were told that she had kidney disease and would need a kidney transplant. Her kidneys were managed until she was three years old, and the Riveras secured a family donor so that they would not have to go through the National Organ Transplant Registry. Chrissy Rivera posted blogs on January 10, 12, and 13, 2012, that expressed her frustration with the transplant team at the Children's Hospital of Philadelphia (CHOP)—after meeting with Mia's doctors about a timeline for a kidney transplant (6 months), they met with members of the transplant team who, according to Rivera, said that she was not eligible for a transplant "because of her quality of life. Because of her mental delays" (2012, para. 14) and that the doctor would not recommend Mia for a kidney transplant.

By January 14, 2012, Not Dead Yet (www.notdeadyet.org), a disability rights group founded in 1996, in response to Dr. Jack Kevorkian's assisted suicide acquittal, picked up the story and provided links to a petition and the fax number and email and snail mail addresses of the Family Relations division of CHOP so that individuals could express their opinions. By January 16, *USA Today* (Painter, 2012) reported that 16,000 people had signed the online petition, hundreds of Rivera supporters posted to the CHOP Facebook page, dozens of bloggers picked up the story, and that the Riveras had been invited back to CHOP to speak with the administration. On January 17, the CBS affiliate in Philadelphia reported on the story, and the story was reported through many disability sites, such as *Disability Scoop* and *Inclusion Daily Express*. On February 15, the Riveras and CHOP released a joint statement in which CHOP administration stated intellectual disability does not determine transplant eligibility and that this event reinforces the importance of communication with families, and both parties reaffirmed that the transplant evaluation process is a long, involved, and multidisciplinary one, and that a single visit does not determine eligibility. The latest post, from March 7, 2012, stated that Mia is getting the medical care that she needs and urged readers to support the "Spread the Word to End the Word" campaign because, "[t]he fact is, language affects attitudes and attitudes influence real world outcomes" (Rivera, 2012, para. 3). As of this writing, Amelia has not yet had a kidney transplant. Without the rapidity with which the original blog post went viral and was picked up by disability-centric media and disability rights organizations, it is doubtful that CHOP would have voluntarily engaged in dialogue with the Riveras so that they could pursue negotiations for Mia's transplant.

Wrongful Birth

On March 9, 2012, Ariel and Deborah Levy won a $2.9 million wrongful birth suit against their Portland, Oregon, health care system based on their assertion that they would have terminated their pregnancy had the hospital told them that their daughter, Kalanit, would be born with Down syndrome, but the doctor was negligent, testing the wrong tissue in making the determination that the baby did not have any chromosomal issues. The 12-member jury took less than six hours to come to a unanimous vote against the health care system (Green, 2012, para. 2). The Levys maintain that they brought the lawsuit to overcome the extra costs of raising and caring for a child with Down syndrome. This is not the first wrongful birth lawsuit (see Hensel, 2005; Weil, 2006), but there are very few wrongful birth cases each year due to genetic testing and termination. Bloom and Miller (2011) cite the first wrongful birth case, *Gleitman v. Cosgrove* (1967), which claimed that the tort was "'be[ing] born to suffer with an impaired body'" and the court reasoned that "children born with disabilities brought fewer benefits to their parents than children born without disabilities" (p. 733). Tort litigation, including wrongful birth claims, relies on medical experts' characterizing disability as tragic, and "making the plaintiff whole" (Bloom & Miller, 2011, p. 721). The Levys lawsuit was won on the back of the eugenics movement, in which Kalanit is reduced to her Down syndrome and the "continued fear and rejection of [ ] disability . . . is manifested in the . . . support of selective abortion as a moral option for dealing with a fetal diagnosis of disability" (Silva, 2011, p. 36).

Burden

Ashley X was born in 1997 with encephalopathy and has severe developmental disabilities. Her parents call her "Pillow Angel," as she usually was placed on a pillow; she cannot walk, talk, or sit up independently. In 2004, when she was six years old, and over the course of two years, Ashley's parents sought growth attenuation treatment, including estrogen therapy to reduce/stop her bone growth, a hysterectomy and breast bud removal to prevent puberty, and an incidental, preventative appendectomy. Ashley's parents maintain that they sought these procedures for their "pillow angel" to reduce the risk of bedsores, sexual abuse/pregnancy (as they maintain that her having breasts would make her vulnerable to sexual abuse), and appendicitis and to make her more comfortable as she ages.

Gunther and Diekema (2006), the doctors who administered this treatment, stated that "[t]he primary benefit offered by growth attenuation is the potential to make caring for the child less burdensome and therefore more accessible" (p. 1016). The doctors dismiss the effects of this treatment, as a non-ambulatory, severely impaired child is not someone who will experience benefits of tall stature and therefore will not suffer their loss if kept short. For an individual who will never be capable of holding a job, establishing a romantic relationship, or interacting as an adult, it is hard to imagine how being smaller would be socially disadvantageous… . it is unlikely that such "infantilization" harms a person whose mental capacity will always remain that of a young child. In fact, for a person with a developmental age of an infant, smaller stature may actually constitute an advantage because others probably would be more likely to interact in ways that are more appropriate to that person's developmental age. (p. 1016)

On March 15, 2012, *The Guardian* ran a series of stories related to the proliferation of the "Ashley Treatment" in the United States and Europe, where at least 12 children have been administered the treatment and at least a hundred more families have expressed interest (Pilkington, 2012). On March 16, Peter Singer, philosopher, bioethicist, and euthanasia and infanticide advocate, dismissed any concern about the treatment's violating Ashley's dignity, equating 14-year-old Ashley with an infant:

Infants are adorable, but not dignified, and the same is true of older and larger human beings who remain at the mental level of an infant. You don't acquire dignity just by being born a member of the species Homo sapiens. (para. 4)

Singer does not believe that the treatment should be banned and instead advocates that hospital ethics committees approve treatments "to ensure they are used only on the most profoundly intellectually disabled patients, where there is no prospect of improvement" (para. 7). In essence, Singer rejects the innate worth, the human dignity, of individuals with significant disabilities and affirms their very existence as something burdensome that must be relieved for their caregivers.

While Ashley's doctors acknowledged that the primary benefit of the treatment was to make caring for Ashley less burdensome, these justifications are framed in ways that present Ashley as the burden—it is her growth and development that is inconvenient for her caregivers; no discussion is considered around accessibility and assistance. It is easier to halt Ashley's growth at 75 pounds and sterilize her than it is to find new ways of moving an adult child with assistance and dealing with an adult female and all that encompasses—breast development and menstruation. And this "quick fix" to the burden of an adult child with very complex needs is growing in popularity.

Control

On April 11, 2012, news affiliates in Boston began reporting on a lawsuit against doctors at the Judge Rotenberg Center in Massachusetts. The Judge Rotenberg

Center (JRC) is a residential school long in the spotlight for using systemized electric shock, graduated electronic decelerator (GED) on students; the United Nations' Special Rapporteur on Torture has determined that this system is indeed torture (see Ahern & Rosenthal, 2010; Hinman & Brown, 2010; TASH, 2011). This particular lawsuit stems from a shock incident in 2002, during which Andre McCollins, identified as "a very disturbed child," with an IQ of 50 (Anderson, 2012, April 11, para. 7), was shocked over 30 times. This lawsuit is significant for two reasons: one, because it is one of the first cases against JRC that has gone to trial—most cases have been settled out of court, and two, because a video recording of the incident, sealed under court order eight years ago, was unsealed and shown in court. The defense maintains that Ms. McCollins knew about the "treatments," and thus her lawsuit has no merit (Anderson, 2012, April 12, para. 10). Articles about this story also lay out an ongoing fight in the houses of the Massachusetts General Court about the use of electric shocks and calling it torture—that the Senate supports a ban on the use of shock therapy but the House refuses to consider such a ban and defends the methods JRC uses on its residents, stating that JRC needs "to do everything within [its] power to ease their pain and suffering" (para. 19).

The Most Dangerous Assumption

Bogdan and Biklen (1977) first identified the paradigm of "handicapism" as "a set of assumptions and practices that promote the differential and unequal treatment of people because of apparent or assumed physical, mental, or behavioral differences" (p. 14). The criterion of the least dangerous assumption "asserts that in the absence of conclusive data educational decisions should be based on assumptions which, if incorrect, will have the least dangerous effect on the student" (Donnellan, 1984, p. 142). Jorgensen (2005) revisits this criterion, defines the prevailing paradigm around students with significant disabilities—based on the presumption that "when we aren't sure that students know, understand, can learn, or have something to say, we presume they don't, can't, and probably never will" (p. 5), and points to a new paradigm, based on the presumption of competence, on the idea that students can "show, when supported, they have learned more than we assumed they were able to learn" (p. 6). However, the set of assumptions inherent in these news stories is the most dangerous one: that children with significant differences have little worth—they are not worthy to be a kidney recipient, or even worthy of life; they are cast as burdens to nondisabled people so that it is then acceptable to perform elective and invasive surgeries on them or to inflict electric shock torture on them to bring their burdensome bodies under control—in essence, their personhood is rejected. Students with significant disabilities, whose worth is often diminished and who are perceived as economic and educational burdens, continue to be marginalized and largely segregated in schools. However, their performance in schools counts in school accountability systems. The irony here is overwhelming.

Accountability and Students With Significant Disabilities: An Ideological, Legislative, and Policy Context

"Policies do not exist in a vacuum; they reflect underlying ideologies and assumptions in society" (Armstrong, Armstrong, & Barton, 2000, p. 7). Barton (2004) considers them to be "a struggle between different interest groups over meaning, participation, and practice" (p. 70). It is this struggle, the heart of the identity crisis in special education, that is the focus of this chapter. As discussed by Haines and Turnbull (Chapter Four, this volume), since PL 94-142 was passed (becoming IDEA in the 2004 reauthorization), researchers, teachers, parents, and lawmakers have been engaged in a struggle over one particular clause of the law, one that some consider to be the principle that is the very basis of the purpose of special education: the Least Restrictive Environment principle (LRE). However, while the law mandates LRE, this principle can also be considered an "escape clause" (Biklen, 1992, p. 85) to the civil rights embodied in this legislation by which schools can segregate those students who have "differences that matter," are characterized as deviant, who are deemed unworthy or burdensome. This escape clause is codified in the federal regulations for IDEIA Part B, which mandates "a continuum of alternative placements." While the mandate is for LRE, the alternative placements continuum clause is the way that burdensome students are regulated out of general education classrooms.

Mirror, Mirror on the Wall, Who's the Most Segregated of Them All?

As described by Morningstar and her colleagues (Chapter Eight, this volume), while postschool outcomes are a major focus of the 2004 IDEIA, NTLS 1 and 2 have documented two decades of poor postschool outcomes, which are foreshadowed by the experiences of students with significant disabilities in schools. Out of the total population of school-aged children, 9.1% are served under IDEIA (U.S. Department of Education, Office of Special Education and Rehabilitative Services, 2011, p. 42), and of this, 8.6% percent are identified with intellectual disabilities (p. 44). In 2006, while 95% of students were educated in general education settings for at least some part of the day, Table 9.1 identifies the disparities in those placements and highlights the segregation of students with significant disabilities.

TABLE 9.1. Time in the General Education Classroom

	> 80%	40%–79%	< 40%	Other environments
All disability labels	53.7	23.7	17.6	5.1
Intellectual disabilities	16.0	28.7	48.4	6.9
Multiple disabilities	13.4	16.7	44.5	25.4

Source: Adapted from 30th Annual Report to Congress on the Implementation of the Individuals With Disabilities Education Act, 2008, by U.S. Department of Education, Office of Elementary and Secondary Education, Office of Special Education and Rehabilitative Services, Office of Special Education Programs, 2011, p. 59.

Twenty-seven years after the passage of PL 94-142, students with significant disabilities are still overwhelmingly segregated from their nondisabled peers by place, affirming that the escape clause of LRE is fully operational. They are also segregated from their nondisabled peers by expectations and instructional and assessment practices, all of which have implications for their equality of opportunity and full participation in life after they leave school.

Competing Ideologies, or, the Same as It Ever Was

Despite the fairly extensive research base on the positive impact—and appropriateness—of students with significant disabilities being educated with their nondisabled peers in general education classrooms on their academic performance (see 20 U.S.C. 1400 § 601(c)(5)(A); Baker, Wang, & Walberg, 1994; Hunt & Goetz, 1997; Jackson, Ryndak, & Wehmeyer, 2008/9; McDonnell, Thorson, McQuivey, & Kiefer-O'Donnell, 1997; Ryndak, Morrison, & Sommerstein, 1999; Ryndak, Ward, Alper, Storch, & Montgomery, 2010), there is still immense pushback to the idea that students with disabilities should be educated with their nondisabled peers to the maximum extent appropriate. The dominant ideology around the education of students with disabilities, particularly students with significant disabilities, holds firm to the "environment" portion of "least restrictive environment" and seeks to maintain the status quo—that special education is a place along a continuum in which services are provided by special education professionals, rather than a continuum of services that should be provided in general education contexts through the collaboration of professionals, both general, special, and related. To this day, those writing the dominant narrative have assailed those who seek to disrupt these hegemonic practices of the dominant ideology. The different "camps" have been called by different terms throughout the decade, and while the "argument" has evolved, the continuing underlying purpose of the rhetoric is to affirm the need for the extant parallel system of education and discredit those who "seek to challenge existing practices in society that devalue and marginalize people based on socially constructed characteristics" (Gabel & Connor, 2009, p. 384).

The Dominant Narrative

That special education is in need of reform is not in question. Advocates of a strong and improved system of special education have perpetuated the schism in the profession by giving names to "opposing" groups and identifying the ideological stance with which they do not align as "radicalizing." The following discussion frames how the dominant narrative approaches the struggle around school reform and fundamental change in teaching students with disabilities.

From High-Incidence/Low-Incidence to IDEA/NCLB

In an article about special education reform in the shadow of Will's REI initiative, Fuchs and Fuchs (1994) identified two competing views on reform, while sustaining their own support of "a strong multifaceted special education system" (p. 296). First, they identified the "'high-incidence [advocacy]' group" as one that maintained that "a stronger general education means a stronger special education" (p. 296). They then identified the "'low-incidence' group" as advocates who had the sole concern of "integrat[ing] children with severe intellectual disabilities into neighborhood schools" (p. 296). From the Fuchses' perspective, this low-incidence group apparently co-opted the REI initiative and "took control" of special education reform. They viewed this as a threat to attention to "[t]he academic needs of low-, average-, and above average achieving students, as well as those with varying disabilities" (p. 303). Brantlinger (1997) noted in a response to this article that "[w]hen an alternate discourse and discourse community began to have power—they constituted a threat to those who had fared well in prior special education scholarly and professional circles" (p. 432).

Fuchs and Fuchs (1998) again wrote about competing visions, addressing the continued focus of the alternate discourse, where they identify themselves as "inclusionists" and made a distinction between themselves and "full inclusionists." The distinctions they made were that the different groups "advocate for different children with different needs" (e.g., children with high-incidence and low-incidence disabilities) (p. 312) and repeatedly use "their" children when referring to the different groups. They further distinguish the groups by asserting that the "full inclusionists" are primarily concerned with "[f]riendship making, attitude change and social skill development" (p. 311) while "inclusionists" want "their" children to get "appropriate academic instruction" (p. 312).

In 2000, there was a moment of détente when Andrews et al. (2000) came together and explored the ways that the field might integrate these perspectives. Now the different perspectives were named the "incremental improvement (of a basically sound system) perspective" and the "substantial reconceptualization (of a fundamentally broken system) perspective" (p. 258). The incremental improvement perspective hinges on the medical model of disability, whereby special education fixes, cures, or accommodates the inherent disability of the student. The substantial reconceptualist perspective, while not "disability-blind," focuses on disability as a social construction and the dominant societal ideology of disability as defect is what has to be contested in the system of (special) education, which is inextricably linked to social justice and societal reform.

In the current climate of the reauthorization of ESEA and IDEIA, the "debate" around the continuum of placements has been resurrected as the identification of "camps" around the nature and purpose of Response to Intervention (RtI): the IDEA and the NCLB camps. The IDEA group holds that "RtI should promote both early intervention and more valid methods of disability identification" (Fuchs, Fuchs, & Stecker, 2010, p. 302) that depends on students' progression through tiers of scientifically based interventions. Fuchs, Fuchs, and Stecker assert that the NCLB viewpoint advocates the unification of general and special education into a system that is standards-driven—but not "standardized testing" or "protocol" driven, and that "with the 'right' general education in place, an additional benefit of meaningful standards for all will be the disappearance of high-incidence disabilities" (p. 303). While both groups support the "preventative intent" of RtI, there are significant divergences, most significantly around placement and services. The IDEA group continues to advocate for a continuum of services on a continuum of placements, while the NCLB group, according to the authors, advocates for a "blurring" of special and general education. Blurring general and special education, then, must implicitly "require a broadened definition of what it means to be a special educator, a role that overlaps considerably, if not completely, with that of other professionals in the school building" (p. 306). The authors lament this loss of special identity: "when special educators were regarded as expert instructors—'go-to' professionals at the building level to whom general educators would take their most difficult-to-teach children. Sadly, over the past quarter century, much of this has changed" (p. 318).

Contesting Hegemony

It is against this very "go-to" mentality—taking the "most difficult-to-teach children" *to* special educators—that critical researchers and educators rail. In the dominant paradigm, the difficult child is brought to the professional/service, typically as pull-out instruction or in segregated spaces; in the counter-paradigm, schools are restructured so that professionals and services are fully integrated in schools and are available to all children who might require the services. In order for this to happen, critical researchers and educators seek to unpack the institutionalized ableism inherent in schools. The dominant narrative, based on a medical model of disability, is an "exceptionalist position" that positions disability as producing "a residue of problems that are not effectively managed by the generally satisfactory mechanisms of the social system," in this case, general education (Ryan, 1976, p. 256), that requires arrangements that are "remedial, special . . . tailored to the individual case" (p. 17). From this viewpoint, human difference is pathologized and meanings attributed to this difference "construct[ ] and sustain[ ] the mutually constituting categorical binaries (for example, normal/abnormal, abled/disabled, general education student/special education student) that serve as the basis for marginalization of the disabled in schools" (Bejoian & Reid, 2005, p. 221).

Beyond Categories

The counternarrative, based on the social model and informed by Disability Studies in Education, takes a "universalist position" that does not put the problems "onto" the individual, but that views the issues that affect individuals as "a function of the social arrangements of the community or the society that . . . are quite imperfect and inequitable" (Ryan, 1976, p. 18). Disability, including the categories used in IDEIA to determine eligibility for special education, is based on an essentialist medical model that defines the norm, and anyone who deviates from that norm and does not function "anatomically, physiologically, intellectually, and/or psychosocially within the limits of what is considered typical" (Artiles & Trent, 1994, p. 424) is disabled. Special education then becomes a "legitimizing device" that perpetuates the dominant paradigm by removing students labeled as disabled from the places that they trouble and moving them to places that purport to address their pathologies and fix them (Skrtic, 1991). It is this systemic framework, based on segregation, oppression, and ableism, that has failed students and that must be interrogated and replaced by a framework that alleviates "the social conditions that produce disability (e.g., inaccessible curriculum or instruction, ability privilege, social isolation, etc.)" (Gabel & Connor, 2009, p. 382).

Beyond the Continuum

A reconceptualized framework for inclusive special education should be a unified one, not bound by rigid markers of categories and services delivered along a continuum. This disrupts the current system, what Ferri (2009) identifies as "a rigid set of normative practices that disempower an ever-increasing number of students . . . [that] paradoxically upholds social injustice and exclusion" (p. 417). In this new system "the lines between general education, special education, Title I, bilingual education, migrant education, vocational education, compensatory education, and other categorical programs become blurred and eventually disappear" (Ferguson, Kozleski, Fulton, & Smith, 2005, p. 7). The general education classroom becomes a "nonrestrictive environment," a space in which services and supports are integrated, where individuals do not have to prove their worth and show that they are ready to join (Taylor, 1988).

Ryndak, Moore, Orlando, and Delano (2008/9) extend the concept of "access to the general education curriculum," a key tenet of IDEIA, to in fact consider general education contexts, not just access to and involvement and progress in the curriculum. They argue that "it is difficult to define access to the general education curriculum in isolation from the general education contexts in which that curriculum is taught and the adults and students involved in that instruction" (p. 203). The very purposes of IDEIA—equal opportunity and full participation, economic self-sufficiency and independent living—and the purposes of the 2004 amendments—further education, employment, and independent living—explicitly denote postschool life in nonrestrictive, integrated spaces. Ryndak et al. assert that students must be prepared for this in ways that support their acquisition of skills through context, content, high expectations, and accountability measures rooted in general education.

A Brief History of Participation in (Alternate) Assessment

When ESEA was originally passed in 1965 as Public Law 89-10, Title II provided for "financial assistance to local educational agencies [LEAs] for the education of children of low-income families." Grants would be awarded to states only if states could satisfactorily ensure in their applications for funding not only a fiscal control and accounting plans, but also the provision of "periodic reports ... evaluating the effectiveness of payments under this title and of particular programs assisted under it in improving the educational attainment of educationally deprived children" (20 U.S.C. § 206(a)(3)(A)). In 1970, the National Assessment of Educational Progress (NAEP) was established, the purpose of which in part "was to authenticate Cold War and War on Poverty education reform efforts" (Stake, 2007, p. 1). Soon thereafter states began passing Education Accountability Acts, the first being Colorado in 1971 and then Florida in 1973, with many states following. Florida was the first state that required annual testing of all students in certain subjects and, in 1978, passing a high school exit exam as one of the criteria for a high school diploma (Herrington, 2005, p. 7).

Students with disabilities, however, were largely exempt from state testing until 1994, when the reauthorization of ESEA identified them as a subgroup whose results were to be disaggregated when reporting on ADEQUATE YEARLY PROGRESS (AYP) in state assessments (20 U.S.C. 2701 § 1111(b)(3)(I)). The act also required "reasonable adaptations and accommodations for students with diverse learning needs, necessary to measure the achievement of such students relative to State content standards" (20 U.S.C. 2701 § 1111(b)(3)(F)(ii)). Shortly thereafter, Maryland and Kentucky were the first states that initiated assessments to measure annual progress, and it is significant that they also developed assessments for students with significant cognitive disabilities who could not otherwise participate, even with adaptations and accommodations (Quenemoen, 2008, p. 3). The 1997 Amendments to IDEA included requirements for states to develop alternate assessments—but not alternate achievement standards, that option is left up to individual states—for students who would not be able to participate in assessment with adaptations and accommodations (20 U.S.C. 1412 § 612(a)(17)(A)(i)). The law also mandated that students with disabilities "be involved and progress in the general curriculum" (20 U.S.C. 1414 § 614(d)(1)(A)(iii)(II)).

The purpose of the 2001 reauthorization of ESEA as No Child Left Behind (NCLB) is "to ensure that all children have a fair, equal, and sufficient opportunity to obtain a high-quality education and reach, at a minimum, proficiency on challenging State academic achievement standards and state academic assessments" (20 U.S.C. 6301 § 1001). The act requires that not less than 95% of each subgroup, including students who take assessments "with accommodations, guidelines, and alternative assessments" be counted in ADEQUATE YEARLY PROGRESS (20 U.S.C. 6311 § 1111(a)(2)(I)(ii)). By 2003, almost all states had developed an alternate assessment, mainly focused on functional skills; two years later, all states moved to or were revising their alternate assessments to assess state content standards (Quenemoen, 2008). Thurlow (2010) reported that by 2008, the participation of students with disabilities in state assessments increased from fewer than 10% to 99%, 98%, and 95% at the elementary, middle, and high school levels, respectively (p. 3). Thus, in a very real way, NCLB asserted the worth of students with disabilities by holding schools accountable for their progress.

Alternate Assessments: The Good, the Bad, and the Ugly

From the 1997 Amendments to the 2004 reauthorization of IDEA, there was a small, but important language change in the findings section. The 1997 Amendments ensure that students with disabilities have access to the general curriculum to the maximum extent possible, but the 2004 reauthorization takes this a step further, by ensuring access to the general education curriculum *in the regular classroom*, to the maximum extent possible (20 U.S.C. 1400 § 601(c)(4)(5)(A), emphasis mine). These findings and assurances are repeatedly iterated throughout both ESEA (2001) and IDEIA (2004), firmly integrating the performance of students with disabilities, including students with the most significant disabilities, in state accountability systems using grade-level academic content and achievement standards, access to which is presumed to be in the general education classroom. Thurlow (2010) maintains that schools should hold "the same high expectations we have for other students" and should be held accountable for assessing students with disabilities, since those assessments in many ways also assess how schools are making sure that students meet those same high expectations (p. 2). Students are now included from a legislative perspective, but the specter of low expectations and its impact on the implementation of legislation remains. For students who have complex needs, who might not be able to use reliable speech or to write or type what they know, it might be difficult to find ways to assess their progress in the general education curriculum. Involving students with significant disabilities in assessments is perceived as a burdensome aspect of schooling, one that "takes away" from the schooling of more worthy, nondisabled students, and this plays out in the ways that schools evade counting students in accountability systems. Students with disabilities continue to be assessed in ways that are less rigorous than the ways their nondisabled peers are assessed, which reinforces the attitudinal and geographic exclusion of students with disabilities (National Council on Disability, 2008).

Characteristics

Alternate assessments, based on alternate academic achievement standards (AA-AAAS), are meant to assess those students who are considered to have the "most significant cognitive disabilities."[1] Approximately half a million students take AA-AAAS (Assistance to States, 2006, p. 46747). Kearns et al. (2011) find that while the students who take these assessments represent a wide range of disability categories, the primary categories represented are intellectual disability (10% of all students receiving special education services), autism (2%), and multiple disabilities (2%) (p. 4). A student's IEP team determines what kind of assessment is appropriate for that student (20 U.S.C. 1414 § 614(d)(1)(A)(i)(VI)(bb)). However, even though IDEIA mandates alternate assessment, ESEA mandates that states develop academic achievement standards, but does not require states to adopt alternate academic achievement standards. Both IDEIA and ESEA require that when states do choose to develop AAAS (and all of them have), that they must be aligned with the state's academic content standards. In addition, ESEA requires that the AAAS promote access to the general curriculum and reflect professional judgment of the highest achievement standards possible.

Since the 2001 reauthorization of ESEA as NCLB, students with disabilities are considered, for the first time, as a discrete subgroup, on which data is reported concerning their achievement in state assessments. Students now, quite literally, need to be counted, and accounted for, in their schools. While this is certainly an immense gain in civil rights for individuals with disabilities, as even the legislation notes, implementation has been—and continues to be—impeded by low expectations.

Minimum N

One of the ways that low expectations, especially for students with significant disabilities, manifests is in states' determinations of how the data on this subgroup are disaggregated. This data reporting scheme is an escape clause used by schools that have found it burdensome to account for students with significant cognitive disabilities, who would potentially lower their AYP calculations. States are prohibited from using "disaggregated data for one or more subgroups . . . if the number of students in those subgroups is insufficient to yield statistically reliable information" (34 C.F.R. § 200.7(a)). Therefore, states must determine the minimum number of students being assessed that would yield statistically reliable information. Any district or school with subgroups smaller than that number is not required to meet the annual measureable objectives for that subgroup; however, their performance is included in the whole-school target (American Institutes for Research, 2012). There is wide variation among states on "minimum N," from 5 in one state to 100 in another (American Institutes for Research, 2012). In the state with $N = 5$, virtually all schools are held accountable for all of their students, with disabilities, while in the state with $N = 100$ (100 students being assessed), any school with fewer than that number may not attend to those students' access to and involvement and progression in the general education curriculum since the school does not have to consider the scores of those students in calculating AYP. In 2006–2007, the latest data available on the percentage of schools required to calculate AYP for each student subgroup, only 30% of schools are held accountable to students with disabilities, African American students, and Hispanic students due to the "minimum n" (U.S. Department of Education, 2010, p. 59). Schools are accountable for only 20% of English-language learners.

The Caps

One percent. States are permitted to count students who score as proficient on the AA-AAAS in calculation of AYP as long as those numbers do not exceed 1% of all students in the grades assessed (34 C.F.R. § 200.13(c)(2)(ii)). There is no cap on the number of students who can be assessed, only on the percentage of students who can be considered proficient for calculating AYP. This 1%-cap represents approximately 9% of all students with disabilities (Lomax, 2011, p. 5). Students with intellectual disabilities make up only approximately 8% of students served under IDEIA, and that category covers a range of students, from what might be considered mild to significant intellectual disability. Students with autism and multiple disabilities only constitute approximately 2% each, and again, the category of autism has a wide span of characteristics. Lomax also points out that there is no federal definition of "most significant cognitive disabilities,"[2] but nonregulatory guidance describes students with the most significant cognitive disabilities as those who receive special education services under one of the disability categories under IDEIA and "whose cognitive impairments may prevent them from attaining grade-level achievement standards, even with the very best instruction" (U.S. Department of Education, as quoted in Lomax, 2011, p. 4). Thus, through such a relatively high cap on counting students who take AA-AAAS, schools have lowered expectations for a great many students with disabilities, especially significant disabilities. States and districts have the further option of raising this cap (and further lowering expectations) by requesting extensions from the Secretary of Education.

Two percent. Since 2007, there has been another way that states have been able to raise the cap to 2%—through developing alternate assessments aligned to modified achievement standards (AA-MAS). This alternate assessment is based on grade-level content standards, but not grade-level achievement standards. For the AA-AAAS, both the grade-level content standard and the achievement standards are adapted. These alternate assessments based on modified achievement standards arose from the concern of states for the "small group of students" with disabilities who were not labeled as having the most significant cognitive disabilities who were not performing successfully in the regular grade-level achievement standards—they considered the grade-level achievement standards too difficult and the alternate academic achievement standards too easy (Title I, 2007, p. 17746). As with the AA-AAAS, there is no limit on how many students can take the AA-MAS, but only those students from "this small group" who score proficient and do not exceed 2% of all students who are assessed at that grade level will count toward AYP. This is approximately 20% of students with disabilities (American Institutes for Research, 2012). Currently, 17 states assess students with disabilities using modified academic achievement standards.

The Department of Education considers this to actually raise expectations for students who had previously been assessed using the AA-AAAS since the AA-MAS assesses more challenging content (but not achievement standards) (Title I, 2007, p. 17767). The Consortium of Citizens With Disabilities (2012, February 6) reports on data that shows that "students who have been assessed based on the AA-MAS cannot be distinguished from English language learners and low-income students assessed on regular assessments" (p. 9). If all of these subgroups are experiencing similar assessment outcomes, this is a matter of equality of opportunity for *all* students to have access to and progress in the grade-level academic content *and* achievement standards; therefore, the focus should be on improved instruction and student engagement, and should not lower the expectations of one group while leaving the other groups to continue to fall behind.

Quick Fixes and Slippery Slopes: The (Dis)Alignment of ESEA and IDEIA and Keeping All Students Safe

Standardized tests do not measure students' progress and ability; they are snapshots of student performance at the time of assessment, and they do not offer a full picture or allow a student to fully demonstrate what he or she knows.[3] However, standardized testing has been the U.S. Department of Education's approach to accountability under the 2001 reauthorization of ESEA, which mandates that all children, including all children in all subgroups, meet or exceed proficiency on state academic achievement assessments by 2014. While the focused attention on previously ignored subgroups is one of the strengths of this legislation, there are also well-documented weaknesses. The punitive approach to accountability has led to, inter alia, "teaching to the test" and a proliferation of scripted curricula that devalues teachers and students and removes innovation and creativity from the classroom. Schools with more diversity related to subgroups are more apt to be identified as in need of improvement, but ESEA is an unfunded mandate that provides minimal real assistance to struggling schools. The underlying social, health, and economic inequities, as well as discrimination, racism, and ableism, are not addressed, and schools operating in communities experiencing these inequities are subject to the harshest sanctions (Bass & Gerstl-Pepin, 2010; Erevelles, 2005; Leonardo, 2007; Raffo & Gunter, 2008).

As Congress is preparing for the reauthorization of ESEA, the Department of Education recognizes that the rigid, punitive accountability approach does not work and has implemented regulatory changes to mitigate the upcoming 2014 deadline for proficiency. Congress is also considering legislation around reauthorizing ESEA and the use of restraints and seclusion in schools, all of which in some ways addresses how to control the "burdens" that students with significant disabilities are considered to bring with them into schools. In this last section, I address some of the "quick fixes" inherent in these regulatory changes and introduced bills that could possibly work to lessen school responsibility for students with significant disabilities, as well as potential slippery slopes that might affect the civil rights of students with significant disabilities.

Quick Fixes: Flexibility Waivers

On February 9, 2012, President Obama signed an executive order that granted states the right to apply for flexibility waivers to avoid the consequences of not meeting the mandated AYP goal of 100% proficiency for all students by 2014 as required by the 2001 reauthorization of ESEA. Through this executive order, the administration essentially bypassed trying to push its education agenda through the reauthorization process in a Republican-controlled House of Representatives. Through these waivers, states are free to develop "new ambitious but achievable" annual measurable objectives (AMOs) to determine AYP.[4] In addition, states are relieved from many of the sanctions related to failing to make AYP, and they have flexibility in how they spend some of their federal (e.g., Title I) funds (U.S. Department of Education, 2011, September 23). As of April 2012, 11 states have been granted waivers and another 27 have applied for waivers. The major components of the waivers are (1) college-and career-ready expectations for all students, (2) state-developed differentiated recognition, accountability, and support, (3) supporting effective instruction and leadership, and (4) reducing duplication and unnecessary burden (U.S. Department of Education, 2011, September 23).

The 1%- and 2%-caps on counting the proficient scores of students with the most significant cognitive disabilities who take AA-AAAS or AA-MAS remain. However, once states have developed and administered "new high-quality assessments" by 2015, they will not be able to use modified academic achievement standards. One of the quick fixes inherent in the waivers is that states that are granted waivers are no longer required to disaggregate their accountability data by the four subgroups in the law (students from major race/ethnicity groups, English-language learners, students with disabilities, and economically disadvantaged students) for all accountability purposes, and the subgroups can now be subsumed into the category of "all subgroups," essentially leaving states two subgroups ("all students" and "all subgroups") on which to report; at least 7 of the 11 states that were granted waivers will base some of their accountability decisions on the achievement of these two subgroups (Riddle, 2012, p. 3). Riddle also observes that "major accountability decisions will no longer be based on whether a school has met all of the performance targets for each of the student groups designated by [ESEA]" (p. 12). In many ways this rolls back the need for schools to be as vigilant to the progress of students with significant disabilities in assessments and in the general education curriculum, since their "worth" in calculations for AYP has been diminished.

Slippery Slopes: ESEA Reauthorization and Keeping All Students Safe

ESEA Reauthorization

The issues around the reauthorization of ESEA as it pertains to alternate assessment have been discussed above, in particular, issues around the general education curriculum and assessment and the 1%- and 2%-caps. These continue to be issues as ESEA approaches reauthorization. Different constituencies have different recommendations for the reauthorization of ESEA as it relates to these issues.

Groups aligned with the special education profession—the Council for Exceptional Children (CEC) and the Council of Administrators for Special Education (CASE)—support maintaining the 1%-cap on counting students who take the AA-AAAS as proficient. They also support maintaining the 2%-cap on allowing students to be assessed against modified academic standards (AA-MAS). CASE also supports the inclusion of student progress on functional goals, which it maintains is a critical component of the IEP. CASE also advocates using alternate assessments for measuring student progress in functional life skills, even though there is a large research base on how functional skills can be embedded into the general curriculum (see Alper, Ryndak, & Schloss, 2001; Browder et al., 2007; Jameson, McDonnell, Polychronis, & Riesen, 2008; McDonnell, Johnson, & McQuivey, 2008). CEC, however, does not support using the IEP for accountability purposes.

Disability advocacy groups largely do not favor an increase to the 1%-cap and recommend that any reauthorization of ESEA do away with the 2%-cap. For example, in a joint statement the National Down Syndrome Society and the National Down Syndrome Congress (2010) recommended that states should develop separate AA-AAAS for each subject tested so that students are not relegated to alternate assessments for every aspect of their schooling, since many students would be able to have higher achievement in some content areas. They also recommend that IEPs not be considered in accountability systems, since accountability should focus on core subject academic achievement, as it does for nondisabled students. In her testimony before the U.S. House of Representatives Education and Labor Committee, Quenemoen (2007) affirms that since IDEIA and ESEA established requirements for students with significant disabilities to be counted in assessment systems, they have experienced increased access to the general education curriculum. She also points out the challenges inherent in moving away from the "pervasive low expectations for the achievement of students with disabilities" and a professional focus on the functional curriculum to one based on standards and academic achievement, with functional skills being embedded in the general education curriculum.

Keeping All Students Safe: Restraints and Seclusion

Students with disabilities are denied their civil rights through being restrained and secluded in schools. There are two bills, Keeping All Students Safe Act: S. 2020, introduced in the Senate Committee on Health, Education, Labor, and Pensions, and H.R. 1381, referred to the House Committee on Education and Labor. The Alliance to Prevent Restraint, Aversive Interventions, and Seclusion (APRIAS) (n.d.) sets out the legal protections against using restraints and seclusion in schools, including the Eighth Amendment barring cruel and unusual punishment and the Fourteenth Amendment that protects "liberty interests in freedom of movement and personal security," and cites the *Youngberg v. Romeo* case where the U.S.

Supreme Court held that "[t]he right to be free from undue bodily restraint is the core of the liberty interest protected by the Due Process Clause." APRAIS also observes that "no specific federal legislation has been passed to establish regulations and procedures for restraints and seclusion in the public schools" (para. 2). The two bills introduced in Congress have the potential to be that federal legislation. However, particularly in the House, lawmakers have taken great issue with the introduction of these bills. Lawmakers repeatedly cite the Tenth Amendment as justification for not passing this legislation. A 2009 report from the Government Accounting Office, *Seclusions and Restraints: Selected Cases of Death and Abuse at Public and Private Schools and Treatment Centers*, entered as testimony before the House Committee on Education and Labor, found evidence of hundreds of cases of alleged abuse and death related to restraints and seclusion in the past two decades and in 2007–2008 in Texas and California alone, more than 33,000 reported incidents of restraint or seclusion (Cardoza, 2010). However, Representative Foxx (R–NC) stated that "the Federal Government has no reliable data on the prevalent use of harmful seclusion and restraint techniques in public and private schools and on whether they result in child abuse, no matter the hyperbole used by people on the other side" (Foxx, 2010, H1039), and she further stated that "[t]his bill is not needed. The states and localities can handle these situations" (H1057).

During the House debates, lawmakers repeatedly referred to the fact that 31 states already have policies and procedures in place to determine when and how restraints and seclusions can be used in schools, and the federal government has no reason to intervene since states are already addressing the issue (even though just under two-thirds of the states have implemented policies). But, as the Consortium of Citizens with Disabilities (2012, March 16) points out, only 14 states limit the use of restraints to physical safety emergencies, and 11 states either ban seclusion entirely or limit its use to physical safety emergencies. Perhaps the most egregious statement on why the federal government should not intervene is from Representative Souder (R–IN). In basing his argument against federal intervention or legislation on the lack of "reliable data on how much use there is of these techniques," Souder asks, "Since when do we get to always determine the speed and kind of satisfactory level of intervention that a State does, particularly since we don't have the data to prove our case?" (2010, H1059). This statement is reminiscent of *Brown*'s vague "with all deliberate speed" order which, as Orfield (2001) and others have shown, has pushed back the promise of *Brown* and has led to resegregation. Souder also believes "there are times, such as in civil rights cases, where there were clear, systemic, systematic, multigenerational interventions that we needed to get in; . . . but what we are looking at today is insufficient data. We're looking at States actually addressing it" (2010, H1059–1060), even though the GAO report clearly identified cases of abuse and death as a direct result of restraints and seclusion. Thus, Souder does not consider the abuse and death of restrained and secluded children to be a violation of their civil rights that demands federal interventions.

On March 9, 2012, the Office for Civil Rights (U.S. Department of Education, 2012) released its civil rights data collection report for the 2009–2010 school year that indicates, among other things, that while students with disabilities represented 12% of the students sampled for the study, they represent 70% of the students who were physically restrained in their schools. That same month, the American Association of School Administrators (AASA) released its own study where it strongly rejected federal intervention in this issue. Without citing a study design or specific data, the AASA determined that 99% of school personnel used restraints and seclusion safely, which effectively refutes the evidence found in the GAO Congressional testimony. Instead, it frames restraints and seclusions as techniques that allow teachers and schools to help students control their behaviors and thus allow students to "remain in [ ] public school setting[s] and not be institutionalized" (Pudelski, 2012, p. 5). However, restraints and seclusion, including the mechanical restraint of electric shock, is also a technique used to control students' behaviors in institutional settings such as the Judge Rotenberg Center. Nonetheless, the AASA supports using restraints and seclusion as necessary ways to control students who are perceived as noncompliant and dangerous.

Conclusion

How students from traditionally marginalized subgroups are counted in school accountability is a statement about their worth in schools. How schools, districts, and states attempt to maneuver around fully accounting for the learning and educational performance of students from traditionally marginalized groups demonstrates how these students are still considered burdens to the system. The Fourteenth Amendment of the U.S. Constitution, along with ensuring equal protection of the law, repealed the three-fifths compromise and affirmed the "counting the whole number of persons" when apportioning representatives in Congress. Equality of opportunity is one of the purposes of IDEIA, as is the mandate to count the whole number of students with disabilities who take alternate assessments—"with the same frequency and the same detail as it reports on the assessment of nondisabled children" (20 U.S.C. 1412 § (a)(16)(D)). However, as this chapter explored, although the intent of NCLB was to fulfill the mandate of IDEIA, through the use of the 1%- and 2%-caps and "minimum N," schools have been able to evade responsibility for the participation and performance of students with significant cognitive disabilities in state assessment systems, thereby eliminating the perceived academic burdens these students present to schools. With the looming reauthorization of ESEA and the potential elimination of the cap and maintenance of minimum N, the worth of students with significant disabilities is even further diminished.

The devaluing of people with significant disabilities that happens in schools generalizes to, or is generalized from, society; people with disabilities who are constructed as academic burdens are also constructed as economic burdens who "are excluded from participating in the market and [ ] become the property of the state" (Erevelles, 2005, p. 73). Society places worth on those individuals who are perceived as able to make productive contributions to the economy and competitive market (Brantlinger, 2004; Erevelles, 2005; Raffo & Gunter, 2008). This diminished worth is evident in the news accounts discussed at the beginning of this chapter. Mia Rivera was not deemed worthy of a kidney transplant even though her family was not going to place her on the national transplant list—she would not have denied anyone who might have been considered able to make more functional contribution the opportunity to get on the list. Kalanit Levy was perceived by her family to be such an economic burden that they sued their doctors for her birth, affirming that she was not worthy of being born from the beginning. The proliferation of the Ashley treatment again signifies the diminished worth that an adult with significant disabilities presents—they are perceived to be difficult for nondisabled people to manage, to be burdens on families and societies so that their very bodies need to be controlled, so their very equality of opportunity to grow and develop as full adults is denied very early in their lives. And finally, Andre McCollins is placed in that class of individuals whose behaviors are perceived to be so dangerous and out of control that they must be managed in ways that the United Nations considers torture. Under the dominant paradigm of schooling and society, these practices are ossified as ways to limit the time and attention that are needed to fully integrate individuals with significant disabilities. Ableism is inherent in decision making around policies related to the school assessment of individuals with significant cognitive disabilities, since they are not deemed worthy to be counted, they "become throwaways (again, or still) and any inventive, desire, need, or value placed on their inclusion in general education classrooms becomes lost" (Smith, 2010, p. 77).

In critiquing the philosophical stance of whom they term *full inclusionists*, Fuchs and Fuchs (1998, p. 310) assert that "there is a limit on how much a given classroom can be expected to change" in order for all students, including students with significant disabilities, to be integrated into general education classrooms. Accepting these artificially constructed limits is not acceptable. Sailor (2008/9) asks, "should we continue to tinker around the edges of a clearly broken system or should we rethink the whole enterprise?" (p. 250). In a reconceptualized, unified system, education is not simply a functionalist market-based issue; but rather, it is a system based on the moral value of all individuals, in which all individuals are perceived as having worth and are recognized for the different ways they contribute to their communities, relationships based on reciprocity, not on utilitarian notions of what constitutes worth (Bogdan & Taylor, 1989; Danforth, 2008; Kliewer, 1998; Raffo & Gunter, 2008).

In the current parallel system, the responsibility for students with significant disabilities is compartmentalized (Burrello, Lashley, & Beatty, 2001). In a reconceptualized system there is shared responsibility for all students. Co-teaching is not fully supported in schools, and most teachers do not use differentiated instruction; indeed, differentiated instruction and universal design for learning is addressed mainly in special education programs (Fuchs & Fuchs, 1998; Fuchs, Fuchs, & Stecker, 2010; Sailor & Burrello, 2009; Smith, 2010). In a reconceptualized system, not only would special education teachers also need to be highly qualified in special education and core academic subjects as is currently required, but general education teachers would also need to be highly qualified not only in their content areas, but also in special education—not just be required to have a 3-credit-hour introductory special education course as is currently required. In this way, responsibility for all students would truly be shared, and students would receive the supports they need, regardless of complexity, in general education settings. In a reconceptualized system, assessments are not given to grade schools, but to assess students' involvement and progress in the curriculum, which is simply "the curriculum," since it is not bifurcated into general and alternate in this reconceptualized system. Kearns et al. (2011) find that alternative and augmentative communication systems (AAC) are not widely used with students who are assessed with the AA-AAAS. In a reconceptualized system, students who have complex needs would have ready, perhaps even mandatory, access to, instruction in, and maintenance of alternative and augmentative communication systems (AAC) so that they would better be able to show their knowledge. In these ways, and others addressed in this book, all students in a reconceptualized system of schooling would enjoy the equality of opportunity, equal protection, and freedom from discrimination provided under the Fourteenth Amendment in fully integrated classrooms.

Notes

The author would like to thank Christine Ashby for her thoughtful discussion around the issues explored in this chapter, Katrina Arndt and Joanne Larson for reading a draft of this chapter, and Barbara Trader, Mary Morningstar, and the members of the TASH Inclusive Education National Action Committee for the rich discussions in our meetings.

1. States are allowed to develop alternate assessments based on grade-level academic achievement standards (AA-GLAAS), in large part because there is limited regulatory or technical guidance for developing these assessments (Shaul, 2005). So far, only Massachusetts and Virginia have developed AA-GLAASs. Therefore, this chapter focuses on AA-AAAS.

2. The original (August 2002) regulations of the 2001 reauthorization of ESEA maintained a 0.5%-cap based on data around prevalence rates of students with the "most significant cognitive disabilities" and defined the cap as: "1) exclud[ing] students with mild [intellectual disability] and other students who were two or fewer standard deviations below the mean, and 2) include[ing] students with intellectual functioning and adaptive behavior three or more standard deviations below the mean" (U.S. Department of Education, n.d., para. 10). The Department of Education removed the definition from the regulations and raised the cap to 1% shortly thereafter, in part because of opposition to the reliance on IQ tests (Lomax, 2011) and to provide states and districts more flexibility.

3. In addition to norm-referenced tests, in order to gain a fuller picture of a student's performance, interviews, observations, and informal assessments should be incorporated into assessment systems (Sattler, 2008).

4. However, according to revised guidance from the Department of Education, states may apply for an optional waiver, whereby they would no longer report AYP determinations, but would have to report on the achievement of all students and all subgroups against the AMOs, participation rates (95% requirement), graduation rates, and other academic indicators, disaggregating by subgroup status and gender and migrant status (U.S. Department of Education, 2012).

References

Ahern, L., & Rosenthal, E. (2010). *Torture not treatment: Electric shock and long-term restraint in the United States on children and adults with disabilities at the Judge Rotenberg Center.* Washington, DC: Mental Disability Rights International.

Alliance to Prevent Restraint, Aversive Interventions, and Seclusion. (n.d.). *Laws and regulations.* Retrieved from http://tash.org/advocacy-issues/restraint-and-seclusion-aprais/resources/

Alper, S., Ryndak, D., & Schloss, C. (2001). *Alternate assessment of students with disabilities in inclusive settings.* Boston: Allyn and Bacon.

American Institutes for Research. (2012). *Reauthorizing ESEA: Making research relevant, students with disabilities: A pocket guide.* Washington, DC: Author.

Anderson, K. (2012, April 11). Mother sues Judge Rotenberg Center over "torture" of disabled son. *WBZ CBS Boston.* Retrieved from http://boston.cbslocal.com/2012/04/11/mother-sues-judge-rotenberg-center-over-torture-of-disabled-son/

Anderson, K. (2012, April 12). Mother's knowledge of son's shock treatments at issue in lawsuit. *WBZ CBS Boston.* Retrieved from http://boston.cbslocal.com/2012/04/12/mothers-knowledge-of-sons-shock-therapy-treatments-at-issue-in-lawsuit/

Andrews, J., Carnine, D., Coutinho, M., Edgar, E., Forness, S., Fuchs, L., . . . Wong, J. (2000). Perspective: Bridging the special education divide. *Remedial and Special Education, 21*(5), 258–260/7.

Armstrong, D., Armstrong, F., & Barton, L. (2000). What is this book about? In F. Armstrong, D. Armstrong, & L. Barton (Eds.), *Inclusive education: Policy, contexts and comparative perspectives* (pp. 1–11). London: David Fulton.

Artiles, A., & Trent, S. (1994). Overrepresentation of minority students in special education: A continuing debate. *Journal of Special Education, 27*(4), 410–437.

Assistance to States for the Education of Children With Disabilities and Preschool Grants for Children With Disabilities, 71 Fed. Reg. 46540 (2006).

Baker, E.T., Wang, M.C., & Walberg, H.J. (1994). The effects of inclusion on learning. *Educational Leadership, 52*(4), 33–35.

Barton, L. (2004). The politics of special education: A necessary or irrelevant approach? In L. Ware (Ed.), *Ideology and the politics of (in)exclusion* (pp. 63–75). New York: Peter Lang.

Bass, L., & Gerstl-Pepin. (2010). Declaring bankruptcy on educational inequity. *Educational Policy, 25*(6), 908–934.

Bejoian, L., & Reid, D. (2005): A disability studies perspective on the Bush education agenda: The No Child Left Behind Act of 2001. *Equity & Excellence in Education, 38*(3), 220–231.

Biklen, D. (1992). *Schooling without labels: Parents, educators, and inclusive education.* Philadelphia: Temple University Press.

Bloom, A., & Miller, P. (2011). Blindsight: How we see disabilities in tort litigation. *Washington Law Review, 86,* 709–753.

Bogdan, E., & Taylor, S. (1989). Relationships with severely disabled people: The social construction of humanness. *Social Problems, 36*(2), 135–148.

Bogdan, R., & Biklen, D. (1977). Handicapism. *Social Policy, 7*(5), 14–19.

Brantlinger, E. (1997). Using ideology: Cases of nonrecognition of the politics of research and practice in special education. *Review of Educational Research, 67*(4), 425–459.

Brantlinger, E. (2004). Confounding the needs and confronting the norms: An extension of Reid and Valle's essay. *Journal of Learning Disabilities, 37*(6), 490–499.

Browder, D.M., Wakeman, S.Y., Flowers, C., Rickelman, R., Pugalee, D., & Karvonen, M. (2007). Creating access to the general curriculum with links to grade level content for students with significant cognitive disabilities: An explication of the concept. *Journal of Special Education, 41,* 2–16.

Burrello, L., Lashley, C., & Beatty, E. (2001). *Educating all students together: How school leaders create unified systems.* Thousand Oaks, CA: Corwin.

Cardoza, D. [CA]. (2010, March 3). H.R. 1381, Keeping All Students Safe Act. In *Congressional Record 156,* H1038. Retrieved from Lexis/Nexis Congressional database.

Clogson, J. (1994). Disability coverage in American newspapers. In J. Nelson (Ed.), *The disabled, the media, and the information age* (pp. 45–58). Westport, CT: Greenwood.

Consortium for Citizens With Disabilities. (2012, February 6). *Letter to U.S. Representative Kline on the draft ESEA reauthorization bill.*

Consortium for Citizens With Disabilities (2012, March 16). *Letter to Congress on Keeping All Students Safe Act, S.2020 and H.R. 1381.*

Danforth, S. (2008). John Dewey's contributions to an educational philosophy of intellectual disability. *Educational Theory, 58*(1), 45–62.

Donnellan, A. (1984). The criterion of the least dangerous assumption. *Behavior Disorders, 9,* 141–150.

Erevelles, N. (2005). Rewiring critical pedagogy from the periphery: Materiality, disability, and the politics of schooling. In S. Gabel (Ed.), *Disability studies in education: Readings in theory and method* (pp. 65–84). New York: Peter Lang.

Ferguson, D., Kozleski, E., Fulton, M., & Smith, A. (2005). *On . . . transformed, inclusive schools: A framework to guide fundamental change in urban schools.* Denver, CO: National Institute for Urban School Improvement.

Ferri, B. (2009). Doing a (dis)service: Reimagining special education from a disability studies perspective. In W. Ayers, T. Quinn, & D. Stovall (Eds.), *Handbook of social justice in education* (pp. 417–430). New York: Routledge.

Foxx, V. [NC]. (2010, March 3). H.R. 1381, Keeping All Students Safe Act. In *Congressional Record 156,* H1039, H1057. Retrieved from Lexis/Nexis Congressional database.

Fuchs, D., & Fuchs, L. (1994). Inclusive schools movement and the radicalization of special education reform. *Exceptional Children, 60*(4), 294–309.

Fuchs, D., & Fuchs, L. (1998). Competing visions for educating students with disabilities: Inclusion versus full inclusion. *Childhood Education, 74*(5), 309–316.

Fuchs, D., Fuchs, L., & Stecker, P. (2010). The "blurring" of special education in a new continuum of general education placements and services. *Exceptional Children, 76*(3), 301–323.

Gabel, S., & Connor, D. (2009). Theorizing disability: Implications and applications for social justice in education. In W. Ayers, T. Quinn, & D. Stovall (Eds.), *Handbook of social justice in education* (pp. 377–399). New York: Routledge.

Green, A. (2012, March 9). Jury awards nearly $3 million to Portland-area couple in "wrongful birth" lawsuit against Legacy Health. *The Oregonian.* Retrieved from http://www.oregonlive.com/portland/index.ssf/2012/03/jury_rules_in_portland-area_co.html

Gunther, D., & Diekema, D. (2006). Attenuating growth in children with profound developmental disability: A new approach to an old dilemma. *Research in Pediatric Adolescent Medicine, 160,* 1013–1017.

Hensel, W. (2005). The disabling impact of wrongful birth and wrongful life actions. *Harvard Civil Rights-Civil Liberties Law Review, 141,* 141–195.

Herrington, C. (2005, June). Educational accountability and assessment in Florida: Where have we been? Where are we going? *Florida Institute of Education Policy Brief, 1.*

Hinman, K., & Brown, K. (2010). UN calls shock treatment at Mass. school "torture." *ABC News Nightline.* Retrieved from http://abcnews.go.com/Nightline/shock-therapy-massachussetts-school/story?id=11047334#.T5FiRhzAPG4

Hunt, P., & Goetz, L. (1997). Research on inclusive educational programs, practices, and outcomes for students with severe disabilities. *Journal of Special Education, 31,* 3–29.

Individuals With Disabilities Education Improvement Act of 2004. 20 U.S.C. § 1400 *et seq.*

Jackson, L., Ryndak, D., & Wehmeyer, M. (2008/9). The dynamic relationship between context, curriculum, and student learning: A case for inclusive education as a research-based practice. *Research and Practice for Persons With Severe Disabilities, 33/34*(4/1), 175–195.

Jameson, J., McDonnell, J., Polychronis, S., & Riesen, T. (2008). Embedded, constant time delay instruction by peers without disabilities in general education classrooms. *Intellectual and Developmental Disabilities, 46,* 346–363.

Jorgensen, C. (2005). The least dangerous assumption: A challenge to create a new paradigm. *Disability Solutions, 6*(3), 1, 5–9.

Kearns, J., Towles-Reeves, E., Kleinert, H., Kleinert, J., & Thomas, M. (2011). Characteristics of and implications for students participating in alternate assessments based on alternate academic achievement standards. *Journal of Special Education, 45*(1), 3–14.

Kleinhammer-Tramill, J., Burrello, L.C., & Sailor, W. (2013). Special education: A critical perspective on reframing public policy for students with disabilities. In L.C. Burrello, W. Sailor, & J. Kleinhammer-Tramill (Eds.), *Unifying educational systems: Leadership and policy perspectives* (pp. 3–20). New York: Routledge.

Kliewer, C. (1998). *Schooling children with Down syndrome: Toward an understanding of possibility.* New York: Teachers College Press.

Leonardo, Z. (2007). The war on schools: NCLB, nation creation and the educational construction of whiteness. *Race Ethnicity and Education, 10*(3), 261–278.

Lomax, E. (2011). *Alternate assessments for students with disabilities.* Congressional Research Service, Report No. R40701. Washington, DC: Congressional Research Service.

Luther, C., Lepre, C., & Clark, N. (2012). *Diversity in U.S. mass media.* Malden, MA: Wiley-Blackwell.

McDonnell, J., Johnson, J.W., & McQuivey, C. (2008). *Embedded instruction for students with developmental disabilities in general education classrooms.* Arlington, VA: Council for Exceptional Children.

McDonnell, J., Thorson, N., McQuivey, C., & Kiefer-O'Donnell, R. (1997). Academic engaged time of students with low incidence disabilities in general education classes. *Mental Retardation, 35,* 18–26.

National Council on Disability. (2008). *The No Child Left Behind Act and the Individuals With Disabilities Education Act: A progress report.* Washington, DC: Author.

National Down Syndrome Society and National Down Syndrome Congress. (2010). *ESEA recommendations.* Retrieved from http://www.advocacyinstitute.org/ESEA/NDSS.NDSC.ESEA.RECS.JUNE2010.pdf

No Child Left Behind Act of 2001. 20 U.S.C. § 6301 *et seq.*

Orfield, G. (2001). *Schools more separate: Consequences of a decade of resegregation.* Boston: The Civil Rights Project, Harvard University.

Pavlides, M. (2005). Whose choice is it, anyway? Disability and suicide in four contemporary films. *Journal of Disability Policy Studies, 16*(1), 46–53.

Painter, K. (2012, January 16). "Team Amelia" backs transplant for special needs child. *USA Today.* Retrieved from http://www.usatoday.com/news/health/wellness/special-needs/story/2012–01–16/Team-Amelia-backs-transplant-for-special-needs-child/52603482/1

Pilkington, E. (2012, March 15). The Ashley treatment: "Her life is as good as we can possibly make it." *The Guardian.* Retrieved from http://www.guardian.co.uk/society/2012/mar/15/ashley-treatment-email-exchange

Pudelski, S. (2012). *Keeping schools safe: How seclusion and restraint protects students and school personnel.* Washington, DC: American Association of School Administrators.

Quenemoen, R. (2007, March 29). *Hearing on how NCLB affects students with disabilities.* Education and Labor Committee, U.S. House (testimony).

Quenemoen, R. (2008). *A brief history of alternate assessments based on alternate achievement standards* (Synthesis Report 68). Minneapolis: University of Minnesota, National Center on Educational Outcomes.

Raffo, C., & Gunter, H. (2008). Leading schools to promote social inclusion: Developing a conceptual framework for analyzing research, policy, and practice. *Journal of Education Policy, 23*(4), 397–414.

Riddle, W. (2012). *Major accountability themes of approved state applications for NCLB waivers.* Center on Education Policy. Retrieved from http://www.cep-dc.org/display Document.cfm?DocumentID=387

Rivera, C. (2012, January 10). *Brick walls.* Retrieved from http://wolfhirschhorn.org/brick-walls/

Rivera, C. (2012, March 7). *Spread the word to end the word.* Retrieved from http://wolfhirschhorn.org/spread-the-word-to-end-the-word/

Rivera and the Children's Hospital of Philadelphia. (2012, February 15). Joint statement. Retrieved from http://wolfhirschhorn.org/joint-statement-of-the-rivera-family-and-the-children's-hospital-of-philadelphia/

Ryan, W. (1976). *Blaming the victim.* New York: Vintage Books.

Ryndak, D., Moore, M., Orlando, A., & Delano, M. (2008/9). Access to the general curriculum: The mandate and role of context in research-based practice for students with extensive support needs. *Research and Practice for Persons With Severe Disabilities, 33/34*(4/1), 199–121.

Ryndak, D.L., Morrison, A.P., & Sommerstein, L. (1999). Literacy before and after inclusion in general education settings: A case study. *Journal of the Association for Persons With Severe Handicaps, 24,* 5–22.

Ryndak, D., Ward, T., Alper, S., Storch, J., & Montgomery, J. (2010). Long-term outcomes of services in inclusive and self-contained settings for siblings with comparable significant disabilities. *Education and Training in Autism and Developmental Disabilities, 45*(1), 38–53.

Sailor, W. (2008/9). Access to the general curriculum: Systems change or tinker some more? *Research and Practice for Persons With Severe Disabilities, 33/34*(4/1), 249–257.

Sailor, W., & Burrello, L. (2009, July 9). *The methods—Best practices in taking inclusive education to scale.* Paper presented by Leonard Burrello under the TASH Congressional Briefing Agenda.

Sattler, Jerome. 2008. *Assessment of children: Cognitive foundations.* 5th ed. LA Mesa, CA: Sattler.

Shaul, M. (2005). *No Child Left Behind Act: Most students with disabilities participated in state-wide assessments, but inclusion options could be improved* (GAO-05–618). Washington, DC: Government Accounting Office.

Silva, V. (2011). Lost choices and eugenic dreams: Wrongful birth lawsuits in popular news narratives. *Communication and Critical/Cultural Studies, 8*(1), 22–40.

Singer, P. (2012, March 16). The "unnatural" Ashley treatment can be right for profoundly disabled children. *The Guardian*. Retrieved from http://www.guardian.co.uk/commentisfree/2012/mar/16/ashley-treatment-profoundly-disabled-children?int cmp=239

Skrtic, T. (1991). The special education paradox: Equity as the way to excellence. *Harvard Educational Review, 61*(2), 148–206.

Smith, P. (2010). *Whatever happened to inclusion?: The place of students with intellectual disabilities in education*. New York: Peter Lang.

Souder, M. [IN]. (2010, March 3). H.R. 1381, Keeping All Students Safe Act. In *Congressional Record 156*, H1059–H1060. Retrieved from Lexis/Nexis Congressional database.

Stake, R. (2007, February 4). NAEP, report cards and education: A review essay. *Education Review, 10*(1). Retrieved from http://edrev.asu.edu/essays/v10n1index.html

TASH. (2011, July 26). *Letter to the Office of the General Counsel Department of Developmental Services, Boston, MA, on proposed amendments to regulations regarding the use of aversive interventions*. Retrieved from http://tash.org/tash-letter-to-massachusetts-department-of-developmental-services/

Taylor, S. (1988). Caught in the continuum: A critical analysis of the principle of the Least Restrictive Environment. *Journal of the Association of Severe Handicaps, 13*(1), 41–53.

Thurlow, M. (2010, April 28). *Hearing on ESEA Reauthorization: Standards and assessments*. Health, Education, Labor, and Pensions Committee, U.S. Senate (testimony).

Title I—Improving the Academic Achievement of the Disadvantaged; Individuals With Disabilities Education Act (IDEA), 35 C.F.R. pt. 200 (2007).

Title I—Improving the Academic Achievement of the Disadvantaged; Individuals With Disabilities Education Act (IDEA); Final Rule, 72 Fed. Reg. 17748 (2007).

U.S. Department of Education. (2011, September 23). *ESEA flexibility*. Retrieved from http://www.ed.gov/esea/flexibility

U.S. Department of Education. (2012). *ESEA flexibility peer panel notes: Florida*. Retrieved from http://www2.ed.gov/policy/eseaflex/approved-requests/fl.pdf

U.S. Department of Education. (2012, February 10). *ESEA flexibility frequently asked questions: Addendum #3*. Retrieved from http://www.ed.gov/esea/flexibility

U.S. Department of Education. (n.d.). *Raising achievement: Alternate assessments for students with disabilities*. Retrieved from http://www2.ed.gov/policy/elsec/guid/raising/alt-assess-long.html

U.S. Department of Education, Office for Civil Rights. (2012). *Civil rights data collection*. Washington, DC: Author. Retrieved from http://www2.ed.gov/about/offices/list/ocr/docs/crdc-2012-data-summary.pdf

U.S. Department of Education, Office of Elementary and Secondary Education, Office of Special Education and Rehabilitative Services, Office of Special Education Programs. (2011). *30th Annual Report to Congress on the Implementation of the Individuals With Disabilities Education Act, 2008*. Washington, DC: Author.

U.S. Department of Education, Office of Planning, Evaluation and Policy Development. (2010). *ESEA Blueprint for Reform*. Washington, DC: Author.

U.S. Department of Education, Office of Planning, Evaluation and Policy Development, Policy and Program Studies Service. (2010). *State and local implementation of the* No

Child Left Behind Act, *Volume IX—Accountability under* NCLB: *Final report.* Washington, DC: Author.

U.S. Senate. 112th Congress. "S. 2020, A bill to protect all school children against harmful and life-threatening seclusion and restraint practices."

Weil, E. (2006, March 12). A wrongful birth? *New York Times Magazine.* Retrieved from http://www.nytimes.com/2006/03/12/magazine/312wrongful.1.html?pagewanted=all

Will, M. (1986). *Educating children with learning problems: A shared responsibility. A report to the Secretary.* Washington, DC: Office of Special Education and Rehabilitative Services, U.S. Department of Education.

10

EDUCATIONAL LEADERS AND THE CAPABILITIES APPROACH

Amy L-M. Toson and Elise Frattura

Leading for Equity and Social Justice

Educational leaders for equity and social justice are often better understood through a human development and capabilities approach. Embedded in a capabilities approach is the manner in which educational leaders view their students, parents, teachers, and the other stakeholders that becomes central to "how" they lead on behalf of all learners, especially those with disabilities. While such school leaders may wrestle with the potential social and political fallout from constituents steeped in a dominant human capital agenda, they move forward on behalf of educational social justice and human dignity and respect for all learners, especially those identified as having a disability.

As discussed in Chapter One, the Capability Approach (CA) is a philosophical one that is concerned with the dignity of all people. It focuses on what people can actually do and how they seek to live their own life. "This approach suggests that if children receive educational and material support, they can be fully capable of human action and expression" (Larson & Murtadha, 2002, p. 155). When used as a leadership framework, the capabilities approach helps us to see that education exists to "expand young people's capabilities and develop opportunities for them to pursue a life they have reason to value" (Hart, 2009, p. 401). It is a promising approach for rethinking social justice agendas in education. However, to date no empirical studies examine the intersection between current leaders in special education, how they address the diverse needs of students with disabilities, and the capability perspective.

The capabilities approach can assist us in examining the current examples of perceived socially just leadership. It begins with the conception that all people are worthy of dignity (Nussbaum, 2006; Terzi, 2008; Walker, 2006). The capabilities of an individual include what he or she is able to do and desires to be and do. It also considers the obstacles that may stand in the way of the individual's ability to function. Evolving out of a theory of economics, social choice, and justice, the capabilities approach is described as a reflection of an individual's "Freedom to achieve valuable functioning. . . . Capability represents a person's freedom to achieve well being" (Sen, 1992, p. 49). This freedom to achieve is dependent on social arrangements that should expand people's capabilities and valuable functions (Alkire & Deneulin, 2009).

The capability approach allows us to assess inequality based upon people's freedom to choose *among valuable functioning* to pursue one's own visions of his or her life. Sen (1992) provides a useful example that helps us to understand the distinction between functionings and capability by comparing the situation of a starving person to that of someone fasting (p. 111). Clearly the person starving is deprived of the capability—that is, the real effective freedom—of choosing whether to eat or to fast, whereas the person who fasts retains her freedom to choose, and hence she has the relevant capability (Terzi, 2005).

When considering the obstacles that might compromise a person's abilities, scholars view impairment, disability, and difference in many ways. Reindal (2009) makes the distinction that disability is conceptualized within an individual model, social model, social-relational model, or capability approach. Within the individual model of difference disability is viewed as a deviation from normal functioning. The social model examines difference as an aspect of human diversity. Reindal (2008) proposes a social-relational model of disability that considers an individual's actual abilities and what he or she is capable of actually achieving and doing in the physio-socio-political context in which he or she is living.

Through the capabilities approach Nussbaum (2011) argues that social arrangements should be designed to ensure that children and their families are granted attributes and rights of human beings, including participation in the common good. She identifies 10 unique human capabilities that apply to all, including a long life; good health; emotional engagement; bodily integrity; senses, imagination and thought; practical reasoning; affiliation; enjoyment of other species; and nature, play, and control over one's environment (politically and materially) (see Nussbaum, 2011, p. 33 for a figure and in-depth discussion of these capabilities). She describes these as comprehensive possibilities and does not disqualify other values a person may hold or wish to pursue.

Nussbaum's contributions to the capabilities approach include the development of a normative and political framework that is fully compatible with the efforts of individuals who have been identified with a disability and who also work to overcome the discrimination and oppression of disabled people in society and secure the recognition of their entitlements as citizens. Nussbaum's approach identifies 10 central human capabilities, which emphasize a role similar to that of human rights, ground government policy standards in the resulting normative concepts, and provide a framework that accords the legitimate demands of people with disabilities through full constitutional recognition (Terzi, 2008).

According to Hincliffe (2007) capabilities therefore point to certain human powers that enlarge possibilities and enable valued accomplishments, given the right conditions.

> Capabilities are not the same as competencies, as generally understood, because whereas the latter can be identified in terms of identifiable outcomes, the development of capabilities permits a range of possibilities. Consequently, capabilities permit the exploration of agency in a way that competencies do not. They do this unforeseen. Capabilities permit agents to take risks. (p. 224)

The key idea here is learning must be worthwhile. He argues:

> In particular, no capability set is advanced through trivial learning: the range of functionings is not opened up as a result of such activities, and no substantive freedoms are developed. To the contrary, the time-consuming nature of trivial learning actually closes down opportunities for functioning. (p. 225)

Differences matter within Nussbaum's theory. In multiple sections of her work she recognizes variability among all children, and, for that matter, adults. Nussbaum (2006) states, "the problem of variability of need is pervasive" (p. 125) and adds, "the question of variability cannot be postponed, it is omni-present" (p. 165). Disability is one component of such human variability, and therefore, such variability does not negate the essential rights of persons with disabilities. Nussbaum (2011) advocates for "a new account of social cooperation that focuses on benevolence and altruism not just mutual advantage" (p. 150).

Situating educational leadership within the capabilities approach allows leaders to see that the equality of meaningful individual capabilities (ability to function meaningfully) is of central importance (Reindal, 2009; Terzi, 2008; Hincliffe, 2007). The concept of capability in education "can assist us in identifying learning that not only yields knowledge, but also yields knowledge that is worthwhile" to one's own life functioning (Hincliffe, 2007, p. 225). By increasing the individual's capacity to function meaningfully in society, one can rethink education as a way of developing individuals to lead a meaningful life of their own choosing. In addition, because the capability approach measures the capabilities of all individuals and the effects of choices on each person, decisions around programming and design are inclusive of all students, including those with low-incidence/high-support needs and other frequently neglected groups.

A Focus on Two Educational Leaders

In the past, we studied a group of five educational leaders who were identi-fied as being highly inclusive and effective (Toson, Burrello, & Knollman, 2012). Each of the five administrators that we interviewed discussed his or her personal view on leadership and disability. Results indicate that each leader was driven by some personal view: instructional leadership in the general education sphere, legal implementation of and compliance with the federal No Child Left Behind Act (NCLB, 2001) and Individuals With Disabilities Education Act (IDEA, 2004), personal commitments and visions around the right of all students to have mean-ingful educational opportunities, and state mandates to increase general education placements for students with disabilities. However, two leaders in particular (the Northeast and Far West) seemed the most closely aligned with the capabilities ap-proach. Therefore, in keeping with the theme of this book, to pose a new vision for a system of education for all children, results presented in this chapter will focus on Candice and Carla (pseudonyms), the two particular leaders whose vision was most closely aligned with the capabilities approach and who made the most sig-nificant changes from segregated to inclusive education for the most students in their districts (see Toson, Burrello, & Knollman, 2012, for complete study).

These two leaders provide a window by which planning for the variability of each student was placed at the forefront of their decision-making process. They emphasized a vision that stresses the importance that all children are equal mem-bers of the school and neighborhood communities, including the students with the most significant support needs. Further, Carla and Candice each spoke to the needs and capabilities of each and every student within the district's boundaries and worked tirelessly to innovatively design their educational system accordingly.

Emerging from the interviews was a series of common themes that further explain the innovative visions and designs of Carla and Candice's educational sys-tems. These themes were (1) understanding of difference and disability, (2) student agency and participation, (3) district influence and visibility, and (4) views on the future of special education. In each section below we will briefly summarize all five leaders' representative perspective on each theme, but we will go into great detail on Carla and Candice's results.

Theme: Understanding of Difference/Disability: Individual Difference Is Normal

We found that all of the five leaders from our sample envisioned disability in one of three ways: a social constructivist lens (2 leaders), a curriculum and instruction/instructional leadership lens (1 leader), and a capabilities approach lens (2 leaders: Carla and Candice). Two of the leaders seemed to align most closely with a social constructivist view of disability. These leaders did not see disabilities as inherent/internal characteristics of the individuals themselves, but instead saw inadequate societal and educational designs and practices as the deficit that was constructing a

disability, or obstacle, for the individual (for an explanation of the social constructivist view of disability see Ferguson, 1987); arguing that the lack of achievement
lies in the conditions that prevent learning from occurring. This leader shared,
"We have created a system of obstacles—the overreliance on textbook learning
being for many the only access point for learning content."

One leader offered a slightly different stance on disability than the first two.
This third administrator, focused on curriculum and instruction in relation to
the educational services provided to students with disabilities in the classroom,
explained that the primary purpose of education was to provide appropriate instruction to match a student's individual needs.

Carla and Candice focused their understanding of disability and difference
through a different lens. Although the capabilities approach was not named, this
perspective on difference and disability as a normal part of human variation was
evident and was partnered with an articulated deep respect for each individual regardless of ability. Candice explained that having a disability is a typical part of life
that doesn't demand you be separated or segregated from your community, "It [in-
dividual exceptionality or difference] is an everyday reality. It's a normal thing . . .
if you have Thanksgiving dinner and an aunt has a significant disability, do you set
aside a separate table when she comes to dinner? No."

Carla suggested that her district's orientation had moved from a deficit orientation to one where it presumed each student was competent to succeed and
achieve at high levels. She offered a description of the district's transformation:

> We start with the Least Dangerous Assumption or presumed competency.
> Kids who historically would have spent their whole career in a secluded
> setting will now be an active member of their community as an adult that
> has potential for a job, diploma.

Carla's and Candice's views on disability/difference translated into an operating framework that followed their unique perspective. First, Carla and Candice
both articulated a nonnegotiable commitment to general education placement
for all students with disabilities, not just ones with high-incidence/mild disability
labels. These two leaders focused on those students who had the most significant/
unique needs (i.e., autism, severe/profound labels, mental illness, etc.). And, while
each leader spoke about struggling with planning and services for students who
most severely challenged the educational program, such as ones who were a true
safety threat to themselves or others, they both spoke of continually working
toward structuring general education to make it accessible for these students, and
not resting until all were included. For instance, when considering the unique
needs and challenges of students with significant support needs, Carla offered
that she primarily focused on building staff who were believers and who listened
to students. Teachers and school site leaders who advocated for the needs of the
most vulnerable and typically neglected students put supports in place, ensuring

their needs were met. Having a staff with a prerequisite conviction that everybody starts inside the school with full membership demands that you believe in each and every child as competent. Carla and Candice talked this talk, making clear that their staff walked the walk with them or took a job elsewhere.

When Carla and Candice were asked if there were other teachers and leaders in the district who espoused similar values about disability, they gave a range of responses that suggested their own values permeated the systems they led. The way they explained their districts' visions and values revealed a consistent focus on ever-increasing access to learning in the age-appropriate general education classroom for all students. They had consistent, stable, and distributed leadership support for a vision of advocacy for all students. Candice said:

> When I'm sitting in cabinet and an issue of disability comes up I don't have to speak up anymore. I'm not the only voice you hear. It's refreshing that my colleagues say, "Oh we can't do that [reference to some form of seg-regated practice]." I'm not the [only] one who has to bring it to the table anymore . . . people used to grind their teeth, roll their eyes, etc. . . . people get tired of hearing it, but I can't stop.

Theme: Student Agency and Participation: Fighting the Fight for All

The second theme that emerged from the coded interviews focused on how the leaders advocated for student agency and participation in the general education classroom and schoolwide activities. Three of the leaders saw the need to maintain specialized education for students with significant support needs in separate programming distinct from general education. Whether this response was a philosophical or legal perspective could not be discerned, but each did offer that parents had a right to select those supports and each of their districts offered settings where these students were clustered, often times on regular school PK–12 campuses, rather than in a separate isolated or segregated center school.

Carla and Candice, on the other hand, purported a consistent action-based stance toward advocacy for all students to be a part of all general education environments. They spoke especially of strong action-based advocacy for those students who are most often neglected from the general education conversations (students with significant disability labels, juvenile delinquents, etc.). By sharing with us that they continually argue for the provision of specialized services for all students within general education classrooms, their commitment to ensure that even the students who seem to challenge school structures the most, those who are often placed in segregated classrooms and schools, are an integral part of the overall general education design, was always their intent.

Carla did share that the primary struggle with inclusion in general education was with students who had a record of violence on school campuses. Currently, these students' education occurred in separate settings, but the district was working with local mental health agencies to find a way to bring needed services into the general education classroom. They just weren't there yet. For instance, when asked specifically about her concerns related to the inclusion of these students, participant Carla noted that the district staff had "not quite figured [it] out yet" and felt that it required a multiagency response that they were working on. What is important to note is that this upset and saddened Carla. She was continually working toward recognizing what students' needs were not currently being met within the general education design and advocating for ways to redesign the classroom and school environments so that all needs would be met.

Carla's district has almost 96% of its students fully included in general education classrooms more than 80% of their school day. The district used to have six special centers and now they have none. When we asked the five respondents why the movement from less to more inclusive placements took place, Carla reported that the state educational agency suggested that they were out of compliance on a set of issues and pressed that they move more students into general classrooms. Whereas, Candice, when asked, reported, "It was the right thing to do."

Carla shared that the increased time in the general education setting was driven by a push from their State's Department of Education, explaining, "The state said we're at the bottom of the barrel." As a general educator with support from the central leadership team and an active partnership group, she started districtwide targeted professional development that focused on the topic of inclusive education practices. As her work continued, she saw the positive results for children. It was from these positive results that moving all students into inclusive educational arrangements became her life's mission. It was no longer just a mandate from the state office.

In her own words:

> I couldn't go fast enough, I was panicked by the idea that we had these kids that were sitting in these settings. Students labeled severe and profound were automatically placed there [special centers] . . . i.e., autism, Down syndrome, etc. . . . It didn't matter who you were individually. It was the label that drove where you went in our district . . . what have we been doing? Where else in society are kids excluded, not church, not restaurants, not the mall, why here? It's a civil rights issue—it's not OK to seclude a child with a disability.

Candice, on the other hand, was not driven by a state mandate. She carried her philosophy of inclusion throughout her life having a physical disability herself and bringing her advocacy for it to each of the three districts that she has worked with over the past 24 years. Where she began her career, she worked in one district that reported having less than 30% of students with support needs receiving services within the general education classroom alongside their peers. The power of her beliefs started the ball rolling toward more inclusive practices. She noted that:

Inclusion is something more than rights. It is humanity. It is life. The law makes people behave in a certain way. But moving beyond that, deep respect for the human being that is before you is called for. Every disabled person has a right to access what everyone else does. In the end, it [inclusion] is an everyday reality, it is a normal thing—it is not a program, it is a way of life.

Both Candice and Carla clearly had an espoused value and built action plans from this value to make general education placement happen slowly and deliberately. For both of them inclusive education was more than a mandate, more than a best practice, it was a core value based on human dignity and human rights.

Theme: District Influence and Visibility: Sitting at the Right Table

A third theme that emerged from our conversation with the school administrators included their strategic placement and influence within the top tier of the district administrative branch. For most of the leaders, this placement within the administrative branch led to the district's commitment to systemwide practices and policies needed to successfully move students with special needs into general education environments.

Three of the five leaders (Carla and Candice included) sat in the superintendent's cabinet. One stated, "Having school board and superintendent support, including a seat at the table working with all senior staff, is crucial to our evolution as a Department." Similarly, Candice stated that she "always had a seat at the table working with all senior staff making collaboration easy."

It is evident from Carla's and Candice's experience that working alongside and with the entire administrative branch of the district in an integrated fashion was paramount to their districts' movement to more inclusive practices. Of particular note, Candice always had a former building principal serve as one of her seconds in command. With the help of this person, she merged her district support staff with curriculum and instruction across all four areas of the district. An integrated curriculum and instruction support team, aligned in vision and mission, now leads all district efforts to improve performance, school by school, across student subgroups regardless of the federal label. With the help of this person, Candice has been a force in removing all staff labels in an effort to integrate district support efforts for all students.

Theme: Future of Special Education

We asked each leader what he or she thought about the future of special education in order to connect their thinking back to the capabilities approach. Two leaders linked the future of special education to structural issues and new role relationships between professionals who work in inclusive classrooms. One of these leaders made the link back to social affiliation for both teachers and students, and the other leader spoke of presumed competency as the starting point for all students. The leader from our smallest district reported that she saw special education's new role as

> Supporting general education to teach a more diverse population. Special education could become a thing of the past—we are moving into one system—when we focus on supporting general education teachers. The only problem is students with significant disabilities that are truly on an alternate path. Always need special education for a small group of kids [including special spaces].

And another stated:

> [The] district view is emerging. We are coming to understand that students have capabilities and are expected to contribute and do contribute. The emphasis is on multiple tiers of support where there are no separated programs, no labels to get kids what they need. [There are] integrated systems of support.

Carla and Candice offered a vision of how special education fit within their districts' mission.

For Carla, a new disposition for all teachers is important:

> Teachers are realizing [the] potential of all children, they are responsible for each child's learning and they can in fact make it happen. Real differentiation—deep content, process, and process that includes—readiness, learning style. We are finding their true potential rather than assumed.

Candice, on the other hand, summarized both her concerns about what is not required of special educators in law and what, in her mind, must happen in the future.

> What's missing [in the law] is how well a school functions when it serves everybody. This perspective gets lost. The numbers don't matter, what does it [student placement numbers] really tell people. What is the quality of education we are giving our kids with disabilities?

> Until the feds take away the option for segregation in the law [the continuum of services], we will always have segregated settings . . . if I had it my way we would move some of the federal government out of the way. IDEA [Individuals With Disabilities Education Act] is for those who deny the rights of the disabled, opening the doors for kids who need it most.

But it is also a law that separates. It does not de-sensitize. It becomes a measure of compliance. It separates. It is something more than rights. It is humanity. Here are the opportunities, [now] how can I help you get there. It is about what they [the students] are achieving. It is about developing the individual's independence. The goal is to have self-advocacy and do something. The whole system needs to believe in and support that level of independence.

Within the capabilities approach human dignity and a person's effort to reach his or her own self-defined goals, such as being mobile or being gainfully employed, are key concentrations (Nussbaum, 2006). By openly discussing humanity, Candice opens doors and focuses on the opportunities for individuals to actualize their abilities to reach their goals. Her statement illustrates the fundamental philosophical tenets from the capabilities approach as part of her rationale for promoting inclusive education.

Discussion and Implications

The purpose of the larger study that these leaders' stories came from (Toson, Knollman, & Burrello, 2012) was to examine whether the capabilities approach was illustrated within five district leaders' personal leadership philosophy. They were interested in whether or not the educational leaders interviewed recognized the value of the capabilities approach, which includes a meaningful self-fulfilled life and human dignity for all students with different needs and disabilities, within their decision-making and district design process. We, however, were particularly interested in how two of the five leaders actively advocated for the protection of human dignity and individual choice, beginning with what Ware (2002) calls the moral conversation with oneself and others about for whom and what you will advocate.

Through our qualitative analysis it became evident that Carla and Candice seemed to most closely articulate a belief about disability that reflected Reindal's (2008) social-relational understanding of difference and Nussbaum's (2011) belief that human variability, and thus disability, is a natural part of humanity. These two leaders stood out in this study, and are the focus of this chapter, because they saw and spoke to the effects of deficit thinking and the historical impact that the continuum of services has had on segregation, getting in the way of a student's access to general education settings. The belief that the capability and the freedom to pursue options, thus the ability to partake in choices, are denied to students who are educated in self-contained placements that separate students and their teachers from their peers based on the student's label was shared by both Candice and Carla. They articulated a position most closely aligned with the capabilities approach and worked via local and district-level advocacy to change practices by directly addressing difference and diversity as a natural part of the student body, rather than seeing disabilities as leading to instructional issues needing to be categorically solved with separate programming. Carla and Candice worked to find ways to design their districts' educational core to meet the needs of all students.

Hincliffe's (2007) argument about avoiding trivial learning is also relevant here. According to Candice and Carla, the greater the separation of programs and supports between students with significant support needs (students with disability labels) and other students without specialized needs (students without disability labels), the more trivial the programming. They advocated for and took continuous action to align and integrate systems of support within general education to meet the needs of all the learners in their districts.

While the authors believe that the other three leaders who participated in the study are concerned about general education programming that meets the needs of many students, they stressed access to the general education curriculum for all but the students with the most significant support needs. Special education was seen for these three leaders as a system with varying degrees of services that are provided to students with significant support needs by specialized personnel in collaboration with their general education colleagues. However, students with significant support needs were either excluded entirely from these partnerships and collaborative decisions, or they were thought of after core educational decisions were made. This often results in the implementation of separate programs all together. Carla and Candice were different. They spoke openly and with a directed focus on why and how they worked to include the students who had the most significant support needs. To Candice and Carla, meaningful general education was curriculum targeting at all students. To these leaders, all really means all (Capper & Frattura, 2009).

Though the leaders were not informed about the capabilities approach framework prior to, during, or after the interview, paramount to both was the idea that all individuals have value and worth and are worthy of respect and quality inclusive education simply because they are human beings. This echoes Nussbaum's underlying tenet of the capabilities within each person, in which she states, "People with disabilities are, however, equals who need to be taken into account from the beginning in designing any scheme of social cooperation" (Nussbaum, 2011, p. 150).

Returning to Nussbaum's (2006) 10 uniquely human capabilities (a long life, good health, emotional engagement, bodily integrity, senses, imagination and thought, practical reasoning, affiliation, enjoyment of other species and nature, play, and control over one's environment), we think about Carla and Candice and what capabilities, if any, may be evident in their practice. Looking at Carla's and Candice's visions of education for students with disabilities and Nussbaum's (2006) 10 unique capabilities, we see four unique capabilities illustrated in our leaders' personal philosophies: affiliation, practical reasoning, control over one's environment, and good health. The first of Nussbaum's capabilities, affiliation, speaks to the importance of each individual, even those with the most significant support needs, being a socially valued member of his or her community. Carla shared her belief that center school placement (a separate educational building for students with specific disability labels) was "harming children because they were not living up to their potential" and that there was absolutely no "opportunity to communicate with peers, only caregivers." Similarly, Candice shared her realization that children who are educated in secluded settings would not ever be active members of "their community as an adult and have the potential for a job or diploma." It was these realizations by both leaders that led them to shift from segregated to inclusive programming. Both leaders express concerns about the need to address their students' affiliation with peer groups in their communities.

Another poignant example of affiliation is the realization of meaningful affiliation as a desired end result and a sought-after educational outcome. One leader shared her excitement on learning that when a student who was "served" in the profound program at a center school transitioned into the general education setting in his neighborhood school, he expressed recognition of his cousin for the first time after a family camping trip. She also shared that after this student was included in a setting where he was a part of the general education community, he, for the first time ever, experienced true affiliation with his community peers. She shared, "He [the student] went from not recognizing that he was in a room with others to recognizing relationships with peers and cousins."

Carla and Candice are two examples of leaders who advanced their advocacy to the forefront of their practice. Their views were most compatible with the capabilities approach, and both espoused a commitment to freedom and agency of all students, including students with significant disabilities. Candice told a story of closing a separate school by transferring each high school student to three or four district high schools and preventing new students from entering it, so that eventually no students were left in the segregated school. They simply aged out of the school and the separate system.

After the students transferred to their new general education schools, Candice was discouraged to see that they had no independent healthy eating choice skills. At the segregated center school the students were served food all day long, never needing to make their own choices. Here, however, the students were allowed to freely choose what to eat (a skill that would carry through into adulthood). Her dismay reached its zenith when she went into the cafeteria and watched these students proceed through the lunch line. They immediately and consistently bought all the candy and sweets and began to fill their stomachs with sugar, with no healthy options to balance their diet. Further, she watched them mill around aimlessly without any sense of the social situation around them or an ability to discriminate between nutritious foods and sweets. She shared, "What we did not teach these students in the separate school [was to make healthy choices] because everything was done for them." Nussbaum's (2006) good health and practical reasoning were underdeveloped capacities for these students. Candice recognized this need for increased good health and practical reasoning (choice) and acted on the need to enhance learning opportunities inclusively to increase the capacities via healthy choice making for these students.

Carla shared similar disgust with segregated school settings. She saw the administration of a group IEP (Individualized Education Plan) daily, a process that is meant to be individualized. She proceeded to move staff and students into inclusive environments as quickly as possible to stop the group planning. When reflecting on the process, she said, "I couldn't do this fast enough." She went on to close six separate campuses and replace at least three principals who could not lead in this direction. Remember, Carla had a mandate as "the bottom of the barrel" to move students and teachers into the mainstream of school life, but her advocacy was largely tied to Nussbaum's affiliation capacity because these students only had access to adult caregivers and only incidentally to their peers before the move.

It appears to us that almost all of Nussbaum's uniquely human characteristics show up through Carla's and Candice's work and their deeply entrenched belief of the human dignity of all individuals. Thus, we see using the capabilities approach in the preparation of all school leaders, especially those concerned with the education of persons with disabilities, as both appropriate and useful. The capabilities approach to leadership may open up possibilities to rethink how to construct the systems of response contained in universally designed and differentiated instruction (aka the common core curriculum and instruction in all classrooms), individual education plans, transition plans, and postschool plans of meaningful community and work life for adults. It reinforces the positioning of the individual student and his or her own unique differences in the conversation. The capabilities approach may be able to open up many possibilities that school leaders should consider to be beyond mere access to general education. That is, it may help leaders to see how putting human dignity at the forefront of their work may lead to an increase in meaningful adult outcomes for all students.

Further, Carla and Candice offered an insight into how leaders apply their personal vision within their decision-making process. This is particularly useful when considering how leadership vision is linked to views on social justice, human dignity, and educational leadership. The capabilities approach has a rightful place in social justice leadership, and there are implications for its practical application in educational leadership and design. Looking at education from a social-relational perspective requires leaders to make instructional design and resource allocation decisions based on acknowledgment of individual difference rather than standardized assessments and curriculums and tests. An individual student's unique abilities that lead to meaningful functionings, with personal agency, must be considered up front; therefore, curriculum, instruction, resource allocation, and assessment must be designed with individual variability in mind.

For us, educational leadership starts with what Carla suggested: "presuming competence in all students" (see Jorgenson, 2007, for a discussion of presumed competence). Presuming competence in all students is a point that we believe is implicit in Nussbaum's (2006, 2011) interpretation, but it is one that needs to be stated as an explicit first step in the design of education. Educational programming and planning must start with the assumption of competence. This presumed competence leads one to come to know what capabilities exist and what need to be developed within the individual student. Thus, presumed competence can lead to a conversation around what the individual student, or trusted advocate, identifies as (1) essential goals to pursue, and (2) what exactly must be planned for based on student capabilities and individual choice. This focus on the individual student's capability to engage meaningfully in life must be considered before any goals, standards, benchmarks, or curriculum and assessment decisions are made. What capabilities are in need of development for an individual student and how will the school staff best do this within general education should be the questions that guide leadership to address the enhancements, differentiations, and resources needed to increase meaningful independent school (curriculum and social) through adult life (community and work engagement) capabilities and functioning for all students.

This research suggests that if the capabilities approach informs leadership practices, individual student variation, as opposed to standards, must guide educational decision making. This focus on individual student variation is the essence of the Individuals With Disabilities Education Act (IDEA, 2004). Therefore, it seems important to consider the possibility that leaders and teachers need to first address getting to know the individual student for who he or she is and to examine each student's individual functionings, capabilities, and needs. By accepting all students' individual variations and leading from the notion that all people are inherently different with inherent dignity, educational conversations on individualized student learning may result in increased capabilities for all students (Nussbaum, 2011). Thus, the impact of being exposed to capabilities approach thinking in educational leadership and teacher training is an area worthy of further exploration and research to examine if increased student outcomes results are needed.

The question for exploration and examination could become this: How do school teams and leadership decide what is best for each individual child based upon his or her own capabilities? This question requires rethinking the standardization movement driven by No Child Left Behind (NCLB, 2001). Instead of grade-level standardization, as mentioned above, the focus will need to be on the variability and individuality of students. Thus, the main policy implication becomes the following: What are the three or four individualized postschool goals that lead to each individual's own capability to live a meaningful adulthood, and how do we get each student there? This implication questions NCLB's focus on standardization and refocuses leaders and teachers on what the pathway to meaningful inclusive adulthood is for each individual student.

Conclusion

We conclude that Carla and Candice seem to be firmly grounded in the capabilities approach. Carla has been able to enact the approach with dispatch in her district of 17,000, and Candice has made steady progress building a community of believers within her district and moving beyond compliance with the law and into meaningful educational design. The capabilities approach did not explicitly inform these leaders, but it was evident in their espoused beliefs and leadership vision.

Based upon this case study, we offer an attempt to use the capabilities approach as a way to guide district leaders in support of equity and social justice by enhancing learning opportunities for students with disabilities through the application of Nussbaum's (2006) 10 tenets of human capability and Reindal's (2009) social-relational model of difference. Educational design that is inclusive of all students' capacities up front may lead to social affiliation, community membership, and improved student outcomes. This in turn may lead to the participation of all people in civic discourse and meaningful membership in their own communities.

References

Alkire, S., & Deneulin, S. (2009). The human development and capability approach. In S. Deneulin & L. Shahami (Eds.), *An introduction to the human development and capability approach: Freedom and agency* (pp. 22–48). London: Earthscan.

Ferguson, P.M. (1987). The social construction of mental retardation. *Social Policy, 18*(1), 51–56.

Hart, S.C. (2009). Quo vadis? The capability space and new directions for the philosophy of educational research. *Studies in the Philosophy of Education, 28,* 391–402.

Hincliffe, G. (2007). Truth and the capability of learning. *Journal of Philosophy of Education, 41*(2), 221–232.

Individuals With Disabilities Education Improvement Act (2004). P.L. 108-446. Retrieved from http://idea.ed.gov/

Larson, C., & Murtadha, K. (2002). Leadership for social justice. In Joseph Murphy (Ed.), *The educational leadership challenge: Redefining leadership for the 21st century.* National Society for the Study of Education. Chicago: University of Chicago Press.

No Child Left Behind Act, P.L. 107-11 (NCLB) (2001). Retrieved from http://www.ed.gov/policy/elsec/leg.esea02/index.html

Nussbaum, M.C. (2006). *Frontiers of justice: Disability, nationality, and species membership.* Cambridge, MA: Harvard University Press.

Nussbaum, M.C. (2011). *Creating capabilities: The human development approach.* Cambridge, MA: Harvard University Press.

Reindal, S.M. (2008). A social-relational model of disability: A theoretical framework for special needs education. *European Journal of Special Needs Education, 23*(2), 135–146.

Reindal, S.M. (2009). Disability, capability, and special education: Towards a capability-based approach. *European Journal of Special Needs Education, 24*(2), 155–168.

Sen, A. (1992). *Inequality reexamined.* Oxford: Clarendon Press.

Terzi, L. (2005). Beyond the dilemma of difference: The capability approach to disability and special educational needs. *Journal of Philosophy of Education, 39*(3), 443–459.

Terzi, L. (2008). *Justice and equality in education: A capability perspective on disability and special educational needs.* New York: Continuum.

Toson, A.L-M., Burrello, L.C., & Knollman, G. (2012). "Educational justice for all": The capability approach and inclusive education leadership. *International Journal of Inclusive Education,* 1–17.

Walker, M. (2006). Towards a capability-based theory of social justice for educational policy-making. *Journal of Educational Policy, 21*(2), 163–185.

Ware, L. (2002). A moral conversation on disability: Risking the personal in educational contexts. *Hypatia, 17*(1), 143–172.

11

THE DANGEROUS POLITICS OF DIFFERENCE

How Systems Produce Marginalization

Elizabeth B. Kozleski, Alfredo Artiles, and Lisa Lacy

In this chapter we explore the ways in which current special education policy and practices in the United States are built upon ideological assumptions around difference, deficit, and disability. These ideological assumptions coupled with decultured views of learning and human development have produced systems of marginalization whose structures constrain opportunities to learn for groups of students who need multiple ramps to support their engagement with formal learning communities such as schools. In particular, we want to describe how these persistent processes flourish through communities of practice in classrooms, schools, school districts, and state education agencies that enact and reconstruct policies through their daily activities.

Rather than referring to *the* system, we conceptualize systems as interconnected activity arenas that traverse micro and macro scales (Artiles & Dyson, 2005; Kozleski, Gibson, & Hynds, in press). Thus, classrooms in schools belong both in activity systems called schools and also in activity systems called school districts. Schools that belong to a single local educational agency (what we call a school district in the United States) constitute a district activity system. Envisioning these networked systems of activity helps to contextualize the localized cultures of practice that emerge from individual activity systems. By describing specific contexts and activities, we intend to explore the ways in which marginalization and countermarginalization narratives evolve and develop. Their connections to the ideological assumptions of U.S. special education policy are analyzed with particular attention to how some local systems contest received policies and sustain those counternarratives over time.

Our focus on special education is not intended to limit our discourse to the marginalization of persons identified as disabled since special education policies and practices provide a nexus for the intersectionality of dis/ability, race, gender, ethnicity, and language (Artiles, 2011). A variety of researchers have reported on the disproportionate representation of students from culturally and linguistically nondominant groups in special education. African American, American Indian, and Latino students are disproportionately identified for special education in some states for some disability categories. The risk that some groups may be identified for special education ranges from more than one and a half times to more than four times more likely to be identified than all other student population groups (Artiles, 2011; Losen & Skiba, 2010). Further, nondominant racial groups are more likely to be served in more restrictive environments (Artiles, Kozleski, Trent, Osher, & Ortiz, 2010). Several studies in the last 10 years have examined the extent to which African American, American Indian, and Latino students have been disproportionately involved in discipline incidents. Losen and Skiba (2010) report that in 18 of the largest U.S. districts, African American students were suspended at anywhere from 11% to 50% more frequently than their White counterparts. Suspension, expulsion, arrest, and dropout rates for students of color continue to plague the nation's schools in spite of increasing surveillance and attention to the data. In 2011, there was an 11% increase in discrimination complaints filed with the Department of Education's Office for Civil Rights (OCR). These data underscore the importance of understanding how our educational systems continue to conflate race and disability in an ongoing process of marginalization that impacts generations of Americans.

Globally, special education has been replaced by a focus on inclusive education, which, in spite of efforts to define it broadly as an educational process of including every child in a unified system of education, is often seen as a disability-focused, educational policy intervention (Kozleski, Artiles, & Waitoller, 2011). In the United States, inclusive education has increasingly been overshadowed by the federal focus on response to intervention (Artiles & Kozleski, 2010). Booth and Ainscow (2000) described inclusive education as a process in which participation is expanded, while, in response, exclusion from mainstream schools dwindles. The key role that participation plays in creating inclusive education is informed by the degree to which equitable opportunities to learn are made available so that the social, participatory nature of learning is contextualized within the cultural, intellectual, and material literacies available in any given learning community (Artiles & Kozleski, 2007). Further, inclusive education is concerned with recognition, redistribution, and representation (Waitoller & Kozleski, in review). Thus, to be engaged in countermarginalization, which inclusive education purports to enact, requires not only an expansion of participation, but also a meaningful focus on understanding and mediating the contexts in which marginalization and inclusivity are produced. Artiles, Kozleski, and Gonzalez (2011) argue that determining who is recognized and accounted for within a community or system embodies the exercise of power that moves individuals and groups into the flow of a system, away from the margins, redistributing identities and power. The warrants for making these moves are embedded within historical notions of race, disease (and thus, disability), difference, and capacity.

By exploring counternarratives, we are also critiquing systems that develop and evolve over time to codify and reify the processes of marginalization. In deconstructing how these systems persist, we are able to explore notions of expansiveness that move individuals beyond dichotomies through the exploration of cultural geographies, notions of practice as inquiry rather than the aesthetics of routinization, and examine the use of responsivity and reflexivity in redesigning practice systems. Moving from marginalization to expansiveness requires disruptions and redirections within activity systems (Engeström & Sannino, 2010).

One avenue that we explore is whether leadership itself can act as a distributive tool to mediate systems and move them from marginalizing to expanding possibilities. Foster (1989) argued early on that leadership resides in the community, and as a communal-based activity, it goes beyond any single person. We offer notions of leadership that are not embodied in individuals, but instead entail social processes that influence the construction and reconstruction of emerging social exchanges and underlying values, attitudes, and ideologies (Bolden, Petrov, & Gosling, 2008). In this way, leadership is no longer an attribute of individuals themselves, but a contextually embedded process emerging from the dynamic relationship between various actors.

How Marginalization Works

Racial, ethnic, gender, and cultural differences can be seen and experienced throughout communities and within schools across the United States, although different contexts produce different forms and patterns of differential treatment, status, and opportunities to learn and develop (Artiles, Kozleski, Trent, Osher, & Ortiz, 2010). Difference is conceptualized and addressed within systems at multiple levels, producing policy levers that intersect within a variety of activity arenas, including classrooms and schools. How these policy levers operate and what they produce is vital information for crafting policy that addresses justice issues. For instance, differences are constructed in classrooms where differential treatment of some students takes place in response to perceived racial, cultural, gender, ability, and other characteristics that are essentialized.

The microanalysis of classroom activity has been studied extensively over the last 30 years (Erickson, 2004). Such studies reveal the ways in which teachers and students construct their classroom cultures, identities, roles, and notions of what it means to learn. One study of teacher talk in inclusive classrooms revealed that teachers use more directives and lower-level questioning with students with disabilities than they do with students who are not identified as disabled (Hestenes, Cassidy, & Niemeyer, 2004). Social and linguistic practices like microaggressions in which teachers or other authority figures directly or indirectly slight students because of racial, gender, or ability stereotypes can create contentious classrooms where students feel personally attacked and threatened (Smith, 2004). Experiencing microaggressions, whether once or repeatedly, can lead to social-psychological stress responses (e.g., frustration, anger, exhaustion, resistance) (Brown et al., 1999). Over time, microaggressions create teacher–student friction that can lead to resentment, resistance, reluctance to participate, and ultimately, overt verbal or physical defiance. In some cases, the end result is student dismissal, suspension, or expulsion from school or referral to special education. More likely and less immediately noticeable is that students may disengage from learning. Thus, tools for discipline and control separate some students out and then push them away from the core work of participation in learning. Academic curricula and materials are examples of other mediational tools that also have embedded sorting agendas (Cobb & McClain, 2006). These patterns are repeated over time, becoming normalized and creating shared explanations among faculty and students for why these patterns persist. The process of marginalization becomes part of the system of practice. Marginalization emerges from the recognition of difference, the production of othering, and is maintained through social interactions (Doehler, 2002). And, yet, it is not only through social interactions that marginalization processes are at play.

We have not yet left behind our assembly-line metaphors. Our systems are laced with reminders to measure, label, categorize, and assign. The common core standards, an innovation at work in the last five years in the United States and funded by the U.S. Department of Education, is an example of how systems seek to describe and name what will be considered the norm or the center from which difference will be gauged (Porter, McMaken, Hwang, & Yang, 2011). Our statistical methodologies are based on assumptions of means and variance that describe the distance between any particular performance and what might be predicted by a norm. Our dominant cultural perspective in the United States embraces this idea particularly in the way that it sorts and categorizes student performance and muddles performance, ability, culture, and ways of knowing. The work of maintaining the core is to determine the degree of variance that can be handled so that most variance fits a predictable pattern. The problem comes when explanations for any given variance don't fit the predicted pattern and the tools for accommodating difference are inadequate. None of this activity occurs in decontextualized spaces. Rather, people with their own particular cultural histories, experiences, and expectations come together in institutional contexts that are veined with historical deposits, and negotiate their activities through the tools available in their settings (Kozleski & Artiles, 2012).

Othering

Once the process of marginalization begins, that is, some students are pushed out to the margins because of the social construction of behaviors, socialization patterns, peer relationships, and learning interests or processes in their classrooms, they are seen as outsiders. Outsiders get lumped together as insiders enact the dominant ideology. The process of identity formation is infused with dominant ideologies and exchange practices, including the use of language and other social artifacts. Since identity is a mutual process of construction, marginalized individuals participate in their identity construction as they share ideologies, values, and practices among themselves (Holland & Lachicotte, 2007). Identities are developed in contrast and in solidarity. Multiple processes work to congeal figured identities, bring social cohesion to insider and outsider groups, and produce the conditions for othering and marginalization. Discourses of power, pathology, and competence with cultural tools are used to make distinctions that lead to othering (Spivak, 1999). In the othering process, members of the dominant group classify and sort the other by several explanatory narratives such as essentializing the characteristics of a particular group and/or employing culturally and racially bound rationales for how language and behavior are produced and can be interpreted. For instance, the identification of students for special education has been practiced for decades with assessments designed for the purpose of special education identification and used widely with groups of students who were not represented in the population samples that were originally used to validate assessments for diagnostic use.

Understanding learning as a change in participation, as Rogoff (2003) suggests, means that the design of learning spaces plays a powerful role in maintaining and facilitating marginalization particularly since culture is deeply embedded in how participation is facilitated and regulated. Students and teachers perform sociolinguistic activities that construct othering as part of their daily activities, even though it is not part of the explicit curriculum. For instance, a common strategy observed in classrooms, organizing students into reading groups, socializes the practice of grouping and is repeated in a variety of ways often based on explicit criteria for what groups are allowed to do when they belong to particular groups. Students and teachers practice these activities with regularity, reinforcing the practice until it becomes part of what is perceived as the natural order, making it almost invulnerable to questions about its function and role in othering.

Special Education as Marginalizing Practice

Various iterations of special education policy and practice illustrate the process of marginalization. The marginalizing process begins with locating problems within an individual. Once problems exist within an individual, their presence requires activating repair strategies so that they can fit, engage, and become part of the community. That means that activity systems need people to fulfill the roles of problem identification and problem fixing. In this example, the context for how local activity systems (like classrooms) operate is informed by larger policy contexts that require narratives of problem identification, cataloging, and fixing. Local boundaries are breeched, new ideologies inserted, and local practices disturbed. Responses to these intrusions are multifaceted. Part of the intent of federal special education law was to push in students to local activity systems (classrooms, schools, and school districts) when they had been denied access (Artiles & Kozleski, 2010). Once on the threshold and even inside, what happens relies on local access to knowledge and resources, how the activity system identifies the goals of the introduced processes, the learning processes of the activity systems, local ideologies, professional identities, and cultural practices. While special education law was intended to create access, local activity systems appropriated special education processes to legitimize ways of marginalizing some students (Zion & Blanchett, 2011) whose differences were read as disability rather than lack of opportunities to learn.

Countering Marginalization Narratives

Countering marginalization narratives is complex work for activity systems located in cultural geographies that continue to maintain and sustain marginalization. In this section, we explore how local systems might examine evidence to expand their understanding of how students are faring in terms of access, participation, opportunities to learn, and accomplishments. More important, they may learn how their systems conflate various kinds of difference and embed processes of marginalization. Consider the experience of a federally funded center that was charged with helping states decrease disproportionate identification by racial and ethnic category of special education students. In 2003, the National Center for Culturally Responsive Educational Systems (NCCRESt) was awarded a $5-million, five-year grant to work with all 50 states and 10 territories on disproportionality data. NCCRESt operated from the premise that culturally responsive educational systems were grounded in an understanding that students learn in race, gender, ability, language, and class-conscious schools that reflect the social order of their communities. Nevertheless, students can excel in academic endeavors if their cultures, languages, heritages, and experiences are valued and connected to the formal learning environments and processes. Culturally responsive practices include the use of curricula with ethnic and cultural diversity content, encouraging the use of communication strategies that build on students' cultures, and nurturing the creation of school cultures that are concerned with deliberative and participatory discourse practices (Gay, 2000). Moreover, culturally responsive educational systems create spaces for teacher reflexivity, inquiry, and mutual support around issues of cultural differences. Key questions that address power and privilege are consistently researched and addressed to develop rich explanations for the (a) differential achievement of minority students, (b) the conceptions of "self" and "others" that inform pedagogical practices, (c) the social relations structured in the cultures of schools and classrooms, (d) the conceptions of knowledge that inform pedagogical, curricular, and assessment practices, and (e) the consequences of these assumptions for academic and social outcomes (Ladson-Billings, 1995; Villegas & Lucas, 2002).

These notions were almost invisible in the special education literature at the time that NCCRESt was funded. Thus one of NCCRESt's challenges from the beginning was to help lay the foundation for understanding how race, ability, gender, class, and culture intersect with the learning conditions and opportunities that are created in classrooms. Educational leaders and practitioners needed much more nuanced understandings of these constructs and how they participated and co-constructed culture. The genesis of minority representation is located beyond the borders of special education, and this problem requires a solid understanding of the intersection of culture, learning, disability, gender, language, and the socio-historical constitution of educational processes and outcomes. The definition of culture is key to practitioner understanding of overrepresentation. A sound definition of culture should encompass both within-group variability and the classroom cultures that are socially created in and shaped by the historically charged contexts of schools (Artiles, 2011). School cultures define what it takes to be competent, what counts as being articulate or smart, and the cultural performances required to navigate and use institutional resources for individual advancement (e.g., how to ask questions, how to negotiate with counselors, course placement decisions, how to be challenging in sanctioned ways). NCCRESt began to cause trouble marginalizing practices through the use of a view of culture that accounts for classroom cultures and the cultures in the classroom (Gallego et al., 2001).

NCCRESt employed a fluid and instrumental view of culture in which students and teachers were not boxed in categorical identities (e.g., poor Latino low-achieving students or White, middle-class teachers). Instead, the Center integrated and disseminated scholarship that (a) took into account students' cultural toolkits and (b) documented how classroom cultures enhance or constrain the implementation of interventions in multicultural classrooms (Artiles, 2011). NCCRESt drew on academic, scholarly work from a variety of related disciplines and areas of study, including the sociology of education, organizational theory, cultural studies, legal studies, political science, social psychology, policy and fiscal studies, urban planning and urban geography, and history. These disciplines assisted the NCCRESt team to help audiences *understand* overrepresentation and promote the *use* of research-based knowledge around aspects such as resiliency in minority students' and families' lives, understandings of institutional processes and factors that can enable or constrain minorities' performance in various school contexts, and leadership issues in the administration of urban and suburban schools in the midst of multiple reforms, among others.

Influenced by the idea of expansive laboratories pioneered by Yrjö Engeström (1999), NCCRESt began by building an extensive set of geographic information system (GIS) maps onto which disproportionality data from all the states were mapped. Data from 2003 on were mapped annually to show state education agencies change over time in the ways in which their policies and intervention strategies impacted their disproportionality data. This visual display not only provided information about each state's status but showed relationships among states, providing a cultural geography of professional practices located at various places and times (Soja, 1996). These maps displayed disproportionality risk ratios by ethnic and racial status as well as disability category and the restrictiveness of the educational environments in which groups of students were placed. Map users could select display options and measure their own progress in comparison to other states depending on the economic, political, policy, and demographic characteristics of interest.

Sets of state teams were invited to inquiry-based meetings to explore their data and develop plans for improving outcomes through professional learning and technical assistance to school districts and schools. In addition to the state maps that masked the variance within states, NCCRESt collaborated with another federally funded center, the National Institute for Urban School Improvement (NIUSI), to produce a set of local GIS maps that looked at disproportionality and placement by racial and disability groups indexed in school systems such as Chicago, Denver, Las Vegas, Memphis, Miami, Madison, and Washington, D.C. Thus, state teams were able to disturb their own space and then, understand how the contours and patterns take very different forms at the local level. This movement in data from macro to micro was continued in a third project also available to states in which data at the school level was also mapped onto building schematics, producing another form of cultural geography at the school level. This work, coupled with mapping endeavors linking school and community social patterns (Artiles, Kozleski, Waitoller, & Luckinbeal, 2011), helped state and local district teams to re-mediate their own assumptions about how disproportionality was distributed and connected to other community patterns like mobility, safety, access to distal community assets, community activism, cultural arts, and proximity to gathering spaces like parks, playgrounds, and shopping centers.

State teams responded to the process of examining data in a variety of ways. We discuss them here because how meaning was extracted, actions were taken, and efforts to change patterns and activity were accomplished is critical to countering marginalization narratives. Of the 50 states, 32 reported their work with NCCRESt. About 18 states that did not cite their work with NCCRESt reported that they changed the threshold for what was considered disproportionate, something that federal statute permitted (Sullivan & Kozleski, 2008). That is, they increased the numerical criteria for what counted as disproportionality, citing lack of resources to offer assistance to local school districts as a compelling reason to loosen the criteria (Sullivan & Kozleski, 2008). Some of the 32 states invested heavily in professional learning efforts to remediate how race, disability, and culture were understood and addressed within local school communities. Other states provided explicit guidance to local systems around their identification procedures. Another group of states focused on moving away from the standard identification processes for determining eligibility for special education to a response to intervention protocol. And, in a few states, these initiatives were intertwined.

The geographic displays of data offered a way for state teams to expand their understanding of intersectionality and to remain in intellectual and creative spaces where traction for change could be achieved by disturbing different layers of their systems simultaneously. Yet, much of the data conversation was grounded in the kind of white innocence that Gotanda (2004) noted in his analysis of *Brown v. Board of Education*. The NCCRESt state teams used the opportunity for exploring their data to both come to new understandings of how the legacies of racism and ableism were deeply embedded in state efforts to support local district practices and to also distance themselves from the reproduction of those legacies through what Gutiérrez (2006) discusses as the "Who Knew? Moment" (p. 1450). By maintaining their White innocence, team members (and NCCRESt staff) were able to both embrace new trajectories but also maintain their own power and authority to make change on behalf of others. This means that paying attention to who is invited to disturb these issues, how they are supported to participate, the degree to which multiple perspectives are engaged, and how action is organized must account for historical differentials in power and position within decision making. In systems where power is concentrated in a few places and tightly connected to fiscal resources, expanding communities and spheres of influence continues to be fraught with questions about power, positionality, and marginalization.

Dangers and Opportunities

Once upon a time a system for cataloging, naming, and sorting plants and animals was developed, a cataloging system for books had to be created, and systems for manufacturing complex machines, like cars, were introduced (Star & Griesemer, 1989). These sorting and managing systems brought many benefits to purposeful analytic activity in which comparisons and contrasts could be drawn. Professional bureaucracies grew up around these systems. People needed to learn how to access, use, manage, tend, and expand our cataloging systems. Sorting and systematizing gained cachet. Modernity was consumed with creating order out of chaos, seeking greater and greater predictability, and managing larger and larger numbers of people (Foucault, 1975). But, the digital age means that managing or curating data is no longer the purview of experts; curation is the everyday practice of people who have access to electronic information, round-the-clock communication, and opportunities to move fluidly in and out of groups, political discourse, and social activism. By curation, we mean the active selection of some kinds of data, artifacts, communication, and evidence for use, storage, or dissemination. Individuals and groups can create curation niches that make their knowledge depositories of particular value for unpredictable amounts of time and space. Further, how these knowledge niches continue to be nurtured and developed can be understood by examining them through the lens of activity theory (Cole, 1996). These new ways of knowing and discovering mean that boundaries between systems are more permeable than ever. It also means that systems will have more difficulty in maintaining binaries (e.g., the center and the margins) because of porous borders and the distributed nature of knowledge development and curation. Active and sustained resistance will give way to reorganized and reassembled knowledge niches as people gravitate toward explanations and discovery that fits their local contexts and capacities.

As we consider the production of marginalization in systems, the loss of a center point from which margins are constructed seems increasingly possible and yet, organized and recognizable work performances will continue in formalized structures for schools. Given both spaces, the formal and bureaucratized spaces of schooling and the free form curated spaces of emerging activities, the work of seeding projects like inclusive education becomes more complex. What these ideas mean for leading change moves far beyond where most of the leadership literature is. That is, if leadership is constituted as a catalyst for change, then, leadership resides not in people or some sets of people, but it is distributed throughout the system so that disturbances in the system produce reflexivity, understanding, and meaning making. Spillane, Halverson, and Diamond (2004) make this point when they discuss the distributive nature of leadership as located between tasks, situations, followers, and leaders. Trite yet useful, the notion that danger and opportunities are two sides of the same coin is a useful trope for summarizing this chapter. Practitioners can use new and indigenous ways of knowing to shape their local activity systems to be responsive to the contexts that surround them while being mindful of the historical and contemporary realities of marginalization within schools.

The new realities that the information age creates for personalized, contextualized learning spaces that are no longer governed by complex hierarchies and formal school structures is thoroughly explored in Chapters One and Two of this book. Notions of distributed knowledge and networks create the very real medium in which educational systems can relinquish notions of global norming (McDermott, Edgar, & Scarloss, 2011) in favor of differentiated pedagogies and outcomes that reflect the needs and preferences of students, their families, their communities, and cultures. In an information age, the needs of students and their families can vary greatly, but not every schooling site needs to function as a repository for all possible variance. Instead, the notion of curated spaces where just-in-time information and knowledge gathering occurs to enhance and expand the human capabilities of students has many implications for what teacher and school leaders need to know and be able to do.

First and foremost, educators must have access to a wealth of information and professional learning in order to respond to local needs. They need the time, space, and material resources to access, learn, apply, and analyze the impact of their approaches. And, they need the dispositions and analytical tools to make this part of their ongoing response patterns. To do this within a team of collaborative educators who bring a cross-section of disciplinary knowledge to meet complex needs must be the goal of a unified system of education. The foundation of these team approaches to supporting and nurturing individual and collective capabilities is grounded in the moral imperative that every child's welfare and well-being contributes to the common good. Further, the work of education is to further the project of democracy, redistributing power and privilege in ways that shatter marginalization and expand our collective understanding of what it means to be in community. In this way, we can reframe how we understand the unique and special educational needs of each student and create an educational system that individualizes and personalizes as a matter of everyday practice for each and every learner.

References

Artiles, A. (2011). Toward an interdisciplinary understanding of educational equity and difference: The case of the racialization of ability. *Educational Researcher, 40,* 431–445.

Artiles, A.J., & Dyson, A. (2005). Inclusive education in the globalization age: The promise of comparative cultural historical analysis. In D. Mitchell (Ed.), *Contextualizing inclusive education* (pp. 37–62). London: Routledge.

Artiles, A.J., & Kozleski, E.B. (2007). Beyond convictions: Interrogating culture, history, and power in inclusive education. *Language Arts, 84,* 351–358.

Artiles, A. J., & Kozleski, E. B. (2010). What counts as response and intervention in RTI? A sociocultural analysis. *Psicothema, 22,* 949–954.

Artiles, A., Kozleski, E.B., & Gonzalez, T. (2011). Beyond the allure of inclusive education in the United States: Facing difficult questions, tracing enduring challenges. *Revista Teias, 12*(24), 285–308. Retrieved from http://www.periodicos.proped.pro.br/index.php?journal=revistateias&page=article&op=view&path%5B%5D=820 [Published in Portuguese].

Artiles, A., Kozleski, E.B., Trent, S., Osher, D., & Ortiz, A. (2010). Justifying and explaining disproportionality, 1968–2008: A critique of underlying views of culture. *Exceptional Children, 76,* 279–299.

Artiles, A. J., Kozleski, E. B., Waitoller, F., & Lukinbeal, C. (2011). Inclusive education and the interlocking of ability and race in the U.S.: Notes for an educational equity research program. In A. J. Artiles, E. B. Kozleski, & F. Waitoller (Eds.), *Inclusive education: Examining equity on five continents* (pp. 45–68). Cambridge, MA: Harvard Education Press.

Bolden, R., Petrov, G., & Gosling, J. (2008). Tensions in higher education leadership: Towards a multi-level model of leadership practice. *Higher Education Quarterly, 62*(4), 358–376.

Booth, T., & Ainscow, M. (2000). *The index for inclusion: Developing learning and participation in schools.* Bristol: Centre for Studies on Inclusive Education (CSIE).

Brown, T.N., Williams, D.R., Jackson, J.S., Neighbors, H.W., Torres, T., Sellers, S.L., & Brown, K. T. (1999). "Being Black and feeling blue": The mental health consequences of racial discrimination. *Race and Society, 2*(2), 117–131.

Cobb, P., & McClain, K. (2006). The collective mediation of a high-stakes accountability program: Communities and networks of practice. *Mind, Culture, and Activity, 13*(2), 80–100.

Cole, M. (1996). *Cultural psychology: A once and future discipline.* Cambridge, MA: Harvard University Press.

Doehler, S.P. (2002). Mediation revisited: The interactive organization of mediation in learning environments. *Mind, Culture, and Activity, 9*(1), 22–42.

Engeström, Y. (1999). Expansive visibilization of work: An activity-theoretical perspective. *Computer Supported Cooperative Work, 8*(1–2), 63–93.

Engeström, Y., & Sannino, A. (2010). Studies of expansive learning: Foundations, findings and future challenges. *Educational Research Review, 5,* 1–24.

Erickson, F. (2004). *Talk and social theory: Ecologies of speaking and listening in everyday life.* Cambridge: Polity Press.

Foster, W. (1989). Toward a critical practice of leadership. In J. Symth (Ed.), *Critical perspectives on educational leadership* (pp. 39–62). London: Falmer.

Foucault, M. (1975). *Discipline and punish: The birth of the prison.* New York: Random House.

Gallego, M.A., Cole, M., & the Laboratory of Comparative Human Cognition (LCHC). (2001). Classroom cultures and cultures in the classroom. In V. Richardson (Ed.), *Handbook of research on teaching* (pp. 951–997). Washington, DC: American Educational Research Association.

Gay, G. (2000). *Culturally responsive teaching: Theory, research, and practice.* New York: Teachers College Press.

Gotanda, N. (2004). Reflections on *Korematsu, Brown,* and White innocence. *Temple Political and Civil Rights Law Review, 13,* 663–674.

Gutiérrez, K. (2006). White innocence: A framework and methodology for rethinking educational discourse. *International Journal of Learning, 12,* 1–11.

Hestenes, L.L., Cassidy, D.J., & Niemeyer, J. (2004). A microanalysis of teachers' verbalizations in inclusive classrooms. *Early Education & Development, 15,* 23–38.

Holland, D., & Lachicotte, W. Jr. (2007). Vygotsky, Mead, and the new sociocultural studies of identity. In H. Daniels, M. Cole, & J.V. Wertsch (Eds.), *The Cambridge companion to Vygotsky.* Cambridge: Cambridge University Press.

Kozleski, E.B., Artiles, A.J., & Waitoller, F.R. (2011). Introduction: Equity in inclusive education. In A.J. Artiles, E.B. Kozleski, & F.R. Waitoller (Eds.), *Inclusive education on five continents: Unraveling equity issues* (pp. 1–14). Cambridge, MA: Harvard Education Press.

Kozleski, E.B., Gibson, D., & Hynds, A. (2012). Transforming complex educational systems: Grounding systems issues in equity and social justice. In J. Aiken (Ed.), *Defining social justice leadership in a global context* (pp. 263–286). Hershey, PA: IGI Global.

Ladson-Billings, G. (1995). Toward a theory of culturally relevant pedagogy. *American Educational Research Journal, 32,* 465–491.

Losen, D., & Skiba, R. (2010). *Suspended education: Urban middle schools in crisis.* Los Angeles: UCLA Civil Rights Project.

McDermott, R., Edgar, B., & Scarloss, B. (2011). Conclusion: Global norming. In A. Artiles, E.B. Kozleski, & F.R. Waitoller (Eds.), *Inclusive education: Examining equity on five continents* (pp. 223–235.) Cambridge, MA: Harvard Education Press.

Porter, A., McMaken, J., Hwang, J., & Yang, R. (2011). Common core standards: The new U.S. intended curriculum. *Educational Researcher, 40,* 103–116.

Rogoff, B. (2003). *The cultural nature of human development.* New York: Oxford University Press.

Smith, W.A. (2004). Black faculty coping with racial battle fatigue: The campus racial climate in a post–civil rights era. In D. Cleveland (Ed.), *Broken silence: Conversations about race by African Americans at predominately White institutions* (pp. 171–190). New York: Peter Lang.

Soja, E.W. (1996). *Thirdspace: Journeys to Los Angeles and other real-and-imagined places*. Oxford: Blackwell.

Spillane, J.P., Halverson, R., & Diamond, J.B. (2004). Towards a theory of leadership practice: A distributed perspective. *Journal of Curriculum Studies, 36,* 3–34.

Spivak, G.C. (1999). *A critique of postcolonialism reason: Toward a history of the vanishing present*. Cambridge, MA: Harvard University Press.

Star, S.L., & Griesemer, J. (1989). Institutional ecologies, translations, and coherence: Amateurs and professionals in Berkeley's Museum of Vertebrate Zoology, 1907–1939. *Social Studies of Science, 19,* 387–420.

Sullivan, A., & Kozleski, E.B. (2008*). Part B annual performance report (APR) analysis: Indicators 9 & 10: Disproportionality*. Tempe, AZ: National Center for Culturally Responsive Systems.

Villegas, A.M., & Lucas, T. (2002). Preparing culturally responsive teachers: Rethinking the curriculum. *Journal of Teacher Education, 53*(1), 20–32.

Waitoller, F., & Kozleski, E.B. (in review). Working in boundary practices: Identity development and learning in partnerships for inclusive education.

Zion, S., & Blanchett, W. (2011). Reconceptualizing inclusion: Can critical race theory and interest convergence be utilized to achieve inclusion and equity for African-American students? *Teachers College Record, 113*(10), 2186–2205.

PART V
Summary and Closing

12

REFLECTIONS AND THE HUMAN CAPABILITY APPROACH

Leonard C. Burrello, Jeannie Kleinhammer-Tramill, and Wayne Sailor

At the outset of this book, Kleinhammer–Tramill, Burrello, and Sailor provided a broad outline for a new policy frame that would remove "the praxis of our efforts to serve students with disabilities from an insular system of services, bound within its own rules and regulations, and to pose a new vision for a system that is fully integrated within the larger context of education" (p. 1). We suggested that special education should become "a temporally bounded instructional support system for any student in the public schools who might need support to achieve his or her full capabilities" (p. 1). We argued that to reconceptualize the system of special education, we need to (a) shift from a human capital agenda to a human capabilities agenda for education, (b) shift from a narrowed vision of what children should learn to a critical pedagogy, (c) create schools that are open systems rather than closed systems, and (d) shift accountability from a legalistic and policy frame to a moral and ethical frame.

As editors of this volume, it is right and appropriate to first thank our authors for the thoughts, creativity, energy, and time that they devoted to assisting our conversation about what it takes to change present policy and practice to one that more closely aligns with a reconceptualized system of education. In Chapter Nine, Julia White reminded us of Madeline Will's proclamation that a system of education that blends "the intrinsic strengths" of both special and general education in a manner that does not do away with special education, but instead, should "deliver the resources and provide the personalized [individualized] instruction each child must have to achieve to his or her greatest potential." She advocated for a collaborative, unified system of shared responsibility and accountability that would "bring the program to the child rather than one that brings the child to the program" (p. 173). The Council of Administrators for Special Education made a unified system part of its futures agenda 20 years ago, which has borne some fruit, and most recently, the concept of RtI, one of our newer policy developments, also facilitates greater attentiveness to instructional effects on student learning before referral to specialized services. RtI, however, has still been largely interpreted in local schools and districts as a means to sort and select. In many cases, it is not changing teacher behavior regarding membership of all students in general education first and foremost and integrating special education resources into the mix of general education thus furnishing expertise with which to plan and execute instructional matches that work for all students. In Chapter Two, Wayne Sailor and Leonard Burrello offer what Sailor (2009) called schoolwide RtI, now more often referred to as multitiered systems of support (MTSS) that seeks to go beyond new assessment practices to instructional development. This theme is echoed by Todd Gravois in his Chapter Six as well.

The policy foundation for what is and what might be was explored by a number of our authors. In Chapter Three, Carl Lashley laid out the legislative birth of programming and services for students with disabilities and the opportunities IDEA and NCLB provide. In addition, to Lashley's framing, Shana Haines and Rud Turnbull take us deep into the values behind the selected policy options and constraints offered in the original authorizing legislation, in Chapter Four. They are particularly adept at laying out the opportunities and the constraints of LRE and the continuum of service mandate in the law that most local and state leadership people have used to provide the release valve, allowing both districts and schools to place students along the continuum of services as needed to avoid placing students first in general education. These two chapters offer us the most complete and current views on options and support needed for a merged system of education as we advocate for changes in IDEA and NCLB.

In Chapter Five, Drs. Rolle, Harris, and Burrello offer us the history of funding options for special education services while providing a means of thought and how to advocate for change in both the types and levels of funding that support a merged system of education. With this reminder, we relaunch into our proposal that a merged and blended system of education is needed if we are committed to creating a public that respects the inherent dignity of each person to pursue his or her own goals and values through education. Special education has been the release valve that continues to provide the place and services to hold a child with mild to significant support needs in the "system." White, and Ryndak, Orlando, and Duran in their Chapter Seven, provide specific arguments and examples of how our most marginalized children and youth, those with significant support needs, should and can participate in a unified system of education. Sailor and Burrello along with Gravois have argued for fleshing out the specifications and operation of the collaborative inquiry to deliver an inquiry process or a means "to figure it out". With this mechanism, teachers and related service disciplines come together to match instructional delivery and supports to the students in a way that moves each student toward his or her educational goals set within a discourse community that includes the family, the school, and its representatives. It is the classic example of what can be done to backward map a relevant process from desired educational outcomes to the present level of functioning.

Under a blended, unified system of educational supports and services with built-in structural systems of collaborative inquiry, Universal Design for Learning (UDL), as discussed by Ryndak et al. and mentioned in other chapters, comes into focus. Ongoing research and development in UDL affords structured as well as instructional procedures for better equipping teachers to address learning challenges of all children.

In Chapter Eight, Morningstar, Knollman, Semon, and Kleinhammer-Tramill reflect on the history of legislation and policy regarding transition services. These exist to ensure that school is about life after school and that outcome data on postschool life needs to be added to systems of accountability for all students in a blended system. We believe the policy question here is "how do we know schooling makes a difference?" By using postschool data on independent living, employment, and postsecondary education measures, can we better ascertain the value of public education for all students? If students with mild to significant support needs have been unable to navigate the policy and program configurations created by past policy and limited financial support during the school years, how are they to achieve independence socially and financially in a competitive, minimum-wage work context without systems of support that include housing, transportation, job coaching, and community engagement? Systems of postschool support like those created in and around Madison, Wisconsin, that employ job and life coaches need to be replicated in communities around the nation. Tax credits to hire people with disabilities could be used to encourage employers across communities to serve their own citizens more independently, thus reducing dependence on families and public agencies with few resources.

Returning to the Human Development and the Capability Approach of Sen and Nussbaum, we are reminded that we got into the discussion of human capabilities trying to find a philosophical base that helps leadership to conceptualize human worth in different terms. In his Theory of Justice, Rawls teaches us about the social contract and the reciprocity between and among people as the basis of social discourse in a civil society and the need for contracts to ensure that economic transactions occur with a spirit of equality and equity. The Capability Approach evolved out of a theory of economics that includes social choice and justice. It is described as a reflection of an individual's "Freedom to achieve valuable functioning. . . . Capability represents a person's freedom to achieve well being" (Sen, 1992, p. 49). It is Nussbaum though who questions the need for reciprocity and argues for a capacity approach since it allows us to assess inequality based upon people's freedom to choose *among valuable functioning* to pursue one's own visions of life. This freedom Toson and Frattura examine (in Chapter Ten) is largely dependent on social arrangements that should expand people's capabilities and valuable functions (Alkire & Deneulin, 2009). The capacity approach affords a context to address next generation questions. What is the nature of those social arrangements? For what and whose desired ends? Who participates in creating those opportunities and arrangements? Who is held accountable for student effort, parent effort, teacher effort, school effort, district effort, state and federal government effort? What is the role of leadership at each level to move the system into a new position to think and act in new ways because the current way marginalizes too many for too long along the lines of class, race, ethnicity, language, ability, gender, and sexual orientation? Toson and Frattura offer examples of what it takes for leaders to advocate for all students to be served with respect and dignity in a unified system.

The Appreciative Inquiry approach to collaborative inquiry discussed by Barrett and Fry (2005) is also highly compatible with the human capability approach. Appreciative inquiry starts with dreams, values, and goals. It is an assets-based or strengths approach that emphasizes capabilities of the students, teachers, parents, school administrators, and community members who collectively envision a future that enables new possibilities to emerge (new functionings and capabilities). Appreciative inquiry begins with the assumption that every human system already has assets and positive success experiences. Problem-solving approaches under RtI are too closely aligned with deficit thinking from the start—what is the problem that we need to resolve?—leading to unintended consequences. Barrett and Fry suggest that these unintended consequences often lead to fragmentation, hopelessness, self-fulfilling deficit thinking, including an overdependence on experts.

We have addressed both the opportunities and constraints posed by the standards-based reform movement and the present accountability system that is narrowly focused on testing reading and numeracy and that reduces school success to annual assessments of student academic achievement. Kozleski, Artiles, and Lacy in Chapter Eleven note "the problem comes when explanations for any given variance don't fit the predicted pattern and the tools for accommodating difference are inadequate. None of this activity occurs in decontextualized spaces. Rather, people with their own particular cultural histories, experiences, and expectations come together in institutional contexts that are veined with historical deposits, and negotiate their activities through the tools available in their settings" (p. 220).

We contend that an outcome-oriented system of education must be broader and more varied. Human variation is both the input and the output expected. We cannot expect the same outcomes and measures to work for everyone. The goal of personalization is within our grasp. We have the technology for personalizing learning within a set of broad goals—enshrined in IDEA's four national outcomes: equal opportunity, independent living, full participation, and economic self-sufficiency. We have yet to design the metrics that will serve as drivers for a blended system, nor have we confronted the need for alternative pathways to graduation.

We recommend that more educators and community members be brought together to reconceptualize special and general education believing in combining assets and pursuing common visions within a transcendent purpose for public education that is inclusive and committed to the value of personalization for each student.

Let us end with two quotes from Kozleski et al.

"Understanding learning as a change in participation, as Rogoff (2003) suggests, means that the design of learning spaces plays a powerful role in maintaining and facilitating marginalization particularly since culture is deeply embedded in how participation is facilitated and regulated" (p. 221).

We believe all educators must come together to educate all students together to figure out how to confront marginalization as both an artifact of separate learning spaces and the result of hegemony-regularized grouping practices within general education. "The foundation of these team approaches to supporting and nurturing individual and collective capabilities is grounded in the moral imperative that every child's welfare and well-being contributes to the common good" (Kozleski, et al. 2013, p. 227). The end result of separating educational spaces and grouping practices within classrooms is, from Sen's and Nussbaum's argument on human development and capabilities, a continuous assault on social justice that is in fact immoral and unacceptable.

References

Sailor, W. (2009). *Making RtI work*. San Francisco: Jossey-Bass.

Rogoff, B. (2003). *The cultural nature of human development*. New York: Oxford University.

Barrett, F.J. and Fry, Ronald (2005). *Appreciative Inquiry*. Chagrin Falls: Taos Institute Publications.

Sen, A. (1992). *Inequality reexamined*. Oxford: Clarendon Press.

Alkire, S., & Deneulin, S. (2009). *The human development and capability approach*. In S. Deneulin & L. Shahami (Eds.), An introduction to the human development and capability approach: Freedom and agency (pp. 22–48). London: Earthscan.

Kozleski, E.B., Artiles, A., and Lacy, L. (2013) *The dangeous politics of difference: How systems produce marginalization*. In Leonard C. Burrello, Wayne Sailor, and Jeannie Kleinhammer-Tramill, Unifying Educational Systems. New York: Routledge.

CONTRIBUTOR BIOGRAPHIES

Alfredo Artiles is Professor of Education in the Mary Lou Fulton Teachers College and Professor of Culture, Society, and Education in the School of Social Transformation at Arizona State University (ASU). Dr. Artiles codirects the Equity Alliance at ASU. Professor Artiles's interdisciplinary scholarship examines the consequences of educational inequities related to the intersections of disability, race, social class, gender, and language. His work aims to inform policies, research practices, personnel preparation programs, and educational systems that enhance the well-being and educational opportunities of multicultural communities.

Leonard C. Burrello, Professor and former Chair of Educational Leadership and Policy Studies and Chair of Adult, Career, and Higher Education at the University of South Florida, has had a long career as a professor and organizational development specialist in the public schools. He has served as a professor at Michigan and Indiana and has consulted with 15 states and more than 40 school districts in his career. He has directed more than 150 dissertations, written 6 books and submitted a 7th, and authored more than 55 articles and produced 30 videos and DVDs as the Executive Director of the Forum on Education at Indiana University, where he is a Professor Emeritus and former head of Educational Leadership. His research interests are in leadership studies, especially school-based leadership, organizational change in schools, and inclusive practices including RtI implementation in schools.

Debra Duran practiced as a registered nurse working with adults and children with multiple and significant disabilities and worked as an administrator in a nonprofit community rehabilitation agency where one of her accomplishments was closing the group home model and transitioning the residents into supported living environments. By blending her nursing experience with years of community service to people with significant disabilities, and her knowledge of disability law and policy, she has spent the last 30 years as an advocate for the rights of people with disabilities.

Elise Frattura is Associate Professor and Department Chair in the Department of Exceptional Education and Administrative Leadership in the School of Education at the University of Wisconsin-Milwaukee. Dr. Frattura researches and publishes in the area of nondiscrimination law, integrated comprehensive services for all learners, and the theoretical underpinnings of educational marginalization through segregation. Dr. Frattura has been a K-12 public school administrator of student services for 12 years. Dr. Frattura is the coauthor of two books, *Leaders for Social Justice: Transforming Schools for All Learners* (2007) and a second edition of *Meeting the Needs of Students of All Abilities: How Leaders Go Beyond Inclusion* (2009).

Todd Gravois is President of ICAT Resources, Inc. As co-developer of the Instructional Consultation Team Model, he and his colleagues have developed and researched ways to support teachers in delivering quality instruction to benefit student achievement. He currently works with over 500 schools in nine states and the District of Columbia. Dr. Gravois has focused his practice and research interests on the reformation of service delivery in schools with an emphasis on applying empirically based instructional practices as part of the consultation process. He is co-author of *Instructional Consultation Teams: Collaborating for Change* as well as author of numerous publications and papers on the training, implementation, and evaluation of consultation based services in schools. He received his Specialist Degree in School Psychology from Nicholls State University and his doctoral degree from University of Maryland, College Park.

Shana J. Haines is a PhD student in the Department of Special Education at the University of Kansas, specializing in disability policy, families, and refugee students.

Pakethia Harris is a PhD student at the University of South Florida. Her research agenda includes examining educational policy with an emphasis on exceptional education, analyzing policy, and exploring the relationship between policy and how it influences the structure of funding mechanisms.

Jeannie Kleinhammer-Tramill is Professor and Coordinator of the Doctoral Program for the Department of Special Education, University of South Florida. Her scholarship focuses on federal policy related to personnel preparation, improving the preparation of general educators to serve students with disabilities, the implications of standards-based education policy for students with disabilities, and personnel preparation for transition services. Kleinhammer-Tramill has written and given scholarly presentations on these topics in multiple forums. Prior to her appointment to the University of South Florida in 2005, Kleinhammer-Tramill was Associate Research Professor at the University of Kansas.

Gregory Knollman is a PhD student in Curriculum and Instruction at the University of South Florida. His area of concentration includes special education policy, leadership, and transition.

Elizabeth B. Kozleski is Chair of the Special Education Program at the University of Kansas. Her scholarship includes examining and theorizing approaches to systems change in urban school systems; exploring how identity, culture, ability, and practice are negotiated in classrooms and schools; and understanding how schools become conscious and purposeful sites for inquiry and transformation related to disability, race, social class, gender, and language. Professor Kozleski works closely with teachers and other school leaders to improve access, participation, and opportunities to learn for students and families from diverse cultural communities.

Lisa Lacy is a former K-6 Special Education teacher. Her research interests are teacher identity and how lived experiences and past schooling events shape and influence teachers' beliefs about inclusive education. She is a special education doctoral student in the Curriculum and Instruction Program at Arizona State University.

Carl Lashley is Associate Professor in the Department of Educational Leadership and Cultural Foundations at the University of North Carolina at Greensboro. He has advanced degrees from West Virginia University and Indiana University. He has been a general and special education teacher, a principal, Director of Special Education and of Curriculum and Instruction. Dr. Lashley's primary intellectual and advocacy interests in equity, justice, and community come from his career-long concerns about poverty, equitable opportunity for all children, and the power of schooling as a mode of social change. His research interests are in education and special education law, policy, and practice; technology; and school leadership preparation.

Mary E. Morningstar is Associate Professor at the University of Kansas. Besides leading federal personnel preparation projects, her research interests include secondary special education and transition to adulthood, online instruction and professional development, and education of students with significant disabilities.

Ann-Marie Orlando is a certified speech-language pathologist with expertise in inclusive education and assistive technology devices for students with significant disabilities. At the University of Florida, her research activities are focused on literacy and communication, including the use of assistive technology to learn and use literacy across contexts. Through her work at the University of Florida,

Dr. Orlando has coordinated agency-funded grants focused on promoting communication for individuals with autism, and coordinated federal- and state-funded grants focused on teacher preparation, doctoral/postdoctoral preparation, and research in inclusive education for students with significant disabilities.

R. Anthony Rolle conducts research that explores and improves relative measures of economic efficiency for public schools. Concomitantly, his research explores and applies measures of vertical equity to analyses of state education finance mechanisms. Dr. Rolle's work is published in numerous books, journals, and monographs such as *To What Ends and By What Means? The Social Justice Implications of Contemporary School Finance Theory and Policy* (2007), *Modern Education Finance and Policy* (2007), *Measuring School Performance and Efficiency* (2005), *Journal of Education Finance*, *Peabody Journal of Education*, *School Business Affairs*, *School Administrator*, and *Developments in School Finance*. In addition his academic work, Dr. Rolle has conducted K–12 education finance and policy research for agencies and commissions in Arkansas, Colorado, Missouri, North Carolina, South Carolina, Tennessee, and Texas.

Diane Lea Ryndak is an internationally recognized professor at the University of Florida on inclusive education and access to the general curriculum for students with significant intellectual and developmental disabilities who have extensive support needs, preservice teacher preparation, and technical assistance for school reform efforts related to inclusive education. She has published more than 50 journal articles and book chapters, coauthored 2 books, and coedited 2 monographs on these and related topics. Several of these works have been republished internationally. Dr. Ryndak has been a Principal Investigator for more than 17 federal- and state-funded projects and focuses on teacher preparation, doctoral/postdoctoral preparation, and research related to meeting the needs of students with significant intellectual and developmental disabilities in inclusive general education classes and schools, and outcomes achieved through such services.

Wayne Sailor is Professor in the Department of Special Education, School of Education, University of Kansas; Senior Scientist with the Institute for Life Span Studies and Associate Director of the Beach Center on Disability at the University of Kansas. The focus of his interests are the full integration of students with severe disabilities through school restructuring processes; and service integration strategies for health, social, and educational services for all children at the school site. He has done extensive research on schoolwide applications of Positive Behavior Support, and in particular, uses of response to intervention logic (RtI) in whole school reform. His most recent research is focused on a structural school reform model called the Schoolwide Applications Model (SAM), which has undergone field testing in the Ravenswood City School District, East Palo

Alto, California; the Washington, DC, School District; and in the New Orleans, Louisiana, Recovery School District. Dr. Sailor's most recent book is *Making RtI Work*, published in 2009 by Jossey Bass.

Sarah Semon is Assistant Professor in the Department of Special Education at the University of Northern Iowa. She currently coordinates the Instructional Strategist I (5-12) and Work Experience Coordinator Programs. Her research interests include investigating inclusive secondary instructional practices, critical discourse analysis of educational policies, and student voice in transition processes.

Amy L-M. Toson has been working with districts and schools, both nationally and internationally, for well over 10 years in the area of inclusive education capacity building and systems change. She began as a K-12 inclusive special education teacher and moved into the role of consultant working with families, teachers, and leaders across the globe facilitating effective inclusion for all learners. Ms. Toson is Adjunct Instructor with the Department of Exceptional Education at the Universities of Wisconsin-Milwaukee and South Florida, teaching courses related to student diversity, inclusive education, and special education foundations. She is currently finishing her doctoral degree with the Departments of Educational Leadership/Policy Studies and Special Education at the University of South Florida-Tampa, researching multidimensional capacity building for effective inclusive school and district reform. Ms. Toson researches and publishes in the area of school systems, leader and teacher capacity building. Her most recent article, "Educational Justice for All: The Capability Approach and Inclusive Education Leadership," is published in the *International Journal of Inclusive Education*.

Rud Turnbull is Distinguished Professor in Special Education, Cofounder and Codirector of the Beach Center on Disability at the University of Kansas, and specialist in policy affecting individuals with developmental and behavioral/emotional disabilities. He has written extensively about special education law and policy, with emphasis on, among other things, integration of students and adults into schools and communities.

Julia M. White is Assistant Professor in the Department of Teaching and Curriculum, and Director of the Inclusive and Special Education Program at the University of Rochester. Her research interests include inclusive education and human rights, Romani Studies, and Disability Studies in Education. She has been published in *The English Journal, Journal of Postsecondary Education and Disability*, and *Disability Studies Quarterly*. She has authored chapters on representations of disability and policies related to inclusive education and is the author of a monograph of the Roma Education Fund, *Pitfalls and Bias: Entry Testing and the Overrepresentation of Romani Children in Special Education*.

INDEX